Contents

Not only is the Universe stranger than we think, it is stranger than we can think.

— Werner Heisenberg

1. Whispers of the Universe: An Introduction to Gravity's Ghosts

Imagine, for a moment, being able to listen to the whispers of the universe, to eavesdrop on the celestial conversations of massive bodies millions and billions of light-years away. With each ripple and wave through the cosmic sea, a story is told—stories of colliding black holes, merging neutron stars, and other cataclysmic events that shape our universe. This is the realm of gravitational waves— the ethereal imprints of massive objects bending the very fabric of spacetime itself.

In "Gravity's Ghosts: Unveiling Gravitational Waves," we embark on a journey to understand these enigmatic specters that dance unseen by the eye. Not long ago, these waves were merely a prediction of Albert Einstein's general theory of relativity. Today, they are a reality, immortalized as one of the most triumphant scientific discoveries of the 21st century.

This book gently guides you through the captivating history, astonishing technological advancements, and profound implications of gravitational wave astronomy. Whether you're a curious reader eager to peer into the mysteries of the cosmos or a seasoned scientist seeking a new perspective, here lies an exciting exploration of a universe that beckons with secrets. Let us venture together, guided by the things which are unseen, to unveil the mysterious voices of gravity.

2. The Seeds of a Revolution

2.1. The Birth of Relativity

In the late 19th and early 20th centuries, the scientific landscape was undergoing a seismic shift. Classical physics, anchored solidly by the laws of Newton, provided a serene understanding of the universe—an understanding grounded in the tangible, measurable interactions of matter and force. However, beneath the surface of this apparent stability, there lay profound questions that classical theories could not satisfactorily answer. The interplay of light, the nature of gravity, and the very structure of space and time remained enigmatic, hinting at deeper complexities that awaited discovery.

Against this backdrop, the seeds of a revolutionary idea began to sprout. Albert Einstein, a young physicist whose unconventional approaches and insatiable curiosity were already beginning to set him apart, was poised to change the course of physics forever. In 1905, he introduced the Special Theory of Relativity, which redefined the concepts of space and time. It asserted that the laws of physics are the same for all observers, regardless of their relative motion, and established the constancy of the speed of light as a universal principle. The implications of this theory rippled throughout the scientific community, creating both excitement and skepticism.

However, it was within this fervor that Einstein envisioned an even broader framework—the General Theory of Relativity, which he published in 1915. This theory would not merely modestly alter the understanding of gravity as something transmitted instantaneously through space, as Isaac Newton had proposed. Instead, it offered a radical interpretation: gravity is not a force at all but a curvature in the fabric of spacetime produced by the presence of mass. Matter influences spacetime, and in turn, the altered geometry dictates how objects move. This profound transformation gave birth not just to a new theory, but to the concept of gravitational waves, ripples in spacetime that could propagate across the cosmos just as light does.

The implications of General Relativity were nothing short of revolutionary. The elegant equations encapsulating this theory suggested that massive objects, such as stars and black holes, would not merely exert gravitational forces but would also create dynamic distortions in the spacetime continuum. These distortions would oscillate and travel outward as gravitational waves, akin to throwing a stone into a pond that sends ripples across the water's surface. This notion not only deepened the understanding of gravitational interactions on an astronomical scale but also revealed an exquisite interconnection between the universe's structure and its most profound phenomena.

Despite its groundbreaking nature, the road from theoretical prediction to empirical verification of gravitational waves was fraught with challenges. While the mathematical foundation of General Relativity was comforting to some physicists, many remained skeptical. The idea of detecting gravitational waves—a phenomenon predicted to be incredibly faint and subtle—seemed impractical, if not impossible. The sensitivity required to measure such infinitesimal perturbations in spacetime was beyond what existing technology could achieve. Waves produced by astronomical events would likely be dwarfed by the cacophony of noise from other physical processes, from seismic activity to thermal fluctuations.

As time marched on, early pioneers in the field continued to wrestle with Einstein's legacy. The interplay between experimental physics and theoretical considerations remained dynamic. Researchers began to explore indirect methods of confirming the existence of gravitational waves. One of the most significant pieces of evidence emerged in 1974 when physicist Russell Hulse and Joseph Taylor discovered a binary pulsar, PSR B1913+16. The pulsar, a highly magnetic, rotating neutron star, emitted precise beams of radio waves. Their observations revealed that the orbit of this binary system was gradually diminishing over time—exactly as General Relativity predicted due to energy lost as gravitational waves.

This landmark discovery opened the door to a new pursuit—the quest for direct detection of gravitational waves. Scientists around the globe mobilized, motivated by a vision that Einstein had set in motion nearly a century earlier. Researchers sought to refine detection technology, hoping to create instruments capable of capturing the faint echoes of gravitational waves as they traveled vast expanses of space. With perseverance, ingenuity, and international collaboration, the groundwork was laid for what would ultimately become the cutting-edge observatories of the 21st century.

The birth of relativity, thus, was not merely an isolated scientific milestone; it represented a paradigm shift that transcended physics, reshaping our understanding of the cosmos and our place within it. Through its lenses, we began to see the universe not merely as a collection of isolated phenomena governed by predictable laws, but as an intricate tapestry, woven together by the reciprocal actions of mass, energy, and the very fabric of spacetime itself. The journey from Einstein's initial equations to the eventual detection of gravitational waves was long and challenging, yet it stands as a testament to human curiosity, the relentless pursuit of knowledge, and the profound mysteries still waiting to be unraveled within the grand expanse of the universe.

As we delve deeper into the narrative of gravitational waves, we recognize that the echoes of that revolutionary birth continue to resonate through modern science, directing our gaze towards the ever-expanding horizons of astrophysical discovery. Each detection of a gravitational wave serves as a reaffirmation of Einstein's vision, a pivotal moment where the whispers of the universe become perceptible to human ears, beckoning us to listen and understand the cosmic dialogue unfolding around us.

2.2. Einstein's Vision

At the heart of Einstein's legacy lies a vision so radical and transformative that it reshaped not only the realm of physics but also our understanding of the universe itself. Einstein's pursuit of a grand unifying theory wasn't merely an academic exercise; it was driven by a deep-seated desire to reconcile the laws governing small-scale particles with the cosmic ballet of large celestial bodies. His work illuminated a path towards understanding not just how gravity operates but why it exists in the context of the very fabric of spacetime.

The General Theory of Relativity, published in 1915, was a culmination of a decade of contemplation, breakthroughs, and rigorous calculations. In this theory, Einstein proposed that what we perceive as gravitational force is no longer a mere pull or push exerted by massive objects, but instead a manifestation of the curvature of spacetime created by those objects. To visualize this concept, one might imagine a heavy ball placed on a taut rubber sheet—it creates a depression that distorts the surface around it. Likewise, both massive stars and planets warp spacetime, and the resulting curvature directs the paths along which other objects travel. This elegant paradox shifted our understanding of gravity from a traditional force to a geometric property of the universe.

Within Einstein's broader vision, gravitational waves emerged as a natural consequence of this warped spacetime. He predicted their existence as ripples caused by the acceleration of massive bodies, comparable to the ripples sent through the surface of a pond when a stone is dropped into it. These waves, traveling at the speed of light, would encode invaluable information about catastrophic cosmic events—namely, the mergers of black holes and neutron stars, the birth of supernovae, and other violent astrophysical processes. Einstein's equations hinted at a universe alive with rhythm and resonance, waiting for humanity to hear its silent songs.

Yet, this profound insight encountered skepticism. The scientific community at the time grappled with the implications of Einstein's ideas, often finding themselves at a crossroads between accepted Newtonian physics and this new, counterintuitive framework. Many regarded the idea of gravitational waves as little more than mathematical musings. The task of detecting such subtle disturbances against the backdrop of colossal cosmic noise seemed insurmountable. This skepticism presented a challenge that only perseverance in research and advancements in technology could alleviate over the decades.

As the years unfolded, the quest for evidence of gravitational waves morphed into a cornerstone of theoretical and experimental physics. Although the groundwork established by scientists like Hulse and Taylor's discovery provided critical validation for the entire framework of General Relativity, it was a mere whisper compared to the symphonies of gravitational waves that awaited detection. With this foundational confirmation, the scientific community rekindled interest in Einstein's predictions and sought innovative techniques and technologies to capture these elusive phenomena.

The vision Einstein had—one that blended theoretical insight with a longing to explore the cosmos—ignited a movement of technological and scientific leapfrogging that culminated in the advent of sophisticated gravitational wave observatories in the 21st century. These facilities, such as LIGO, represented not just a testament to decades of hard work and dedication but a realization of an idea that originated from the mind of a single physicist. The critical marriage of engineering excellence and theoretical groundwork turned Einstein's abstract concepts into practical tools for investigating the mysteries of the universe.

What followed in the wake of LIGO's unprecedented discoveries—where collisions of black holes and neutron stars sent shockwaves through spacetime—was the unlocking of a new window into the cosmos. The gravitational waves detected were not merely ripples; they became messengers carrying stories of cosmic events that shaped the universe. With each detection, scientists gained insight into phenomena that had eluded mankind's understanding for centuries, including the formation and behavior of black holes and neutron stars, the origin of heavy elements forged in cataclysmic mergers, and even the very fabric of cosmic history itself.

Moreover, Einstein's vision extended well beyond the boundaries of gravity and spacetime. His insistence on a cohesive unity within physics inspired future generations to pursue interdisciplinary collaboration, blending astrophysics, engineering, computer science, and philosophy to unravel the intricacies of the universe. The pursuit of understanding gravitational waves has not only illuminated individual cosmic events; it has allowed scientists to challenge and refine existing cosmological models. In doing so, it has ushered in fresh perspectives on dark matter, dark energy, and the fundamental nature of the universe.

Thus, Einstein's vision, initially dismissed as an extravagant notion, persists as a silent guide driving scientists to probe the deeper questions of existence. His ability to intertwine complex mathematical reality with an imaginative perspective on the cosmos emboldens the current generation of physicists in their journey toward the unknown. The ongoing exploration of gravitational waves is a reaffirmation of Einstein's audacious foresight—the realization that elusive whispers of the universe, captured in gravitational waves, pave the roads of discovery leading us toward a more profound comprehension of the cosmos.

In conclusion, as we continue to tune into the frequencies of the universe, we honor Einstein's original vision. Each detection of gravitational waves is not merely a scientific achievement; it is an echo of our collective curiosity and determination to decipher the messages woven into the very fabric of reality. It is an invitation to keep listening, to remain inquisitive, and to acknowledge that the universe speaks not only in the language of light but also in the melodic waves of spacetime that gently carry its secrets across the cosmos. Through meticulous effort and a commitment to understanding, we strive to unveil the symphony of gravitational waves as we listen closely to the whispers of the universe.

2.3. Challenging Newtonian Ideas

The advent of gravitational wave astronomy has given scientists a new lens through which they can understand the workings of the universe, and in this context, the challenge to Newtonian ideas presents itself as a pivotal moment in the continuity of physics. For centuries, Isaac Newton's laws of motion and universal gravitation formed the bedrock of classical mechanics, providing a robust framework for understanding the movements and interactions of celestial bodies. These principles dictated a predictable and ordered cosmos, where forces acted instantly at a distance and gravity was perceived as a force emanating from masses, drawing them together.

However, as physicists delved deeper into the realms introduced by Einstein's theories, it became necessary to re-evaluate and ultimately challenge the classical notions encapsulated in Newtonian physics. One of the most significant arguments against Newtonian gravity was the idea that it does not account for certain relativistic effects, particularly those that arise in extreme conditions such as near massive bodies or during high-velocity interactions. Einstein's work unveiled a universe where time and space are intertwined, bending under the influence of mass and energy, thereby introducing concepts that would forever alter humanity's comprehension of the cosmos.

The notion of gravitational waves, anticipated as perturbations that travel through the fabric of spacetime, inherently challenged the instantaneous nature of gravitational interactions posited by Newton. In Newtonian theory, if one were to suddenly remove a massive object, the effects of that removal would be felt instantaneously by surrounding entities. This presents a paradox when considering relativistic conditions, where changes in gravity would propagate at the speed of light, establishing a limit on how swiftly gravitational influence could be transferred across distances. Thus, the idea that gravitational waves would carry information regarding celestial events—traveling through spacetime with a finite speed—illustrated a remarkable departure from classical physics and an embrace of a more intricate universe.

As the groundwork for gravitational wave detection solidified, it demonstrated that massive celestial events, such as the merger of black holes, would generate ripples in spacetime that could be measured even billions of light-years from their origin. These ripples, vibrating through the very structure of spacetime, encapsulate information about their progenitors, revealing insights into their masses, spins, and orbital dynamics—all phenomena that had no place in the Newtonian model and beckoned towards a more nuanced understanding allowed by Einstein's general relativity.

Moreover, gravitational waves not only inform us about the behavior of massive bodies but also create an avenue for examining the limits of general relativity itself. By observing the phenomena accompanying gravitational wave events, scientists are provided with opportunities to discern the fundamental nature of gravity, especially as it interacts with quantum mechanics. This intersection presents a fertile ground for inquiry, as understanding how gravity behaves under these extreme conditions might one day lead to a unified theory bridging the gap between the macroscopic laws governing galaxies and the microscopic behaviors of particles.

The implications extend further into the realm of cosmology, where gravitational waves can offer vital clues about the early universe, dark matter, and dark energy. By investigating the signatures left by these elusive waves, researchers can probe phenomena that are fundamentally absent from traditional observations of light, thus addressing gaps in cosmological models long held lauded under the Newtonian lens. In short, gravitational waves prompt an exploration of questions that transcend the capabilities of classical physics and elucidate the complexities of the universe's fabric.

As we journey through the cosmos, utilizing the instruments developed to detect these waves, it becomes increasingly evident that our understanding is perpetually evolving. The interplay of gravitational waves and their dynamic encoding of information reflects a universe in constant flux, wherein the fabric of reality encourages us to challenge established ideas and venture down paths unimagined. In doing so, we enter into a dialogue with the universe, where past certainties must yield to new discoveries grounded in both observational prowess and theoretical innovation.

Ultimately, challenging Newtonian ideas is not merely an academic pursuit; it represents a philosophy of exploring the unknown, embracing complexity, and acknowledging the limitations of established thought. As we stand on the precipice of a new era in astronomy, propelled by the whisperings of gravitational waves, we find ourselves grappling with not just the mechanics of the universe but with profound questions of existence, connection, and the fundamental principles that govern all that is. The journey into the depths of gravitational waves serves increasingly as both a scientific expedition and a philosophical undertaking, inviting future generations of scientists and explorers to continually refine their understanding and redefine the very nature of reality itself. Each wave detected echoes with the invitation to listen more closely, to engage with the universe's complexities, and to proceed with curiosity as we unravel the serene mysteries lying beneath the fabric of spacetime.

In reframing our perspectives on gravity, matter, and the very interplay of forces at work in the universe, we are reminded that the journey toward understanding is an ongoing process—one ripe with revelations and challenges that beckon us toward greater truths. As they traverse the cosmos, gravitational waves stand as both evidence and heralds of a breathtakingly rich and interconnected reality, compelling us to boldly inquire and evolve beyond the intellectual boundaries of the past, propelling us into a future rich with infinite possibility and discovery.

2.4. The Quest for Unseen Waves

The quest for unseen waves is a narrative woven with ambition, innovation, and tenacity, echoing the very essence of humanity's desire to explore and understand its universe. The pursuit of gravitational waves represents not merely a chapter in the annals of science but a vivid journey of discovery, bridging the realms of abstract theoretical physics with the concrete realities of experimentation and observation.

At the heart of this quest lies a profound challenge: how does one observe something that is inherently elusive? Gravitational waves, predicted nearly a century ago by Einstein's theory of general relativity, were originally viewed as a theoretical curiosity, an elegant but seemingly unattainable aspect of spacetime physics. The theoretical prediction alone ignited a flicker of hope and curiosity, but the significant obstacles to detection loomed dauntingly large. Early enthusiasts faced the seemingly insurmountable task of measuring distortions in spacetime that would be imperceptibly small, fraught with challenges rooted in both the faint nature of the waves and the noise produced by the world around us.

Throughout the years, the scientific community evolved its conception of diligence. Theoretical physicists labored to refine and consolidate mathematical models, while experimentalists set about attempting to design the tools necessary for detection. This duality of effort underscores gravitational wave astronomy's dependence on collaborative innovation across disciplines, encompassing physics, engineering, and computer science. Within the trajectory of this quest, pioneers such as Kip Thorne, Rainer Weiss, and Barry Barish emerged, weaving together a vision that would breathe life into gravitational wave detection.

As the aspirations crystallized into ambition, the next critical step was conceptualizing detection methodologies that could isolate gravitational waves from the cacophony of environmental noise. This necessitated the invention of ultrahigh-sensitivity instruments capable of measuring minute changes in distance on the order of one-thousandth the diameter of a proton. The concept of laser interferometry emerged as a powerful technique where lasers would be employed to measure the minute changes in the length of two perpendicular arms —an endeavor that would profoundly elevate experimental physics to a new epoch.

The Laser Interferometer Gravitational-Wave Observatory (LIGO), constructed during the 1990s and operational by 2002, epitomized this ambitious endeavor to hear the echoes of the universe. The workshop of human ingenuity came alive as engineers crafted devices that were poised to detect the minutest fluctuations in spacetime. From the calibration of intricate optics to the stabilization against seismic vibrations, each element of LIGO was meticulously engineered to enhance sensitivity and specificity. The legendary moment arrived on

September 14, 2015, when LIGO successfully detected its first gravitational waves from the merger of two black holes. This moment was not merely a scientific triumph; it was a historical milestone, one that echoed across the universe and embedded itself into the consciousness of humanity.

But the story did not end with the initial detection—rather, it was just the beginning of a new era in astrophysics. The enthralling experience of capturing even a single gravitational wave opened the door to a wealth of information about the cosmos. Researchers quickly realized the potentialities inherent in gravitational wave astronomy, leading to the establishment of global collaborations aimed at expanding the network of observatories. Facilities such as Virgo in Europe and KAGRA in Japan sprung up, each contributing to the collective endeavor of enhancing sensitivity and correlating observations across different locales to refine the obtained data.

In this intricate dance of discovery, the implications of gravitational wave astronomy extended far beyond detection. Each wave provided a unique insight into the lifecycles of massive stars, the nature of black holes, and the nascent universe itself. The ability to measure the frequencies and amplitudes of these waves translated to vital information about their origins, enabling astrophysicists to piece together events—an interstellar narrative told through mathematical expressions of form and resonance. The collisions of black holes, neutron star mergers, and even the formation of exotic matter enriched the scientific vocabulary, giving rise to complex conversations encompassing physics, cosmology, and even philosophy.

Yet, every step in this journey has not been without its challenges. The early skepticism surrounding gravitational waves lingered for years. Many in the scientific community questioned if such feeble signals could ever be detected amid the symphony of noise produced by the earth itself. Moreover, convincing funding agencies and the world at large about the feasibility and necessity of building immensely complex observatory infrastructures required a combination of visionary persuasion and empirical credibility. The path to acceptance was dotted with obstacles, requiring not just scientific rigor, but a compelling narrative about the significance of unlocking the universe's secrets through gravitational waves.

In navigating this quest, the resilience of the scientific community illuminated a salient truth—the pursuit of knowledge is a collective endeavor, fueled by curiosity and shared aspirations. The collaborative spirit witnessed in the realm of gravitational waves reflects the beauty of human inquiry, reminding us that challenges can transform into triumphs when minds and efforts unite around a common goal.

Today, as gravitational wave astronomy stands at the intersection of continued exploration and burgeoning technological advancements, we are inspired to dream of new possibilities. Observatories poised for the next generation will refine our understanding further, transforming gravitational wave detection from a frontier science into a cornerstone of our cosmic exploration toolkit. The quest for unseen waves is an ever-evolving saga, one that beckons scientists and dreamers to listen closely to the universe's whispers, unearthing truths entwined in the delicate fabric of spacetime.

As we continue navigating this cosmic sea, the achievements realized thus far offer not merely a reflection of what we can accomplish, but a promise of the limitless potential that lies ahead. Each detected wave represents more than a mere measurement; it encapsulates the very aspirations of humanity to bridge the chasm between the known and the unknown, reminding us that the universe, in all its grandeur, persists as a vast ocean of mysteries waiting to be unfurled. With each wave, we inch closer to unveiling the profound stories embedded within the cosmic tapestry—a quest that invites us all to join the voyage and embrace the unfathomable wonders that dwell in the space beyond our sight.

2.5. The Early Theorists

As the 20th century dawned, the realm of physics found itself fertile ground for innovation and upheaval, and it was within this charged atmosphere that the early theorists began to redefine our understanding of the universe. Their contemplation of gravity, space, and time was not merely an academic pursuit but a passionate quest that would yield insights reshaping how humanity perceives the cosmos. At the forefront of this intellectual revolution was Albert Einstein, whose audacious ideas would challenge the foundational concepts established by Isaac Newton for over two centuries.

The early stages of gravitational research can trace their roots back to pioneers like Galileo and Newton, whose landmark contributions provided rigor to classical mechanics. However, as the scientific community advanced, its pursuit of deeper truths led to discontent with the limitations of established paradigms. The observations of celestial objects, including the anomalies in Mercury's orbit, left scientists yearning for a more comprehensive framework. This curiosity would soon coalesce into the revolutionary theories that emerged from the minds of early theorists.

Einstein's initial foray into modern physics began with the Special Theory of Relativity in 1905, which introduced the mind-bending concept that space and time are woven into a single continuum rather than separate entities. Yet it was General Relativity, published in 1915, that introduced the concept of gravitation as a curvature of spacetime, fundamentally shifting how gravity was perceived. Unlike Newton's perspective of gravity as an instantaneous force acting at a distance, Einstein's formulation positioned gravity as a geometric property dependent upon mass's influence on the fabric of spacetime. This radical reinterpretation inspired the notion of gravitational waves— ripples in spacetime moving at the speed of light, carrying crucial information about astronomical events.

In the shadow of this monumental shift, several early theorists worked tirelessly to expand upon and validate Einstein's visionary framework. One of the critical figures in this early landscape was Hermann Weyl, whose investigations into the sufficiency of empirical observation and the philosophical considerations of relativity encouraged further exploration of the universe's structure. The voices of these early theorists, echoing in support of or skepticism towards

Einstein, created a dynamic atmosphere where ideas were vigorously tested and refined.

Moreover, the implications of General Relativity were not confined solely to theoretical conjectures; they inspired a growing emphasis on empirical validation. As researchers like Karl Schwarzschild formulated solutions to Einstein's field equations, predictions about black holes, singularities, and the warping of light around massive objects came to fruition. However, many theoretical concepts faced resistance; scientists grappled with the abstract nature of an unseen phenomenon like gravitational waves.

In this context, a pivotal moment occurred in the mid-20th century with the discovery of radio pulsars by Jocelyn Bell Burnell and her collaborator Antony Hewish. Their work not only expanded our understanding of neutron stars but laid groundwork that would later validate General Relativity. The precision of pulsar timing provided indirect evidence supporting the existence of gravitational waves; namely, using binary pulsars to measure energy loss—which correlated with predictions derived from General Relativity.

Simultaneously, theorists delved into the interplay between gravity and quantum mechanics, an area where bold thinkers such as John Archibald Wheeler ventured into concepts of geometrodynamics and the implications of quantum foam, implicitly tying Einstein's legacy to realms then untouched. These reflections revealed the gravity well's mysterious depths: the enormity of the universe coupled with tiny quantum fields presented an opportunity to unify disparate realms of physics, which, though dreamlike, remained tantalizingly just out of reach.

As the scientific community forged ahead, the resonance of early theorists' voices became a symphony of inquiry and skepticism. Their collective challenges molded the framework for future gravitational research, as decades of work culminated in the establishment of direct detection programs. Although gravitational waves were initially seen as a dream beyond the grasp of empirical science, the relentless pursuit of truth propelled researchers forward, fuelling a quest destined to redefine humanity's understanding of the universe.

The vibrations of these dreams began to materialize into realities with advanced instruments designed to capture the subtle nuances of spacetime distortions. Research institutions and observatories, inspired by the pioneering spirit of early theorists, saw the establishment of projects like LIGO—a project that would not merely seek to confirm Einstein's predictions but unearth a plethora of knowledge about cosmic events.

Looking back at the early theorists reveals a narrative rich with ambition, resilience, and ingenuity. They stood as the forerunners, planting critical seeds that would grow into theories and technologies crucial for unveiling the gravitational waves pulsating through the cosmos. Their contributions, however cryptic at the time, have ultimately beckoned humanity to listen more closely to the enigmatic whispers of the universe, guiding future generations to probe the depths of spacetime and discover the tales woven into the fabric of reality.

As we reflect on this journey, it becomes clear that the evolution of gravitational physics is a legacy rooted in the fervor of inquiry. The whispers of the universe indeed echo the thoughts of those early theorists, calling scientists to remember their foundational contributions while striving for deeper understanding amidst the profound mysteries that characterize our celestial home. In this ongoing exploration, from the abstract realms of theory to the tactile world of measurement, lies the unending quest of humanity to comprehend the cosmos and our place within it, driven by the echoes of voices long past but not forgotten.

3. Echoes from the Past

3.1. Historical Theories and Predictions

In the realm of scientific inquiry, the echoes of historical theories and predictions resonate strongly, illustrating the evolution of thought surrounding gravitational waves through the years. This subchapter invites readers to traverse the journey from the early musings of ancient scholars to the bold assertions driven by the scientific revolutions of the 20th and 21st centuries, where predictions were forged into empirical realities that now illuminate our understanding of the universe.

Long before Einstein's revolutionary insights, ancient civilizations sought to comprehend the cosmos. Babylonian astronomers meticulously tracked celestial movements, while Greek philosophers like Aristotle proposed a geocentric universe governed by comprehensible laws. Their inquiries were foundational yet limited to observable phenomena—gravity was understood as a force that attracted objects towards the earth, with little depth concerning its underlying nature. According to Aristotle, the heavier the object, the faster it would fall, a notion that dominated Western thought until the Renaissance.

This prevailing mindset began to shift with Copernicus and Galileo, whose observations laid the groundwork for a more profound understanding of planetary motion. Galileo's thought experiments questioning Aristotle's assertions marked a paradigm shift in scientific thought. He proposed that objects fall at the same rate regardless of mass, challenging conventional dogma. However, it was Isaac Newton who synthesized these insights into a coherent framework, culminating in his landmark work, "Philosophiæ Naturalis Principia Mathematica," published in 1687. Newton articulated the laws of motion and universal gravitation, providing a mathematical description of gravity as an attractive force acting instantaneously over a distance. His formulation, while revolutionary, wove gravity into the fabric of classical physics, anchoring it firmly within a decidedly mechanical view of the universe.

As the scientific revolution progressed into the 19th century, challenges to Newton's framework began to surface. Observations such as the precession of Mercury's orbit could not be wholly reconciled with Newtonian predictions. These discrepancies sparked an intellectual firestorm, prompting theorists to search for deeper explanations beyond the established laws. The dawn of the 20th century brought forth the work of Albert Einstein, a physicist whose ideas not only contradicted Newton's laws but invited humanity to view gravity and spacetime through a novel lens.

Einstein's introduction of the Special Theory of Relativity shifted the paradigm by asserting that the speed of light is constant, creating a unified framework for understanding space and time. Building upon this revolutionary idea, Einstein announced his General Theory of Relativity in 1915, which radically transformed the conceptualization of gravity from a force acting at a distance to a curvature of spacetime. According to Einstein, massive objects like stars and planets warp the very fabric of spacetime, creating a dynamic landscape through which other bodies move. Thus, gravity was no longer perceived as a simple attraction but as a relationship entwined with the geometric properties of the universe. These concepts provided fertile ground for the predictions of gravitational waves—ripples generated by the acceleration of massive bodies, propagating through spacetime like waves across a cosmic sea.

The announcement of Einstein's theories marked a watershed moment in physics, sparking a flurry of theoretical exploration and empirical validation. Nevertheless, the detection of gravitational waves remained, for nearly a century, an elusive dream. Scientists likened the quest to detecting the faintest whisper of the universe amid a storm of noise. Early theorists, facing skepticism from their contemporaries, grappled with the computational challenges of Einstein's equations, leading to a drive for both theoretical innovations and practical technologies that could facilitate detection.

As the decades rolled on, various predictions made by Einstein's theory while tantalizingly close, faced severe skepticism. Notably, an empirical realization of gravitational waves was profoundly hindered by the technological limitations of the time. The sheer faintness of the waves meant that the sensitivity required for detection exceeded the capabilities of existing instrumentation. Nevertheless, the groundwork was being laid as researchers like Russell Hulse and Joseph Taylor made significant discoveries in pulsar studies that indirectly confirmed Einstein's proposal regarding energy loss due to gravitational waves.

The 21st century became the stage for a dramatic transformation in gravitational wave astronomy. With the construction of LIGO, an exquisite instrument designed to detect incredibly subtle changes in distance, the predictions of Einstein began to cross the threshold from theory into observation. On September 14, 2015, the historic detection of gravitational waves from the merger of two black holes marked a triumphant moment in scientific history, substantiating a phenomenon that had been speculated upon and theorized for nearly a century. This empirical validation not only reaffirmed Einstein's legacy but also opened wide the gates to new explorations in astrophysics, allowing us to listen to the celestial symphony of the universe.

Historical theories and predictions regarding gravitational waves reflect a rich and intertwined narrative that encapsulates the evolution of human understanding. As scientists peer through the lenses of sophisticated technology and refined theoretical frameworks, they uncover the intricate connections between past predictions and present discoveries, revealing a universe more complex and harmonious than previously imagined. Each new wave detected not only serves as a reminder of the journey from theory to reality but reinforces the ongoing dialogue between scientific inquiry and the majestic being of the cosmos itself.

Thus, the echoes from the past guide us as we press onwards into the future, nudging humanity to remain inquisitive and humble as we unveil the mysteries of gravitational waves—enigmas that continue to whisper through spacetime, instilling both wonder and enlightenment in our quest for knowledge. In embracing the historical tapestry forged by visionary thinkers and astronomers, we harness both a legacy of exploration and the promise of new revelations, compelling us to persist in listening to the universe's murmurs as we advance towards the horizons of understanding.

3.2. Gravitational Interactions

Gravitational interactions form the backbone of the grand narrative explaining how celestial bodies influence one another across vast distances in the universe. The essence of these interactions lies in the framework established by Einstein's General Theory of Relativity, which radically redefined our understanding of gravity as a geodesic in the multidimensional fabric of spacetime. Rather than conceptualizing gravity as a mysterious force acting instantaneously across distances—an idea rooted in Newtonian mechanics—Einstein presented it as the natural result of gravitational fields shaping the geometry of spacetime itself.

In this context, gravitational interactions become a dance where massive bodies like stars, black holes, and galaxies influence the trajectories and behaviors of one another through the curvature they induce in spacetime. Imagine a heavy bowling ball placed on a rubber sheet. The ball's weight distorts the sheet, creating a well that smaller marbles placed nearby can spiral towards. Similarly, significant masses cause ripples and warps in the fabric of spacetime, dictating how other objects move and interact.

At the heart of gravitational interactions are the concepts of attraction and collision. For instance, during stellar formation, dense clouds of gas and dust experience gravitational collapse, drawing material inwards until nuclear fusion ignites, creating a new star. As these bodies accumulate mass over time, the gravitational influence extends, attracting additional matter and establishing more complex interactions. It is a dynamic and accumulative process marked by both the synergy of attraction and the competition of forces at play.

One particularly fascinating aspect of gravitational interactions is their role in the formation and evolution of binary systems, such as binaries composed of neutron stars or black holes. In these systems, two massive objects orbit around a common center of mass. The gravitational forces at play lead to intricate orbital dynamics, influencing each star's spin, decay rates, and, ultimately, their fates. When such binary systems spiral inwards due to the emission of gravitational waves—mechanisms predicted by Einstein—they eventually lead to dramatic events such as mergers, producing powerful gravitational waves detectable across vast cosmic distances.

Consider two black holes merging, a phenomenon that dramatically illustrates gravitational interactions in action. As they spiral towards each other, the gravitational attraction grows stronger, leading to increasingly faster orbits, culminating in a final collision. This cataclysmic event sends ripples through spacetime itself, producing gravitational waves that carry information about the masses, spins, and other properties of the black holes. These waves, although faint, can be measured by advanced observatories like LIGO and Virgo, allowing scientists to decode the tales of distant cosmic events.

Moreover, these interactions serve as the foundation for understanding phenomena like gravitational lensing, where massive objects act as lenses, bending the light from objects behind them. This effect not only provides insights into the distribution of dark matter but also offers stunning visual evidence of the universe's richness and complexity, bending our perceptions of reality while reinforcing the interconnectedness of all celestial bodies through gravitational ties.

As we delve deeper into gravitational interactions, we also confront the enigma of gravity's nature itself. Gravitational interactions differ fundamentally from electromagnetic forces, for example, because they produce a warping of spacetime rather than merely acting at a distance. This nuanced understanding prompts essential questions surrounding the integration of general relativity with quantum mechanics, focusing on how gravity operates at subatomic scales and whether gravitational interactions will yield unifying theories bridging the vastness of cosmic phenomena with the smallest constituents of matter.

The quest to unravel these questions is deeply tied to the future of gravitational research. As technology advances, next-generation observatories promise to enhance sensitivity, allowing scientists to observe waves generated by more varied sources—such as the remnants of the Big Bang, or the echoes produced by events occurring at the edges of black holes. Such advancements can lead to improved models of cosmic evolution, elucidating not only how celestial bodies interact but also how the universe itself expands and evolves over time.

Importantly, understanding gravitational interactions is not solely an academic exercise; it holds profound implications for humanity's understanding of reality. Each interaction captured and characterized deepens our insight into nature's workings and nurtures our collective curiosity. Investigating these interactions propels science forward, fostering innovations that resonate beyond astrophysics, influencing technology, engineering, and even philosophy.

In summary, gravitational interactions encapsulate the interplay between cosmic bodies within the greater tapestry of the universe. They reveal the complexities and intricacies of how mass shapes spacetime and ultimately govern the fabric of reality as we comprehend it. As we continue to observe and decipher the language of gravitational waves, we are reminded that each revelation extends an invitation to explore the awe-inspiring phenomena that govern our cosmos—an eternal journey characterized by complexity, beauty, and a relentless pursuit of understanding the whispers of the gravitational forces that bind everything together.

3.3. Beyond the Visible

In our exploration of gravitational waves and their significance, we reach a realm that transcends mere visibility. While we are accustomed to perceiving the universe primarily through photons, the reality of the cosmos extends far beyond what our eyes can detect. Gravitational waves serve as gateways into this hidden domain, allowing us to glean insights into cosmic events that unfold silently, revealing truths buried deep within the fabric of spacetime.

The journey into this unobservable territory is marked by profound revelations. Traditional astronomical observations, which depend heavily on electromagnetic radiation—light of various wavelengths—restrict our comprehension of the universe to occurrences that emit, reflect, or interact with light. This limits our perspective to relatively few sources, largely overlooking phenomena that either absorb light or emit it in such varying conditions that it becomes exceedingly difficult to analyze. Moreover, events of vast magnitude, like black hole mergers or neutron star collisions, generate gravitational waves —mysterious ripples in spacetime that elude the direct observation of traditional telescopes yet massively impact the cosmic landscape.

The significance of detecting gravitational waves lies not just in confirming Einstein's predictions but in uncovering an entirely new way of listening to and understanding the universe. Gravitational waves offer a complementary approach to astrophysical investigations, expanding our toolkit for probing the cosmos. They enable scientists to observe and analyze events that might otherwise remain invisible. For instance, phenomena such as black hole mergers, which produce no light, emit powerful gravitational waves that carry intricate information about the properties of the colliding objects.

Listening to these waves requires not just sophisticated technology but a paradigm shift in our understanding of observation itself. The detection is akin to tuning into a frequency of the universe that has gone unnoticed until now. Each event that generates gravitational waves contributes a piece of a cosmic puzzle, providing new avenues for inquiry. For instance, the waves emitted from the collision of two neutron stars not only signify the merger itself but also serve as a probe for our understanding of the dense matter physics and the creation of heavy elements like gold and platinum through such cosmic events.

This engagement with the unseen leads to rich scientific discussions, challenging existing theoretical frameworks while simultaneously nurturing the ongoing dialogue between proven science and emerging concepts. Each detection opens avenues for further research, compelling scientists to consider how gravity behaves under extreme conditions and how it intertwines with the fundamental forces of nature. This broader inquiry often extends beyond astrophysics, touching fields such as particle physics, cosmology, and even philosophy, nurturing critical interdisciplinary interactions that represent the very essence of scientific exploration.

Yet, as we probe these unseen waves, we navigate through challenges of interpretation and classification. The data obtained from gravitational wave observatories, whether LIGO, Virgo, or future facilities, represent sound waves filtered through intricate mathematical language. Scientists meticulously sift through raw data to identify genuine signals among a cacophonous background noise that includes terrestrial vibrations and other astrophysical phenomena. Each successful interpretation emerges from a collaborative effort not just in technical expertise but in conceptual understanding of wave mechanics and astronomy.

The insights gleaned from these waves have important implications for cosmological models, particularly in illuminating dark matter and dark energy—the elusive components that govern the large-scale structure and expansion of the universe. By analyzing how gravitational waves interact with these components, researchers can gain new perspectives on the fundamental makeup of reality, leading to revised models that elongate the fabric of our understanding.

Furthermore, exploring beyond the visible portends exciting possibilities for cosmic discovery, as we grow adept at interpreting signals from distant galaxies. Extragalactic gravitational waves contain stories baked into their wavelengths, informing us about the processes and histories of galaxies billions of light-years away. As our observational capacity deepens, we can better understand the nature of cosmic evolution, relating the remnants of the early universe to the structures that populate the modern cosmos.

These advances will not occur in isolation. The endeavor requires a fusion of technologies, methodologies, and international collaboration. The future of gravitational wave astronomy involves amplifying these global networks, enhancing sensitivity through advances such as space-based observatories. Future missions aim to lift detectors beyond Earth's atmosphere, allowing them to circumvent terrestrial noise entirely and offer unprecedented insight into waves unmuted by atmospheric interference.

As we stand on the precipice of this expanding frontier, it is essential to recognize the broader implications of what lies beyond the visible. Gravitational waves are a reminder that our universe is cloaked in significant mysteries, awaiting discovery by those who dare to look past conventional limitations. The complex interplay between visibility and invisibility sharpens our resolve to listen more closely, to engage more openly with the universe's subtle cues, and to embrace the unquantified vastness of knowledge that lies in wait.

In this pursuit, we become part of a grand narrative that connects past theorists, modern-day pioneers, and future explorers. Gravitational waves resonate not just through spacetime but through the very fabric of human curiosity and inquiry. Every wave detected is a testament to our quest for understanding, a movement toward a reality where we acknowledge that the universe has so much more to offer than what is merely visible to the naked eye. In this enticing realm, we are called to listen, to decipher, and to embrace the hidden camouflages of existence we have yet to unveil. Each whisper of gravitational waves echoing from the depths of the cosmos serves as an invitation to venture further into the great unknown, forging connections that tether us to both the past and the infinite potential of discovery that lies ahead.

3.4. Deciphering the Cosmos

In the quest to decode the mechanics of the universe, the notion of deciphering the cosmos through gravitational waves emerges as both an enthralling challenge and an unparalleled opportunity. Gravitational waves represent a language of the universe that offers whispers of cataclysmic events, allowing us glimpses into regions and phenomena that remain obscured by distance, light, or mere human limitation. Understanding these waves involves not just observing phenomena but interpreting the stories and mysteries they carry, revealing insights that transcend traditional astrophysical inquiry.

Gravitational waves are born from the most violent and energetic events in the universe—the mergers of black holes, the collisions of neutron stars, and even the catastrophic deaths of massive stars. When these colossal bodies accelerate or collide, they send ripples through the very fabric of spacetime, distorting it and allowing for the propagation of these waves across vast cosmic distances. Much like sound waves vibrating in air, gravitational waves extend through the vacuum of space, carrying information about their origins.

To decipher these waves is to engage in a multi-faceted endeavor that couples advanced physics with the latest in engineering and technology. The first step involves the detection of gravitational waves. Instruments such as LIGO utilize laser interferometry to measure the minuscule distortions created by these waves as they pass through Earth. Imagine a long tunnel with mirrors at either end. As a gravitational wave travels, it stretches one arm of the tunnel while compressing the other, causing a change in the distance measured by light pulses bouncing between the mirrors. This delicate measurement demands extraordinary precision—LIGO's detectors are designed to identify changes in distances as small as a fraction of the wavelength of light, equivalent to less than a proton's diameter.

Once detected, the challenge of interpretation begins. The encoded information within these waves reflects the dynamics of the astronomical events that created them—such as the masses, spins, and trajectories of the colliding bodies. That information is deciphered using complex mathematical models that connect the encoded signals to their physical sources. Researchers use sophisticated algorithms and data analysis techniques to sift through noise and identify the characteristic "chirp" signatures produced by the gravitational waves of colliding binary systems. Each detectable event becomes a key to unlocking mysteries; for instance, the observation of binary black hole mergers that yielded insights into their population and formation pathways.

Much like deciphering an ancient script, this process requires a deep understanding of both the underlying theory and the empirical data that come from observations. Through this intricate interplay of physics and technology, scientists have begun to assemble a coherent picture of the universe's evolution and the behaviors of its most enigmatic objects.

Beyond just detection and interpretation, the implications of gravitational waves ripple through the entire field of astrophysics and cosmology. They serve as tools that augment our observational capabilities, providing insights that traditional electromagnetic observations cannot. By venturing into the realm of the "invisible," gravitational wave astronomy fosters a new wave of inquiry that expands our understanding of cosmic phenomena.

This newly discovered capacity to "listen" to the universe reshapes our understanding of fundamental concepts such as gravity itself, cosmological structures, and the lifecycle of stars. The ongoing analysis of gravitational waves leads to questions of their potential to probe the mysteries surrounding dark matter and dark energy, which both comprise a significant portion of the universe yet largely elude our understanding. For instance, the properties of gravitational waves might give clues about the nature of these enigmatic components, propelling us towards more profound revelations about the fundamental forces that govern the cosmos.

The story of deciphering gravitational waves is still unfolding, with significant prospects on the horizon. Technological advancements promise to enhance our sensitivity and detection capabilities, leading to the identification of more diverse sources and a richer tapestry of gravitational wave events. International collaborations, such as efforts to create a global gravitational wave observatory network, will provide a comprehensive framework to explore the universe on a grand scale. This collaborative spirit mirrors the very essence of scientific inquiry—where individuals contribute unique skills towards unlocking the shared enigma of cosmic existence.

Furthermore, the philosophical implications rippling through society as gravitational wave astronomy progresses cannot be ignored. Each discovery holds profound ramifications for humanity's understanding of its place in the universe and the fundamental nature of reality. As we glean insights through the melodies of gravitational waves, we deepen our appreciation for the interconnectedness of all matter and energy, reinforcing our commitment to exploring the cosmos.

Ultimately, as we venture into this uncharted territory, we are driven by an insatiable curiosity—a desire to listen more closely to the universe's whisperings and to learn the stories hidden within the waves that traverse spacetime, bridging the gaps between knowledge and the unknown. The endeavor to decipher the cosmos is not solely a scientific pursuit; it is a universal calling that binds the threads of inquiry, imagination, and discovery. Each wave detected reverberates through time and space, echoing humanity's quest for understanding —reminding us that within the vastness of the universe lies an endless menu of mysteries yet to be revealed. As we continue to unravel these cosmic tales, we are offered a grand invitation to explore the marvels of existence, always listening, always decoding the beautiful and intricate language of gravitational waves that speak to us across the gulfs of space and time.

3.5. Early Challenges and Skepticism

The early challenges and skepticism surrounding gravitational waves were critical in shaping the trajectory of gravitational wave astronomy, demonstrating the interplay between theoretical innovation and practical reality in the scientific process. The journey from the initial prediction of gravitational waves to their eventual detection was marked by a series of notable obstacles that pushed the boundaries of technology, theoretical understanding, and acceptance.

Despite the tremendous theoretical framework developed by Albert Einstein in the early 20th century, particularly with his General

Theory of Relativity, many in the scientific community remained skeptical about the existence of gravitational waves. The notion that massive objects could not only warp spacetime but also generate ripples detectable across cosmic distances was daunting—both technically and philosophically. The inherent limitations of the technology available in the early years compounded this skepticism, making the concept of detecting these faint ripples appear almost whimsical.

The skepticism was further exacerbated by the philosophical implications of Einstein's theories. At its core, General Relativity challenged not only the prevailing Newtonian mechanics but the very way scientists understood the mechanics of the universe. The notion that gravity was not a force transmitted through space but rather a manifestation of spacetime curvature was radical, and many found it difficult to reconcile with the foundational principles established by Newton. Tension between established traditions and the new ideas proposed by Einstein created an atmosphere of rigorous debate, leading to hesitation among scientists to whole-heartedly embrace the implications of gravitational waves.

As decades passed, the issue of detection remained paramount. The early theoretical predictions suggested that any gravitational waves produced would be exceedingly faint, jeopardized by a cacophony of noise created by various terrestrial and astrophysical phenomena. This posed significant hurdles for experimental physicists eager to make a tangible connection between the theoretical predictions and observable reality. Despite pervasive skepticism, a small group of scientists remained adamant in their belief that gravitational waves could be detected, given the right technology.

In the latter half of the 20th century, significant advancements paved the way for a more optimistic outlook regarding gravitational wave detection. Nonetheless, challenges persisted. Experiments designed to detect gravitational waves confronted an array of practical obstacles. The necessary sensitivity to measure changes in distance smaller than a proton seemed insurmountable. Strikingly sensitive equipment must be insulated from an array of disturbances: seismic activity, thermal fluctuations, and ambient noise, creating an engineering challenge of monumental proportions.

Critical breakthroughs began to emerge through the work of pioneering scientists. The discovery of the first binary pulsar by Russell Hulse and Joseph Taylor in 1974 was a landmark moment that indirectly confirmed the existence of gravitational waves, as the binary system exhibited orbital decay exactly as predicted by Einstein. The energy lost to gravitational radiation was compelling evidence supporting the theoretical framework that underpinned gravitational waves. This discovery rejuvenated interest in direct detection efforts, inspiring an array of researchers to embrace gravitational wave projects and to develop innovative solutions to the technological and conceptual problems that had plagued earlier endeavors.

The path to the eventual success of LIGO (Laser Interferometer Gravitational-Wave Observatory) was not merely the result of refined engineering or theoretical advancements; it also stemmed from a collaborative spirit among scientists. This collaboration transcended disciplines, drawing astrophysicists, astronomers, engineers, and computer scientists together into a cohesive unit, working tirelessly towards a common goal. Organizations formed, cross-institutional partnerships were built, and a vibrant community of scholars emerged, dedicated to overcoming the persistent challenges and skepticism surrounding gravitational waves.

Each step forward, from endurance through skepticism to breakthrough successes, was marked with intellectual risk-taking and profound passion for understanding the universe. The launch of LIGO in 2002 exemplified this spirit; it was an ambitious undertaking born from the vision shaped by early theorists and the myriad of challenges overcome in the face of continued doubt. The initial detection of gravitational waves in September 2015 was an epochal moment in science, ushering in a new era of astronomy where previously unseen phenomena were finally brought to light.

In conclusion, the early challenges and skepticism were not merely hindrances to the search for gravitational waves but rather pivotal moments that fomented a rich dialogue within the scientific community. They catalyzed groundbreaking collaborations, inspired relentless innovation, and ultimately reinforced a commitment to the pursuit of knowledge. As the scientific community transformed doubt into a clarion call for exploration, gravitational wave astronomy was born—an endeavor that continues to reveal the nuanced whispers of the universe, inviting us all to listen closely and engage with the cosmos in ways previously thought impossible. The journey from skepticism to validation serves as a testament to human perseverance, illuminating not only the waves woven through spacetime but also the boundless potential of scientific inquiry that perpetuates throughout history.

4. Modern-Day Pioneers

4.1. Reviving Einstein's Theories

In the landscape of scientific inquiry, the revival of Einstein's theories stands as a beacon of intellectual pursuit, illuminating the path from theoretical speculation to empirical reality. This renaissance is particularly evident within the realm of gravitational wave astronomy, which has breathed new life into concepts that once resided firmly in the realm of abstraction. As we delve into the intricacies of this revival, we uncover the layers of thought that connect Einstein's original insights to the extraordinary advancements in modern astrophysics, paving the way for unprecedented discoveries.

The underpinning of this revival began with the realization that Einstein's General Theory of Relativity not only redefined gravity but also proposed a dynamic interplay between space, time, and mass. Central to this theory was the idea of gravitational waves—ripples in spacetime generated by the acceleration of massive objects. Initially, these waves were considered an elegant implication of Einstein's equations, yet they faced skepticism that stemmed from both theoretical and experimental challenges. For decades, the pursuit of empirical evidence for gravitational waves was fraught with obstacles, as the faint nature of these signals meant that their detection required sensitivity beyond what was achievable with existing technology.

Yet, Einstein's vision persisted, echoed through the voices of early theorists and the collective aspirations of modern scientists. After the 1974 discovery of a binary pulsar by Russell Hulse and Joseph Taylor provided indirect evidence supporting gravitational radiation, momentum began to build within the scientific community. This marked a turning point, demonstrating that the fascination with gravitational waves was not merely theoretical; it could manifest into reality. As excitement surged, the groundwork was laid for ambitious endeavors to directly detect these elusive signals.

The establishment of LIGO (Laser Interferometer Gravitational-Wave Observatory) represented both a culmination of Einstein's ideas and a testament to human ingenuity. It wasn't simply an engineering marvel; it was a physical manifestation of a profound theoretical understanding, drawing connections between relativity, advanced engineering, and an appetite for exploration. When LIGO made its historic detection of gravitational waves in September 2015—a signal from the merger of two black holes—it marked a pivotal moment in the legitimization of Einstein's audacious predictions. The scientific community erupted in celebration, as the waves confirmed not only the existence of this phenomenon but also the robustness of the theories that had long ago been relegated to speculation.

However, the revival of Einstein's theories extends beyond mere affirmation; it opens new realms of inquiry and inquiry. Each detection of gravitational waves invites scientists to seek a deeper understanding of cosmic events, examining the parameters of black hole mergers, neutron star collisions, and even the fabric of spacetime itself. For instance, the ability to measure the mass and spin of black holes through gravitational waveforms brings unprecedented insights into stellar evolution and the dynamics of high-energy astrophysical phenomena. The waveforms serve as cosmic fingerprints, encoding information that was once unattainable and challenging existing paradigms about the lifecycle of stars.

The resurgence of interest in Einstein's theories catalyzed collaborations across disciplines, as physicists, engineers, and astronomers united around a shared goal. The creation of a global network, comprising facilities like Virgo in Europe and KAGRA in Japan, embodies the spirit of collaboration propelling the modern understanding of gravitational waves. Each new observatory enhances the collective ability to triangulate data, leading to a more comprehensive visualization of the universe's gravitational heartbeat. Moreover, this unified approach facilitates the sharing of knowledge, technology, and methodologies, providing a richer context within which to interpret the celestial signals.

As we probe deeper into the implications of gravitational waves, we encounter profound philosophical questions that echo throughout the scientific community. The revival of Einstein's theories invites contemplations about the nature of knowledge, the very fabric of reality, and humanity's relationship to the cosmos. This ongoing inquiry challenges us to reflect on the limits of our understanding, compelling us to acknowledge that even the most comprehensive theories can be vibrant, living entities subject to evolution through observation, experimentation, and innovative thinking.

In this continual process of revival and refinement, the legacy of Einstein shines brightly. It serves as a reminder that scientific knowledge is not static; rather, it thrives in the dynamic interplay of ideas, methodologies, and empirical validation. Each new discovery represents a chapter in an ever-evolving narrative as humanity strives to understand its place in the universe. The whispers of gravitational waves echo, beckoning us to listen more closely, to appreciate the interconnectedness of phenomena, and to engage in the pursuit of knowledge that transcends individual disciplines.

As technology advances and observational capacities grow, we can anticipate the emergence of new scientific revelations. The aspirations of young theorists today reflect the enduring impact of Einstein's vision, charting a course toward uncharted territories beyond the gravitational waves we currently observe. The revival of Einstein's theories serves not only to clarify past truths but also to unearth future inquiries that may redefine our understanding of the cosmos once more.

In conclusion, reviving Einstein's theories is not simply a retrospective affirmation but an active, vibrant dialogue that propels modern science forward. As we continue to explore the enigmatic world of gravitational waves, we honor Einstein's legacy while simultaneously positioning ourselves to confront the challenges and opportunities that lie ahead. Each wavering ripple across the fabric of spacetime reminds us that we are participants in an ongoing cosmic symphony —a testament to the profound beauty of discovery, curiosity, and the unyielding quest for understanding that defines humanity's relationship with the universe.

4.2. The Rise of Astrophysics

The journey of astrophysics has progressed through dynamic chapters marked by groundbreaking discoveries, innovative thinking, and an irrepressible curiosity about the universe. Emerging largely in the 20th century through the union of astronomy and physics, astrophysics seeks not only to observe celestial phenomena but also to explain the underlying mechanisms governing them. Among its many endeavors, the rise of astrophysics has been fueled by the quest to understand gravitational waves, ripples in spacetime emitted by some of the universe's most violent events, which serve as both evidence and harbingers of the interactions between massive cosmic bodies.

Astrophysics, as a distinct discipline, began coalescing as scientists grappled with reconciling celestial observations with the theoretical frameworks emerging from physics. The initial foundations were laid by early astronomers, whose meticulous records of celestial movements challenged existing models, leading to the rejection of the geocentric interpretations espoused by Aristotle and Ptolemy. Instead, Copernican heliocentrism illuminated a cosmos rich with possibilities. This transition laid the groundwork for Isaac Newton's classical mechanics, which synthesized gravitational theory and motion into a coherent description of how celestial bodies interact, thus shaping the course for future inquiry.

However, the classical paradigm would soon be challenged as scientists ventured beyond Newtonian mechanics toward a more profound understanding of gravity offered by Einstein's Relativity. Unveiling a cosmos tinted with geometric complexity, Einstein's theories imposed a new conceptual framework—gravity became understood as the curvature of spacetime influenced by mass. This radical departure from classical assumptions encouraged the scientific community to expand its horizon, paving the way for the emergence of a rigorous astrophysical science that aimed to unveil the cosmic order.

The burgeoning field of astrophysics drew heavily upon the technological advancements of the 20th century. The development of spectroscopy, radio telescopes, and later, the advent of space-based observatories transformed our understanding of the universe, allowing scientists to glean intricate details about stellar compositions, planetary systems, and cosmic microwave backgrounds. Each new instrument unveiled facets of the cosmos that had been concealed, inching humanity closer toward a comprehensive understanding of celestial processes.

In these formative years, the connections between gravity, mass, and light coalesced into a tapestry that revealed the universe's evolution. The notion of gravitational waves, while articulated in theory by Einstein, remained elusive for decades. As scientists sought to more profoundly understand catastrophic events such as supernovae and black holes, the idea of detecting the gravitational waves generated by such phenomena gained traction. However, skepticism lingered; many considered the detection of gravitational waves impossible due to their predicted faintness, lost amid cosmic and terrestrial noise.

It was the pioneering spirit of modern astrophysics that compelled researchers to undertake the monumental challenge of designing instruments capable of measuring these minute fluctuations in space-time. Initiatives like LIGO sprang to life, spearheaded by the vision of scientists who recognized the potential to listen to the universe in ways previously thought unattainable. The labor of countless interdisciplinary teams laid the groundwork for one of the most profound scientific inquiries of our time—the quest to prove the existence of gravitational waves and, by extension, unravel the stories of celestial dynamics.

The culmination of this effort materialized on September 14, 2015, as LIGO made history with its first successful detection of gravitational waves emanating from the merger of two black holes. This landmark moment heralded a new age in astrophysics, where gravitational waves transformed the way scientists engage with the universe. No longer confined to merely observing light, researchers now had access to a novel pathway for inquiry, enriching their understanding of cosmic events, stellar life cycles, and the intricate fabric of spacetime itself.

The rise of astrophysics, particularly highlighted by this newfound capability, serves as a reminder of the indefatigable human spirit that propels inquiry into the unknown. Each gravitational wave detected during subsequent observations unveils a tapestry of information that shapes our understanding of black hole formations, neutron star mergers, and even the genesis of mass itself, sparking debates around the Nature of reality, the origins of elements, and ultimately, the fate of the universe.

As we stand on the shoulders of giants from Einstein to LIGO's modern pioneers, we recognize that the evolution of astrophysics is an ongoing story—one that continues to be written as new observations challenge existing paradigms. Every whisper of a gravitational wave enhances our comprehension of the cosmos, revealing an intricate dance interwoven with physics and more profound questions about existence itself.

The ascent of astrophysics embodies a symbiotic relationship between theory and observation, advancing through each challenge, triumph, and new frontier reached. Placed in the overarching narrative of our understanding of the universe, the field strengthens the call to innovate and collaborate—a journey not undertaken alone but hand-in-hand with those who, like us, seek to unveil the mysteries that gravitational waves and all cosmic phenomena present. In this exploration of the universe's myriad secrets, we remain humble, attentive, and ready to listen to the gravitational echoes that resonate across the vastness of space and time, guiding us ever deeper into the mysteries of existence itself.

4.3. The LIGO Dream

The landscape of modern physics is illuminated by the groundbreaking exploration of gravitational waves, a pursuit that represents humanity's collective dream to understand the fabric of the cosmos. Central to this journey is the Laser Interferometer Gravitational-Wave Observatory (LIGO), an engineering marvel that translates abstract theories into tangible discoveries. The "LIGO Dream" embodies the aspirations and realities of unlocking the universe's most profound secrets using the whispers of gravitational waves, which are heralds of cataclysmic cosmic events.

The dream began as a theoretical concept, rooted in Albert Einstein's General Theory of Relativity, which posited that massive objects warp spacetime and that ripples—gravitational waves—should emanate from these events. However, for decades, this notion remained a tantalizing hypothesis, shrouded in skepticism and challenged by the limitations of contemporary technology. Scientists grappled with how to detect these incredibly subtle disturbances in the very structure of spacetime, as theorized by Einstein, illuminating a path woven with ambition, innovation, and determination.

As the scientific community sought to bring the dream into reality, researchers faced immense challenges. The physics underlying gravitational waves suggested that any detectable signal would be staggeringly weak, decaying rapidly over cosmic distances to be swallowed by the noise of the universe. Factors such as seismic activity, thermal fluctuations, and even human interference created a backdrop of noise that threatened to obscure the faint signals of gravitational waves. For experimental physicists, the task of designing instruments capable of discerning minute changes in distance was monumental, requiring an unprecedented level of sensitivity.

The visionaries behind LIGO embarked on this formidable journey, drawing together experts from diverse fields, including physics, engineering, and mathematics. Construction of the observatory began in the 1990s, with its two facilities located in Hanford, Washington, and Livingston, Louisiana, working as an interconnected network. The design hinged on the principle of laser interferometry, where beams of light travel down two perpendicular tunnels measuring over four kilometers in length. As a gravitational wave passed through Earth, it would stretch one arm while compressing the other, producing incredibly tiny fluctuations—a mere fraction of the diameter of a proton.

As the LIGO project progressed, enthusiasm for the endeavor swelled. Yet, profound skepticism lingered. The scientific community continued to debate the feasibility and practicality of detecting such faint signals. Concerns remained not only about the effectiveness of the technology but also whether gravitational waves could be observed at all. It was only through determination, rigorous experimentation, and iterative improvement of the instruments that the dream transformed into a magnificent reality.

The watershed moment for LIGO arrived on September 14, 2015, when the observatory triumphantly announced its first detection of gravitational waves originating from the merger of two black holes —an event occurring 1.3 billion light-years away. The signal, characterized by a distinctive "chirp," marked a revolutionary confirmation of Einstein's predictions and propelled the field of astrophysics into a new epoch. The scientific community celebrated this achievement, not merely for the successful detection itself but for what it represented—the validation of decades of theoretical work, engineering ingenuity, and the collaborative spirit that embraced the LIGO dream.

But LIGO's achievement transcended a singular discovery; it opened the doors to a wealth of new knowledge about the universe. Researchers began to interpret the data, gaining insights into the masses, spins, and dynamics of colliding black holes. Gravitational wave astronomy introduced a novel means to probe the hidden corners of the cosmos, revealing phenomena previously unreachable through electromagnetic observations alone. With each subsequent detection, scientists unearthed new narratives about the life cycles of stars, the formation of galaxies, and the nature of spacetime itself.

As the global community expanded, additional collaborations emerged. Facilities like the European Virgo and the Japanese KAGRA joined the network, enriching the observational capabilities and triangulating data for more accurate detections. The interconnectedness of these observatories embodied the spirit of scientific unity—a testament to the collective dream of unveiling the cosmos. Each collaboration not only enhanced sensitivity but also enabled researchers to cross-correlate events, gathering greater context regarding the astrophysical phenomena being observed.

While the LIGO dream initially focused on the mechanics of detection, the implications extend far beyond the initial scope. The ability to capture gravitational waves offers profound insights into the nature of dark matter, dark energy, and the fundamental mechanics of gravity itself. As researchers continue to investigate the implications of their findings, the pursuit remains inexhaustible. The network of observatories acts as a global "ear" tuned to the universe, inviting the scientific community to explore the mysteries that gravitational waves reveal.

The LIGO dream symbolizes more than just a scientific accomplishment—it is an inspiration for emerging generations of scientists and dreamers. It represents the culmination of human curiosity, perseverance, and ingenuity. The whispers of the universe beckon those willing to listen closely, bridging the gap between theory and reality and inviting us to engage in a shared conversation with the cosmos.

As we gaze forward into the unknown, we stand on the threshold of exciting possibilities. Plans for next-generation observatories promise to enhance detection capabilities, examining stellar phenomena at even greater resolutions. New technologies and theoretical developments will propel the narrative of gravitational waves, ensuring that the dream of comprehending the universe continues. The quest is unending, resonating with the essence of exploration, investigation, and the profound realization that the universe holds many more secrets, waiting patiently for curious minds to decode its whispers.

Within this extraordinary journey lies a vital lesson in the importance of collaboration, adaptation, and dedication to inquiry. The LIGO dream serves as a reminder that while we may pursue the unseen, we must do so together—unearthing the timeless narratives intertwined in the cosmos, waiting to be unveiled through the exquisite language of gravitational waves. The adventure remains, beckoning all who dare to listen, explore, and dive into the enigmas woven into the tapestry of existence itself.

4.4. Key Scientists and Discoverers

The landscape of gravitational wave astronomy is defined not only by its recent advancements but also by the array of brilliant minds that have shaped its trajectory. Key scientists and discoverers have laid the essential groundwork, enabling humanity to venture further into the mysteries of the universe through the lens of gravitational waves. Their contributions span a broad spectrum of scientific inquiry, theoretical prediction, and experimental ingenuity, culminating in the vibrant field that we witness today.

At the forefront of this transformative journey stands Albert Einstein, whose General Theory of Relativity fundamentally redefined our understanding of gravity. Published in 1915, Einstein's theory introduced the concept of spacetime—a four-dimensional fabric influenced by mass and energy. Crucially, it predicted the existence of gravitational waves: ripples generated by the acceleration of massive bodies that propagate through spacetime. Although Einstein himself doubted the practicality of ever detecting these waves, his theoretical vision served as a catalyst, inspiring generations of scientists to pursue their detection.

Following in Einstein's footsteps, early 20th-century physicists such as Hermann Weyl, Karl Schwarzschild, and Arthur Eddington further explored the mathematical implications of relativity. Their contributions elucidated various aspects of gravitational interactions and cosmic phenomena, setting the stage for future theoretical advancements and empirical tests. The debates and exchanges of ideas among these early theorists fostered a rigorous intellectual environment, paving the way for modern physics to embrace the complexities of gravitational waves.

Despite the momentum generated by these foundational theories, skepticism regarding gravitational waves persisted for several decades. Many in the scientific community found it challenging to reconcile the abstract predictions with tangible observational realities. This prevailing skepticism was partly rooted in the technological limitations of the time, which made the prospect of detecting such weak signals seem improbable. The convergence of theorists and experimentalists seeking empirical validation became increasingly important, catalyzing efforts aimed at overcoming the challenges tied to gravitational wave detection.

A notable breakthrough in this context emerged in the 1970s with the discovery of the binary pulsar PSR B1913+16 by Russell Hulse and Joseph Taylor. Their observations revealed that the orbit of the pulsar was decaying, precisely as predicted by Einstein's theory—an indirect confirmation of gravitational waves. This moment marked a turning point, rekindling interest in their existence and catalyzing a renewed commitment to the search for direct detection. Hulse and Taylor were awarded the Nobel Prize in Physics in 1993 for their remarkable work, which provided essential evidence supporting the theoretical framework laid out by Einstein.

As a collective vision for detecting gravitational waves gained traction, a new generation of scientists and engineers began to envision the technologies required. Pioneers such as Kip Thorne, Barry Barish, and Rainer Weiss emerged, each playing a vital role in translating the dream of LIGO into reality. These individuals not only possessed a deep understanding of theoretical physics but also exhibited extraordinary engineering prowess and collaborative spirit. Their teamwork and dedication fueled the establishment of the Laser Interferometer Gravitational-Wave Observatory, which would later achieve groundbreaking successes.

Kip Thorne, a gravitational physicist at Caltech, became instrumental in developing the scientific framework that guided LIGO's design. Thorne's foresight and leadership inspired rigorous theoretical studies that shed light on the gravitational waves expected from various cosmic events. Meanwhile, Rainer Weiss and Barry Barish contributed immeasurably to the engineering and implementation of the LIGO detectors, employing sophisticated laser interferometry techniques that would ultimately enable the detection of faint ripples in space-time.

The culmination of these efforts materialized on September 14, 2015, when LIGO made history by successfully detecting gravitational waves from the merger of two black holes. This monumental achievement not only confirmed Einstein's predictions but also elevated gravitational wave astronomy into a new realm of astrophysical inquiry. The scientific community celebrated this landmark moment, marking a transformative shift in our understanding of the universe.

Following LIGO's success, the global gravitational wave community expanded, welcoming other observatories like Virgo and KAGRA. This collaborative ecosystem altered the landscape of astrophysics, creating opportunities for researchers to share data, insights, and adopt unified approaches for further discoveries. By triangulating gravitational wave events with multiple observatories, scientists could better characterize the properties of the sources and unveil unprecedented details about their origins and life cycles.

Throughout the journey from theory to detection, the contributions of key scientists and discoverers have echoed through the corridors of physics—each insight building upon those before it. The complexity of gravitational waves necessitates an interdisciplinary approach, drawing upon the expertise of physicists, engineers, astronomers, and computational scientists. This collaborative spirit, propagated by the foundational figures in gravitational wave astronomy, continues to shine brightly as the field advances toward future discoveries.

Looking ahead, the scientific community remains poised to explore the vast richness encoded within gravitational waves. As we prepare to engage with the mysteries of the cosmos, the legacies of those pioneers who forged the path forward remind us that the quest for knowledge is ever-evolving—rooted in the collective ambition to understand the fundamental workings of our universe. The whispers of gravitational waves beckon us onward, urging future generations to listen carefully and unravel the intricate tapestry of celestial stories woven into the fabric of spacetime. Each new discovery carries with it the weight of history, fulfilling the promises made long ago by the visionary thinkers who dared to gaze into the void and imagine the unimaginable.

4.5. The Road to Validation

In the evolving narrative of gravitational wave astronomy, the road to validation has been paved with challenges, persistence, and milestones that have led to one of the most exciting paradigms in modern physics—the ability to listen to the very whispers of the universe. As we delve into this journey, we uncover the significant progress, excitement, and debates that have shaped our understanding of gravitational waves and their implications for astrophysics.

The theoretical groundwork for gravitational waves was laid by Albert Einstein, who proposed in 1916 that massive accelerating objects create ripples in the fabric of spacetime. These ripples, or gravitational waves, travel through the cosmos at the speed of light. Despite the elegance and groundbreaking nature of this theory, skepticism permeated the scientific community for decades. Many physicists barely engaged with gravitational waves, considering them as mere mathematical artifacts of a complex theory that held little bearing on observable reality.

As the 20th century progressed, experimental validation became the rallying cry for a group of dedicated scientists. They sought to bridge the gap between theoretical predictions and empirical observations. The challenge was immense; gravitational waves were predicted to be incredibly weak signals, drowned amidst the backgrounds of cosmic and terrestrial noise. Validating Einstein's vision demanded unprecedented technological advancements and innovative engineering solutions.

The search for indirect evidence began with notable breakthroughs. Perhaps the most significant was the discovery of the binary pulsar PSR B1913+16 by Russell Hulse and Joseph Taylor in 1974. The orbital decay of this pulsar system, as observed by the duo, closely matched the predictions made by Einstein's equations regarding gravitational radiation. This provided a crucial piece of evidence supporting the concept of gravitational waves, reigniting interest in the quest for direct detection and transforming the skepticism surrounding gravitational wave predictions into cautious optimism.

With this renewed interest came the realization that if gravitational waves existed, they could convey critical information about some of the universe's most dramatic events—such as the mergers of black holes or the collisions of neutron stars. These cosmic phenomena would, in theory, emit gravitational waves strong enough to be detected on Earth, serving as messengers from the depths of space. This notion galvanized a plethora of scientists and engineers, united by a common goal: to construct instruments capable of detecting these elusive signals.

This collaborative spirit found its crystallization in the Laser Interferometer Gravitational-Wave Observatory (LIGO). Initiated in the 1990s, LIGO represented a monumental engineering endeavor. Scientists, engineers, and theorists had to combine their expertise to develop a technology capable of measuring infinitesimal changes in distance—distortions on the order of one thousandth of the diameter of a proton—resulting from passing gravitational waves.

LIGO's two facilities, located in Hanford, Washington, and Livingston, Louisiana, operated as an interconnected network, utilizing laser interferometry. Here, lasers traveled down two arms arranged in a perpendicular L-shape. As a gravitational wave passed through the Earth, one arm would elongate while the other shortened, leading to a measurable change in the path of the laser beams. This ingenious design exemplified the interplay between theoretical understanding and technical achievement.

The anticipation reached a crescendo on September 14, 2015, when LIGO made its historic first detection of gravitational waves originating from the merger of two black holes, an event that took place 1.3 billion light-years from Earth. The signal, characterized by a specific "chirp," confirmed not only the existence of gravitational waves but also provided an experimental validation of Einstein's century-old predictions. The scientific community erupted in celebration, marking a watershed moment in modern physics. This verification was not simply a triumph for LIGO or gravitational wave science; it signified an important validation of Einstein's legacy, reaffirming the relevance of his theories in a contemporary context.

Following this groundbreaking detection, the excitement extended beyond LIGO. The global gravitational wave community rapidly expanded to include observatories like the European Virgo and Japan's KAGRA. These collaborations fostered a culture of shared knowledge and data analysis, allowing scientists to triangulate observations and enhance the understanding of cosmic events—each detection painting a clearer picture of the universe's most profound phenomena.

The implications of successfully validating gravitational waves extend far beyond one event. Every subsequent detection carries with it rich opportunities for scientific inquiry, illuminating aspects of black hole formation, neutron star interactions, and the evolution of galaxies. It has transformed not just our approach to astrophysics but also instilled a new appreciation for the interconnected nature of all celestial bodies, reshaping the framework within which we understand the cosmos.

At every step of the journey, the road to validation was fraught with skepticism, challenges, and a resolute dedication to overcoming them. Each success paved the way for new questions and explorations, while lingering uncertainties reminded the scientific community of the vast unknown still to be explored. As we advance in this field, the narrative continues to evolve, merging the theoretical with the empirical, and uncovering a universe rich with stories waiting to be told through the graceful motions of gravitational waves.

The journey through the road to validation serves as a testament to the human spirit—curiosity driven by an unwavering desire to understand the universe. As we listen to the cosmic whispers carried by gravitational waves, we are compelled to explore further, driven by the promise of discovery and the mysteries yet to unfold. Each echo from the cosmos is not just a signal but a reminder of the complexities that define our existence—a call to venture forth into the wonderful unknown that lies just beyond our reach.

5. The Mechanics of Mystery: Gravitational Waves Explained

5.1. Understanding Spacetime

Understanding spacetime is essential to grasping the broader implications of gravitational waves and their role within the universe. At its core, spacetime unifies the three dimensions of space with the dimension of time into a single four-dimensional continuum. This revolutionary shift in perspective, introduced by Albert Einstein through his theories of relativity, fundamentally altered how we understand not just gravity, but the very fabric of reality itself.

In classical physics, as characterized by Isaac Newton, space and time were viewed as separate entities. Space was an immutable three-dimensional stage upon which events occurred at distinct moments in time. Each concept functioned independently, allowing for a model where forces acted instantaneously across distance, unmarred by the constraints of the cosmos. However, Einstein's insights shattered this Cartesian dichotomy, weaving time into the very structure of space, thus creating a new framework where gravity manifests through the curvature of spacetime.

Einstein posited that massive objects, like stars and planets, do not simply exert gravitational force; rather, their mass warps the surrounding spacetime, creating wells in the four-dimensional fabric. To visualize this, one can imagine a trampoline with a heavy bowling ball placed in the center. The ball creates a depression, causing smaller marbles placed nearby to roll towards it, illustrating how masses influence the paths of other objects. This depiction serves as an elegant metaphor for how gravitational interactions unfold in the universe—where spacetime curvature dictates the motion of celestial bodies.

The implications of this theory are profound. Firstly, spacetime curvature informs our understanding of orbits, revealing that objects in motion are not merely following forces but are traveling along geodesics—paths defined by the curvature of spacetime itself. When celestial bodies influence each other's movement, they create dynamic relationships deeply rooted in the geometry of their environment. This revelation allows us to comprehend why planets orbit stars in predictable patterns, why comets take elongated trajectories, and why gravity governs the dance of galaxies.

Beyond mere mechanics, Einstein's conception of spacetime also intertwines with the evolution of the universe. As the cosmos expands, events shaping its history—from a supernova explosion to the merger of two black holes—send ripples through spacetime, giving rise to gravitational waves. These waves are generated during significant astronomical events where massive objects accelerate, akin to throwing a stone into a pond, resulting in concentric ripples that propagate outward.

The detection of gravitational waves then offers a direct means to observe interactions at cosmic scales, transforming how we gather information about the universe. By understanding the waveforms produced by colliding black holes or merging neutron stars, researchers can glean considerable insights into these events, including details about their masses, spins, and dynamics. The ability to detect these waves transcends traditional electromagnetic observations, which often rely on light. Gravitational waves provide access to previously unseen phenomena, thus expanding our observational capacity for understanding the universe.

Yet, the study of spacetime is not merely an academic pursuit; it possesses philosophical implications as well. The intertwining of space and time prompts us to reconsider our conception of reality itself. Can time exist independently of events occurring within spacetime? As we delve deeper into the mysteries of the cosmos illuminated by gravitational waves, we confront existential questions about the nature of causality, the limits of human understanding, and our place within an ever-evolving universe.

Furthermore, understanding spacetime invites inquiry into its properties under extreme conditions, an area where contemporary physicists are working diligently. Here, efforts aim to reconcile general relativity, which describes gravity on large scales, with quantum mechanics, which governs the behavior of particles at the subatomic level. The intersection of these two theoretical frameworks holds tantalizing possibilities for a unified theory that could reshape our understanding of forces governing the universe.

As we advance in our research, the continuing study of spacetime underpins many of the challenges faced within modern gravitational wave astronomy. Building new instruments capable of detecting ever fainter signals requires precision in measuring distortions in spacetime and understanding the implications of those distortions when related to cosmological events.

In conclusion, understanding spacetime serves as the backbone of gravitational wave astronomy, uniting concepts of motion, gravity, and cosmic evolution under a single framework. The way in which massive bodies interact, generating ripples through spacetime, not only reshapes our understanding of the cosmos but also unlocks new pathways for inquiry transcending traditional boundaries. The expanding knowledge of spacetime promises to reveal deeper truths about the universe—truths that echo through the cosmic ocean, continually beckoning humanity to listen closely and engage with the profound mysteries that remain intertwined in the fabric of reality itself.

5.2. Wave Mechanics

The concept of gravitational waves, which are ripples in the fabric of spacetime, represents a transformative leap in our understanding of the universe. To fully appreciate the complexities of these phenomena, one must first grasp the intricate mechanics that govern their behavior. This section delves into the fundamental principles of wave mechanics as they pertain to gravitational waves, exploring their generation, propagation, and interaction with the surrounding environment.

At its core, wave mechanics provides the framework for analyzing how waves, including gravitational waves, behave in various media.

In classical physics, waves are typically understood as disturbances that propagate through a medium, transferring energy from one location to another without transporting matter. This concept is epitomized in mechanical waves—such as sound waves in air or water waves on the surface of the ocean—which rely on the availability of a material medium to convey their energy. However, gravitational waves diverge from this traditional definition by requiring no medium; they travel through the vacuum of spacetime itself, defying conventional notions of wave propagation.

Gravitational waves arise as a consequence of significant changes in the distribution of mass within the universe, particularly when massive bodies accelerate. According to Einstein's General Theory of Relativity, when objects such as black holes or neutron stars collide, they create disturbances in spacetime that unfold as gravitational waves. These waves are produced by the quadrupole moment —the distribution of mass in a specific configuration—resulting in non-spherical motion. The world of gravitational wave generation is dominated by astrophysical processes characterized by extreme masses and velocities, leading to energetic events that launch waves across the cosmos.

The fundamental properties of gravitational waves can be classified according to their amplitude and frequency. While most astronomical events involving gravitational waves produce low-frequency signals, typically measured in Hertz (Hz), the actual amplitude—namely, the strain created in spacetime by the passing waves—can be extraordinarily small. For reference, the gravitational waves detected by observatories like LIGO have amplitudes on the order of 10^{-21}. To illustrate, this minuscule distortion corresponds to change in distance that is one-thousandth of the diameter of a proton over the entire length of a LIGO arm, which measures four kilometers.

Furthermore, gravitational waves carry vital information about their sources. Each wave's waveform—characterized by its frequency, amplitude, and phase—encapsulates a unique signature that provides insights into the nature of the cosmic events that generated it. For example, the "chirp" pattern seen in the waveform emitted during the coalescence of binary black holes reflects the dynamics of their fusion: a gradual increase in frequency and amplitude, followed by a sudden decrease as the merger completes. The detailed study of these waveforms empowers scientists to infer the properties of the source events, including masses, spins, and even distances to the originating systems.

As gravitational waves travel through spacetime, they exhibit remarkable resilience. Unlike electromagnetic waves, which can be absorbed or scattered by matter, gravitational waves pass through objects without interacting with them in any significant way. This characteristic grants gravitational wave astronomy an unparalleled advantage, allowing detectors located on Earth to capture signals emitted from events occurring billions of light-years away. The ability to "listen" to the universe via these waves opens a new frontier in astrophysics, providing direct access to and understanding of cosmic phenomena that would remain hidden to traditional electromagnetic observation.

The interaction of gravitational waves with spacetime also raises interesting questions regarding their propagation speed. Gravitational waves travel at the speed of light, consistent with the predictions of Einstein's theory. This fundamentally ties the behavior of gravitational waves to the principles of causality, wherein signals cannot travel faster than light, ensuring that perturbations in spacetime maintain a causal relationship with events that initiate them. The implications of this are profound; it means that gravitational wave signals can serve as real-time messengers from the depths of the universe, allowing scientists to gain insights into events as they unfold.

In summary, understanding wave mechanics within the context of gravitational waves reveals the astonishing intricacies of these cosmic messengers. The connection between their generation, propagation, and behavior embodies a fascinating interplay of energy and spacetime, challenging preconceived notions while reinforcing the astonishing predictability of the universe governed by the principles of relativity. Such insights not only invigorate our grasp of gravitational waves but also foster an ongoing dialogue between theory and experimentation—one that continues to flourish as we strive to unlock the mysteries of the cosmos. As we enhance our capabilities to detect and interpret gravitational waves, we inch closer to understanding the profound cosmic tales woven into the very structure of reality.

5.3. Types of Gravitational Waves

In the context of gravitational waves, they can be categorized into distinct types based on their origins, the dynamics involved in their generation, and the characteristics of their propagation through spacetime. Understanding these categories not only informs scientists about the nature of the sources but also enhances our ability to decipher the information encoded within the waves themselves.

One of the primary distinctions among gravitational waves involves their frequencies, which correspond to the type of astrophysical events generating them. For instance, low-frequency gravitational waves are typically produced by the slow-motion interactions of massive bodies, such as the gradual inspiral of binary neutron stars or black holes that orbit each other over extended periods. These waves may travel vast cosmic distances with relatively small amplitudes, requiring highly sensitive detectors to capture their subtle signals. Conversely, high-frequency gravitational waves, often associated with more dynamic events, manifest during catastrophic occurrences —such as the final moments of a black hole merger—leading to rapid oscillations and sharper signals.

In addition to the frequency classification, gravitational waves can be differentiated according to the specific astrophysical processes that exemplify these interactions. The mergers of black holes stand as quintessential sources, particularly noteworthy due to the immense energy released during such events. When two black holes spiral toward each other, the gravitational waves emitted encode critical information about their masses, spins, and the dynamics of their interaction. This process not only represents a fascinating area of study but also unveils broader implications for understanding the evolution of galaxies and the population of black holes in the universe.

Another notable source of gravitational waves arises from the collision of neutron stars. These dense remnants of supernova explosions exhibit unique properties, as their extremely high masses and compact nature create considerable gravitational effects. When neutron stars merge, they can give rise to both gravitational waves and electromagnetic signals—an event that is particularly exciting because it allows for cross-disciplinary studies. The detection of gravitational waves from neutron star mergers has already provided insights into the origins of heavy elements like gold and platinum, revealing the role that such cosmic events play in the broader narrative of stellar synthesis.

Moreover, the oscillations of pulsars also contribute to our understanding of gravitational waves. In binary systems, the precise timing of radio emissions from pulsars—rapidly rotating neutron stars—can be used as a tool to detect gravitational waves indirectly. Changes in the timing signatures of the pulsar's emissions may signal a dynamically evolving system influenced by gravitational waves, effectively allowing scientists to observe the effect of these waves on visible astronomical objects.

The mechanics of gravitational waves also allow researchers to categorize them based on their polarization states. The two predominant polarization modes, known as "plus" and "cross," inherently arise from the curvature of spacetime during wave propagation. Each mode produces distinct patterns of strain in spacetime, which can be analyzed through detection techniques, aiding scientists in identifying the nature of the source and determining its orientation relative to the observer.

With these classifications in mind, scientists can utilize advanced detection techniques to capture the delicate signals from varied sources, enhancing our comprehension of the universe. Observational strategies involve sophisticated modeling and data analysis that take into account the specific characteristics of the signals expected from different gravitational wave sources. Each wave detected can yield rich information, telling stories of catastrophic events that shaped the cosmos, and offering insights into the fundamental physics governing these interactions.

Ultimately, the study of gravitational waves is not merely an exercise in classification; it represents an expansive realm of inquiry, inviting scientists to explore beyond our current boundaries. As the technology improves and our understanding deepens, the exploration of diverse types of gravitational waves promises to broaden our comprehension of the cosmos, unveiling the interconnectedness of phenomena that have lain hidden for millennia. Each wave detected becomes a key to unlocking the mysteries of the universe, compelling us to listen closely to the stories they carry, and inviting us to venture into a narratives woven into the fabric of spacetime itself.

5.4. Sources of Gravitational Waves

Gravitational waves, as envisioned through the lens of modern astrophysics, arise from some of the most cataclysmic events in the universe, offering vital clues to understanding the complex dynamics of celestial bodies. These waves are generated by a variety of processes involving the acceleration and interaction of massive objects. Each source of gravitational waves adds a layer to the intricate tapestry of our cosmos, revealing the underlying physics that govern stellar behavior and cosmic evolution. Understanding these sources not only affirms the principles outlined by Einstein's general relativity but also opens new avenues for exploration and inquiry.

One of the most significant sources of gravitational waves is the merger of binary systems, particularly those involving black holes and neutron stars. When two massive objects orbit each other, their gravitational interaction gradually causes them to lose energy, spiraling inward until they ultimately collide. This process can generate immense gravitational waves, with the most notable signature being the "chirp," a characteristic rising and falling tone that reflects the increasing frequency and amplitude of waves emitted as the objects approach their inevitable merger. The recent observations of black hole mergers have confirmed the existence of these waves, linking the phenomena directly to the dramatic processes unfolding at the heart of black hole creation.

Neutron star collisions represent another fascinating source of gravitational waves. Neutron stars, the remnants of supernovae, possess extraordinary density, resulting in considerable gravitational effects. When two neutron stars spiral toward each other, they create gravitational waves that can be detected by facilities such as LIGO and Virgo. The 2017 detection of the merger of two neutron stars not only confirmed the presence of gravitational waves but also coincided with electromagnetic observations of a kilonova, shedding light on the origins of heavy elements like gold and platinum. This convergence of gravitational and electromagnetic phenomena underscores the importance of multi-messenger astronomy, where the combination of different observation methods enriches our understanding of cosmic events.

Furthermore, rapid changes in mass distribution—such as supernova explosions—can also generate gravitational waves. In these instances, the asymmetric explosion of a massive star leads to rapid acceleration of the surrounding mass, producing gravitational waves that carry information about the explosion dynamics and the structure of the progenitor star. By studying the gravitational waves emitted from these cataclysmic events, scientists can glean insights into star formation processes, the lifecycle of massive stars, and the role of supernovae in galactic evolution.

Another intriguing source lies in the pulsar population. Pulsars, which are highly magnetized, rotating neutron stars that emit beams of electromagnetic radiation, can be employed in gravitational wave detection through timing measurements. When pulsars exist in binary systems, their precise rotation can be affected by passing gravitational waves, leading to observable changes in their timing signals. While these signals may be faint and indirect, they offer another avenue for validating theories surrounding gravitational waves and expanding the catalog of potential sources.

Additionally, gravitational waves can emanate from the early universe, particularly from phenomena associated with cosmic inflation or phase transitions during the Big Bang. These primordial gravitational waves, although challenging to detect, hold clues to the very origins of our universe, influencing theories regarding cosmological growth and the formation of large-scale structures.

As we continue to enhance our detection capabilities—including improvements in interferometry and the development of future space-based observatories—the potential to discover new sources of gravitational waves grows exponentially. Continuous advancements in technology will not only refine our existing measurement tools but also elevate our understanding of these celestial phenomena, shedding light on the events that shape the very fabric of spacetime.

In summary, the sources of gravitational waves are diverse and profound, each revealing key insights into the operations of the cosmos. By studying the intricate dynamics associated with these waves, researchers are piecing together a richer narrative of cosmic evolution, deepening our understanding of the fundamental forces that bind our universe. Gravitational waves serve as both messengers from the cosmic distance and key components for unraveling the complex interplay of events that have defined the evolutionary course of our universe. As we remain attentive to these cosmic echoes, we stand poised to discover even larger stories hidden within the fabric of spacetime, waiting to be uncovered through the whispers of gravity.

5.5. The Mathematical Language

In the realm of physics, particularly in the study of gravitational waves, mathematics serves as the fundamental language through which the intricate workings of the universe can be articulated. The mathematical framework of gravitational waves is embedded deeply in the structure of Einstein's General Theory of Relativity, which provides the necessary tools to describe the curvature of spacetime and the dynamical phenomena resulting from massive bodies and their interactions. This subchapter seeks to delineate the essential mathematical concepts that underpin our understanding of gravitational waves, elucidating how these abstract structures manifest in the physical world.

To begin with, the cornerstone of gravitational wave theory resides in Einstein's field equations. These equations, expressed as $G\mu\nu = 8\pi G T\mu\nu/c^4$, relate the geometry of spacetime (represented by the Einstein tensor $G\mu\nu$) to the energy and momentum of matter within that spacetime (described by the energy-momentum tensor $T\mu\nu$). Here, G is the gravitational constant, c is the speed of light, and μ and ν denote different spacetime coordinates. Within this elegant equation lies the profound insight that gravitation is not simply a force; rather, it emerges through the fabric and structure of spacetime itself.

In order to extract meaningful predictions from these equations concerning gravitational waves, we utilize a linearized approach. This involves perturbing the metric tensor $g\mu\nu$ that describes spacetime into a flat Minkowski background metric and a small perturbation $h\mu\nu$, such that $g\mu\nu = \eta\mu\nu + h\mu\nu$, where $|h\mu\nu| \ll 1$. The perturbation represents gravitational waves traveling through spacetime, and by substituting this form into the field equations, we derive linearized equations that describe the propagation of these waves. Importantly, it leads to the conclusion that gravitational waves propagate at the speed of light, confirming one of Einstein's critical predictions.

To characterize the waves themselves, we analyze their polarization states, which are inherent in the tensor nature of gravitational waves. Mathematical analysis reveals two distinct polarization modes: the 'plus' (h+) and 'cross' (h×) polarizations. Each polarization manifests itself in how spacetime is stretched and compressed as the waves pass through. For a gravitational wave traveling in the z-direction, these polarizations can be described mathematically as follows:

$h+(t, z) = A(t-z/c)$ and $h\times(t, z) = B(t-z/c)$,

where A and B are functions related to the amplitude of each polarization, incorporating temporal changes. This representation effectively captures how gravitational waves oscillate in spacetime, producing characteristic changes in the distances between objects on Earth when such waves traverse our planet.

Moreover, the mathematical characteristics of gravitational waves can be studied through Fourier analysis. The Fourier transform allows us to express the time-varying signal of detected gravitational waves, converting the signal into a frequency domain representation. This transformation reveals vital information about the frequency and amplitude spectrum of the waves, enabling scientists to differentiate and analyze various sources of gravitational waves, such as merging black holes or neutron stars.

The detection of gravitational waves via laser interferometry, the technique employed at observatories like LIGO, roots itself firmly within mathematical methodology. The interference pattern of light beams manipulated by minute changes in arm lengths due to passing gravitational waves can be modeled using linear algebra and wave principles. The fundamental change in the path length is represented mathematically and translates to observable data that researchers analyze to infer events occurring billions of light-years away.

Furthermore, the study of gravitational waves has necessitated advanced statistical methodologies for signal processing. Given that many sources of noise can interfere with gravitational wave signals, the analysis requires keen statistical techniques to discriminate between genuine signals and background noise. This has led scientists to employ Bayesian inference and other probabilistic approaches to establish the likelihood of events, ensuring that the claims made regarding gravitational wave detection are robust and verifiable.

The evolution of the mathematical language surrounding gravitational waves does not exist in isolation. It has implications for interconnected disciplines within physics. The dialogue between mathematics and physical realities fosters advancements in theoretical physics, astrophysics, and cosmology, ultimately reflecting a beautiful reciprocity: as we deepen our mathematical understanding, we gain more profound insights into the mysteries of the universe.

Importantly, the mathematical language employed to describe gravitational waves also extends into philosophical realms. Questions about the nature of reality, the dimensionality of spacetime, and the very fabric of existence stem from the mathematical frameworks we have developed. Engaging with these principles incites consideration not just of what we can observe, but of the very mechanisms that underlie the existence of the cosmos and its governing laws.

In summary, the mathematical language underpinning the study of gravitational waves is essential for articulating the complexities of spacetime interactions caused by massive bodies and their cataclysmic events. It serves as both a tool for detection and a bridge to deeper philosophical considerations about our place in the universe. As we continue to refine our mathematical constructs and apply them to the vast array of gravitational phenomena, we shape our understanding, listen intently to the whispers of the cosmos, and remain ever mindful of the intricate, interwoven stories that gravitational waves tell about the fabric of reality itself.

6. Eavesdropping on the Universe

6.1. Gravitational Wave Observatories

Gravitational wave observatories stand as testaments to human ingenuity, embodying the convergence of theoretical physics, innovative engineering, and collaborative spirit. These facilities are meticulously designed to detect the faintest ripples in the fabric of spacetime, allowing us to unlock previously hidden stories of the universe. The pioneering endeavor to establish these observatories took shape due to the revolutionary predictions made by Albert Einstein in his General Theory of Relativity, which posited that the collision and merger of massive cosmic bodies could create detectable gravitational waves. What initially began as theoretical speculation has evolved into a formidable scientific enterprise.

The first major gravitational wave observatory to come online was the Laser Interferometer Gravitational-Wave Observatory (LIGO), which became operational in the early 2000s. LIGO consists of two facilities located in Hanford, Washington, and Livingston, Louisiana, each designed to work in tandem. Utilizing laser interferometry, LIGO measures changes in distances between mirrors placed at the ends of two perpendicular arms, each spanning 4 kilometers. The fundamental principle involves sending laser beams down these arms; if a gravitational wave passes through Earth, it will cause a minuscule difference in the distances, resulting in a measurable interference pattern. LIGO's sophisticated engineering has placed it at the forefront of gravitational wave detection, allowing it to first confirm the existence of gravitational waves in 2015 when it captured the waveforms from a binary black hole merger.

Following LIGO's groundbreaking achievements, other gravitational wave observatories were established around the globe. Notable among them is the Virgo observatory, located near Pisa, Italy. Virgo operates under similar principles to LIGO but with increased sensitivity, aided by its larger size (3 kilometers per arm) and advanced technology. Its collaboration with LIGO creates a network of observatories that aids in refining the parameters of gravitational wave sources, improving the precision of detections and the subsequent analysis of cosmic events.

The GEO600 observatory, located in Germany, further complements this network. Though smaller in scale, GEO600 employs state-of-the-art techniques to enhance sensitivity. Its contributions to the calibration and refinement of detection methods are invaluable, serving as a testbed for innovations that can be integrated into larger observatories like LIGO.

As gravitational wave astronomy advances, the methodologies employed in detection are continuously refined. Stringent detection methods are vital to discern genuine signals from the pervasive background noise created by seismic activity, thermal fluctuations, and even human activities. Techniques such as feedforward control, where noise is actively mitigated using advanced algorithms, enhance the observatories' capabilities, allowing physicists to detect gravitational waves more effectively.

The global network of gravitational wave observatories exemplifies a spirit of scientific collaboration. This interconnected system strengthens the ability to achieve what individual observatories cannot, as information from multiple locations contributes to better mapping the sources of gravitational waves. When a gravitational wave event is detected by one observatory, the data can be supplemented and confirmed by others, creating a robust classification of the cosmic event and enabling a deeper understanding of the phenomena involved.

In addition to these terrestrial observatories, future plans for space-based gravitational wave detectors, such as the Laser Interferometer Space Antenna (LISA), aim to provide even greater sensitivity over a broader frequency range. This future observatory will revolutionize our ability to study low-frequency gravitational waves, potentially unveiling new sources such as those from the early universe or supermassive black hole mergers.

The evolving landscape of gravitational wave observatories represents not just a technological marvel, but a profound enterprise that reshapes our understanding of the cosmos. Each detection leads to a cascade of insights—teasing apart the mysteries of black hole formation, neutron star behavior, and cosmic evolution. As these observatories continue to listen to the whispers of the universe, they underscore a central theme of modern science: through collaboration and innovation, humanity can uncover the profound stories hidden within the cosmic tapestry, pushing the boundaries of knowledge ever further into the depths of spacetime.

6.2. The LIGO Breakthrough

The breakthrough achieved by the Laser Interferometer Gravitational-Wave Observatory (LIGO) in 2015 marked a monumental milestone in the field of astrophysics and heralded the dawn of a new era in gravitational wave astronomy. This revolutionary endeavor was not merely a scientific achievement; it symbolized humanity's enduring quest to listen to the whispers of the universe and unravel the complexities of its most enigmatic phenomena. The detection of gravitational waves from the merger of two black holes unleashed a torrent of excitement, validating a century-old prediction from Albert Einstein and unveiling a wealth of knowledge about the intricate workings of the cosmos.

LIGO's first detection on September 14, 2015, was the culmination of years of collaborative effort, ingenuity, and unwavering dedication from a community of scientists, engineers, and researchers. The gravitational waves emitted during the merger of these massive black holes carried vital information encoded in their waveforms—the frequencies, amplitudes, and patterns spoke to the characteristics of the colossal bodies involved and their cataclysmic interactions. As the signals arrived at Earth, they were meticulously analyzed, revealing the masses of the black holes and their distance from our planet, cementing the significance of this extraordinary achievement.

The event ignited a new branch of astrophysics, one that emphasizes the study of violent cosmic events through the lens of gravitational waves. Just as electromagnetic spectrum observations have enriched our understanding of the universe, the detection of gravitational waves promises to provide new insight into the life cycles of stars, the formation of black holes, and the mysteries surrounding supernova explosions. The ability to detect such waves opens avenues to investigate phenomena that were previously unnoticed, allowing scientists to probe deeper into the fabric of reality itself.

LIGO's breakthrough revolutionized the scientific landscape and initiated an era of collaboration among gravitational wave observatories worldwide. Observatories such as Virgo in Europe and KAGRA in Japan joined the network, creating an interconnected web that enhances detection capabilities. This global collaboration enriches the pursuit of knowledge and fosters a collective spirit of inquiry, bridging continents and disciplines.

In addition to the excitement surrounding detection, the implications of LIGO's breakthrough extend into fundamental physics. Gravitational waves bring into question established theories and challenge scientists to refine their models of the universe. Through the analysis of waveforms and the data derived from multiple observatories, researchers seek to better understand the intricacies of black hole dynamics and the gravitational interactions that govern the cosmos.

Furthermore, LIGO's accomplishment has propelled gravitational wave astronomy to the forefront of public consciousness. It serves as a symbol for future generations of scientists, embodying the profound potential of curiosity and scientific exploration. The success of LIGO not only represents a validation of years of hard work but also inspires a sense of wonder, inviting a broader audience to engage with astronomical discoveries and participate in the journey of unveiling the universe's secrets.

As LIGO continues to operate and new discoveries arise, the potential for further breakthroughs remains immense. Each detection of gravitational waves heralds a new chapter in our understanding of the universe, promising to elucidate the mysteries surrounding the formation and evolution of celestial bodies while providing crucial insights into the fundamental laws governing reality. The whispers of the universe, once silent, are now being heard. The breakthroughs realized through LIGO and its successors stand as a testament to the enduring journey of scientific discovery—an invitation to listen, explore, and join the cosmic dialogue that persists across the vastness of spacetime.

The LIGO breakthrough not only reshaped our understanding of gravitational waves but also laid the groundwork for future explorations. As the scientific community delves into the cascade of data produced by these observations, each detection becomes a guidepost, pointing toward new inquiries and fostering a collaborative spirit that transcends borders and boundaries. The waves, once theoretical, have now become tangible echoes of cosmic events, beckoning us to continue questioning, exploring, and listening closely to the universe's symphony. As we stand at the precipice of discovery, propelled by the lessons learned from the LIGO breakthrough, we glimpse a future rich with possibilities, awaiting those brave enough to listen and unveil the mysteries woven into the very fabric of existence.

6.3. Virgo and GEO600

Virgo and GEO600 represent critical threads in the tapestry of gravitational wave observatories, each contributing to the rich narrative surrounding the detection and analysis of gravitational waves. These observatories not only bolster the existing framework established by LIGO but also usher in new possibilities for understanding the intricate resonances of the universe.

Virgo, located in Italy near Pisa, is a prominent member of the global network of gravitational wave detectors. With its design closely following LIGO's, Virgo features a similar laser interferometry technique to detect ripples in spacetime. However, its innovative design incorporates some unique features aimed at improving sensitivity and reducing noise. The observatory is larger than its LIGO counterparts, boasting arms that span 3 kilometers, and has been engineered to minimize seismic vibrations and thermal fluctuations that could obscure potential gravitational wave signals. This emphasis on enhanced sensitivity enables Virgo to work in tandem with LIGO, providing complementary data that enriches the understanding of gravitational wave events.

The collaboration between LIGO and Virgo fosters a powerful synergy in gravitational wave astronomy. When a signal is detected by one observatory, the second can verify the event, improving the accuracy of measurements and providing triangulated information regarding the location and characteristics of the source. This cooperation is nothing short of essential; many of the key detections in recent years have emerged from joint observations, allowing scientists to better map the events taking place across vast expanses of the cosmos.

Similarly, the GEO600 observatory in Germany has emerged as an important player in this expanding network. While physically smaller than Virgo and LIGO, GEO600 employs cutting-edge technology designed to push the boundaries of detection sensitivity. The facility utilizes advanced techniques, including highly sensitive optical components and innovative suspension systems, which are crucial for canceling out noise and enhancing the observatory's capacity to detect minute signals. It acts as a testbed for new methodologies and technologies, providing valuable insights that can be applied to larger observatories.

Each of these observatories plays a vital role in addressing the challenges inherent in gravitational wave detection. The collaborative efforts among LIGO, Virgo, and GEO600 exemplify a spirit of unity and shared ambition within the scientific community. This global network not only enhances the methodologies utilized for detection but also promotes an interdisciplinary exchange of ideas and expertise, facilitating the advancement of gravitational wave physics and the underlying principles of astrophysics.

As researchers strive to elevate detection capabilities, the explorations of Virgo and GEO600 merge into broader plans for the future —such as the establishment of additional observatories and space-based detectors like LISA (Laser Interferometer Space Antenna). The significance of these initiatives cannot be understated; as detection sensitivity improves, areas of the universe previously obscured by limitations in our observational toolbox may emerge into clarity.

Indeed, the evolution of gravitational wave observatories like Virgo and GEO600 exemplifies the relentless pursuit of knowledge within the astronomical community. Each facility contributes to a collective mission history that encompasses both the observation of spectacular cosmic events and the subsequent analysis that informs our understanding of the fundamental laws governing the universe.

In summary, Virgo and GEO600 are more than mere observatories; they represent vital components within the ever-expanding framework of gravitational wave astronomy. Through innovation, collaboration, and continuous refinement of detection methods, these facilities stand poised to transform our perceptions of the cosmos, inviting the scientific community—and humanity at large—to listen ever more intently to the gravitational rhythms that ripple through the very fabric of spacetime. Through this collective endeavor, the voices of the universe are no longer merely whispers; they are bold proclamations, urging us to understand and explore the grand narrative stretching across the vast cosmos.

6.4. Stringent Detection Methods

In the realm of gravitational wave astronomy, stringent detection methods are at the forefront of transforming theoretical predictions into observable realities. These methods embody a disciplined blend of physics, engineering, and mathematics, designed meticulously to unravel the faint whispers of gravitational waves traversing the fabric of spacetime. To appreciate the sophistication and complexity of these detection mechanisms, we must delve into the intricate methodologies that have emerged to confront the challenge posed by the exceedingly subtle signals of gravitational waves, positioning them against a backdrop of relentless terrestrial noise.

At the heart of gravitational wave detection is the fundamental principle of laser interferometry, a technique that serves as the backbone for facilities like LIGO and Virgo. Laser interferometers measure changes in distance with extraordinary precision, making them exquisitely sensitive instruments for detecting minute variations in spacetime caused by the passage of gravitational waves. When these waves travel through Earth, one arm of the interferometer stretches while the other compresses; the result is an interference pattern indicative of a change in the relative length of each arm. However, the amplitude of the waves expected from astronomical events is so minuscule—often less than the width of a proton—that specialized techniques are essential to distinguish genuine signals from the background noise.

Detecting gravitational waves necessitates rigorous engineering and innovative designs aimed at minimizing environmental interference. These observatories must contend with various noise sources, including seismic activity, thermal fluctuations, and even fluctuations in the laser light itself. To mitigate these disturbances, a combination of sophisticated vibration isolation systems and active noise cancellation techniques are employed. Seismic isolation employs pendulum systems, which shield sensitive equipment from ground vibrations, while advanced feedback systems dynamically adjust parameters to counteract detected noise, ensuring the clarity of the signals received.

The quest for heightened sensitivity has driven researchers to optimize various components of detection systems. One area of significant focus is the laser source itself. Utilizing high-power, frequency-stabilized lasers enhances the signal-to-noise ratio and enables the observatories to capture the faintest waves. Additionally, the design of the mirrors, which must withstand both the intense gravitational forces and maintain stability, is curated with extreme precision—a measure that directly impacts detection capabilities.

Temperature control also plays a crucial role in the accuracy of measurements, particularly in the context of quantum noise. Observatories maintain ultra-cold environments to ensure the thermal noise does not obscure potential gravitational wave signals. Advanced cooling systems utilize cryogenic technologies that lower the temperature of the mirrors and suspensions, significantly enhancing their performance. The combination of lower thermal vibrations and improved optical quality leads to optimal measurement conditions that elevate sensitivity to potential gravitational wave events.

Moreover, the advent of quantum sensing has emerged as a game-changer in the arsenal for gravitational wave detection. Utilizing the principles of quantum mechanics, scientists are developing techniques like squeezed light—where the uncertainty in one quantum property (either position or momentum) is reduced, thereby enhancing measurement sensitivity. This innovative approach addresses the seemingly insurmountable challenges posed by quantum noise, opening new avenues for capturing faint signals from distant astrophysical events.

As gravitational wave astronomy continues to evolve, ongoing advancements in detection methodologies promise to push the boundaries of what is possible. The development of next-generation observatories, such as the proposed LISA (Laser Interferometer Space Antenna), aims to venture into space, further enhancing sensitivity and expanding the observable frequency range of gravitational waves. A space-based configuration is advantageous, as it circumvents many terrestrial noise sources, allowing scientists to probe phenomena that were previously unreachable.

In summary, stringent detection methods lie at the intersection of scientific ingenuity and engineering prowess, transforming the abstract concepts of gravitational waves into concrete observations. Each refinement in technique enhances our capability to listen to the universe, unveiling the hidden stories woven into the fabric of space-time. As we continue to grapple with and refine these methodologies, we ultimately reaffirm humanity's profound desire to understand the cosmos, translating the elusive whispers of gravitational waves into profound insights that resonate across the universe. The relentless pursuit of discovery underscores the spirit of scientific exploration, driving us to innovate continually as we endeavor to decipher the complex melodies that gravitational waves impart.

6.5. The Global Network

In today's interconnected scientific landscape, the pursuit of knowledge transcends geographical borders, forming an intricate web of collaboration and shared intellect that fuels the exploration of gravitational waves. The global network of gravitational wave observatories stands as a testament to human ingenuity and collective ambition, integrating resources, expertise, and technological advancements into a cohesive effort to unlock the secrets of the universe.

As the foundational endeavor for direct detection of gravitational waves, the Laser Interferometer Gravitational-Wave Observatory (LIGO) has catalyzed the formation of this global community. LIGO, with its facilities in Hanford, Washington, and Livingston, Louisiana, serves as the flagship observatory, its successful detections laying the groundwork for other institutions around the world to engage in similar pursuits. The announcement of the first detection of gravitational waves in 2015 sparked unprecedented interest and collaboration, leading to the establishment of a broader international network of observatories.

Key among these is the Virgo observatory, situated in Italy, which employs laser interferometry akin to LIGO but is designed with unique enhancements to mitigate environmental noise and improve sensitivity. The synergy born from the collaboration between LIGO and Virgo allows for simultaneous observations, improving the accuracy of measurements and expanding the capacity to triangulate the location of gravitational wave events. This cooperative effort exemplifies the principle of synergy in scientific discovery—together, the observatories achieve results far surpassing what could have been accomplished in isolation.

Another important player in this global concert is KAGRA, located in Japan, which features a unique underground design and cryogenic technology aimed at reducing noise and enhancing sensitivity. By integrating advanced instrumentation and employing innovative approaches, KAGRA represents the next evolution in gravitational wave detection, demonstrating how international collaborations transcend individual institutional efforts. The scientific community recognizes that each observatory, with its unique architectural adaptation and technological advances, contributes distinctly to the shared mission of unveiling cosmic phenomena.

The foundation of the global network goes beyond hardware and infrastructure; it encompasses the pooling of intellectual resources, data sharing, and collaborative research efforts. When a gravitational wave event is detected, observatories can analyze and compare their data, cross-referencing findings to ensure robustness and reliability. Each instance of cooperation between LIGO, Virgo, KAGRA, and other emerging observatories enhances the collective ability to probe the depths of spacetime, mapping out the intricate tapestry of cosmic interactions that give rise to these ephemeral signals.

The significance of this global framework extends to outreach and education as well. Engaging with the public fosters interest in gravitational wave astronomy and science more broadly, drawing upon the power of citizen science programs. By harnessing the collective enthusiasm of individuals across the world, the scientific community can promote a deeper understanding of the cosmos, encouraging a new generation of aspiring scientists to participate in this grand endeavor.

Moreover, the philosophy of scientific unity embodied in the global network of gravitational wave observatories is not without its challenges. Efficient data sharing requires the ongoing development of robust systems and agreements to maintain cybersecurity and protect proprietary research. Navigating the complexities of international collaborations can also present logistical hurdles, necessitating careful communication and aligned goals among global partners. These challenges must be actively managed to foster continued collaboration as the field evolves.

A future filled with potential lies ahead for the global gravitational wave network. As technological capabilities expand, aspiring observatories are being developed in various locales, all aiming to join this vibrant community, increasing detection capacity and sensitivity. The next generation of observatories, such as proposed space-based detectors like LISA (Laser Interferometer Space Antenna), promises to enhance detection capabilities dramatically while opening new frontiers in our understanding of the universe.

The essence of the global gravitational wave network is rooted in its capacity to connect scientific minds and forge stronger paths toward discovery. It illustrates the idea that when scientists unite against the backdrop of the cosmos, they can achieve remarkable feats of exploration and understanding. The global endeavor invites collaboration, enabling scientists to learn from each other while sharing knowledge, data, and resources to address the ultimate questions of existence—questions that have lingered since the dawn of humanity's curiosity.

As we listen to the gravitational waves generated by cataclysmic cosmic events, we are reminded of our place within the vast universe. The echoes of these waves reverberate not just through spacetime but through the interconnected network of scientific exploration, inviting us all to join in this extraordinary journey of discovery, transcending borders as we come together to unveil the mysteries of gravity's ghosts. The collaborative spirit embodies a profound vision: that through unity, humanity can aspire to explore and understand the celestial spheres, listening attentively to the complex interplay of forces that shape the cosmos.

7. Technological Marvels: Engineering the Future

7.1. Innovations in Detection

In the evolution of gravitational wave detection, innovative techniques have emerged that have fundamentally changed our understanding of these enigmatic phenomena. Each advancement has built upon the insights and objectives driving scientists toward the ambitious goal of detecting and interpreting the whispers of the cosmos. The journey through innovations in detection focuses on not just technological achievements but also conceptual breakthroughs that have collectively forged the path for this cutting-edge field.

One cornerstone of detecting gravitational waves is laser interferometry, which forms the framework of leading observatories like LIGO and Virgo. This technique leverages the principle of light interference to measure incredibly small variations in distance, allowing researchers to sense the distortions caused by passing gravitational waves. At its heart, the method utilizes two long, perpendicular arms, where lasers are sent down each path and reflected back by highly polished mirrors. When a gravitational wave reaches the Earth, it stretches one arm's length while compressing the other, leading to observable shifts in the interference pattern of the combined light beams.

This innovative approach was revolutionary; however, creating a detector capable of capturing such faint and fleeting signals posed significant technical challenges. The quest for high sensitivity led to advances in optics, where researchers developed sophisticated laser systems capable of achieving exceptional power and stability. In particular, frequency-stabilized lasers have become instrumental in enhancing the signal-to-noise ratio, allowing for clearer signal detection amidst the tumult of environmental noise.

As the search continued, researchers turned to super-sensitive equipment designed to tackle the significant challenges imposed by noise. Terrestrial vibrations, thermal noise, and even gravitational noise from distant cosmic sources contribute to an overwhelming background that can obscure gravitational wave signals. Reducing these interference factors has become crucial for successful detection, leading to the implementation of cutting-edge noise-reducing mechanisms, such as seismic isolation systems. These systems employ pendulum designs to decouple the mirrors from the ground, preserving their stability and protecting against fluctuations that could distort measurements.

In tandem with these efforts, the observatories' operational environments have been carefully controlled, with a keen focus on maintaining cooler temperatures. The presence of thermal noise can obscure faint signals, prompting experiments aimed at cooling various components using advanced thermal management systems. Cooling techniques enhance the detectors' overall performance, achieving conditions that allow for reduced vibrations, improving the likelihood of capturing gravitational waves.

Quantum sensing, an area undergoing rapid development, has also emerged as a promising frontier for gravitational wave detection. By utilizing the principles of quantum mechanics, researchers explore novel methodologies like squeezed light, which reduces uncertainty in measurements by manipulating the quantum state of light. Squeezed states enhance sensitivity, enabling scientists to discern gravitational wave signals that would otherwise vanish into background noise.

Continued advancements in technology also hold potential for the future of gravitational wave detection. Proposals for next-generation observatories aim to enhance sensitivity and expand the range of detectable frequencies, allowing scientists to observe a broader array of events. Space-based observatories, such as LISA (Laser Interferometer Space Antenna), will offer a significant leap forward by circumventing terrestrial noise altogether. By positioning detectors in space, researchers hope to capture low-frequency gravitational waves from supermassive black hole mergers and other cosmic phenomena that remain largely inaccessible from the ground.

As we venture further into this ambitious journey, the future of gravitational wave detection brims with opportunities and challenges. The innovations in detection reflect not only the human endeavor to push the boundaries of knowledge but also the collaborative spirit that drives intense interdisciplinary exploration. By integrating advancements across engineering, physics, and computer science, researchers continue their quest to listen closely to the universe, discerning the cosmic symphony of gravitational waves that resonate through the vastness of spacetime.

This narrative of innovation encapsulates the essence of discovery—an invitation to explore, to question, and to evolve. Each breakthrough brings us closer to unveiling the intricate stories hidden within the fabric of reality, reminding us that the cosmos holds profound mysteries just waiting to be revealed, echoing softly through the tendrils of gravity's whispers. In this realm of relentless pursuit, we are propelled not only by technological aspirations but by a fundamental curiosity that propels humanity to understand its place in the universe and the secrets that lie beyond.

7.2. Laser Interferometry

Laser interferometry is a pivotal technique in the realm of gravitational wave detection, formed through an intricate interplay of scientific principles, cutting-edge technology, and engineering ingenuity. At its core, this method utilizes the fundamental properties of light and relies on the precise measurement of distance changes induced by gravitational waves as they propagate through spacetime. The emergence of laser interferometry has not only brought forth the capability to detect these elusive cosmic ripples but also transformed our understanding of the universe itself.

The foundation of laser interferometry lies in the manipulation of laser beams to perform interferometric measurements. Specifically, configurations like LIGO and Virgo employ a design where coherent light beams are split and sent down two long, perpendicular arms of equal length. The interference of these beams allows researchers to detect changes in distance so minuscule that they are paradoxical to our sensory experiences. When a gravitational wave passes through, it warps spacetime, altering the lengths of these arms differently—one arm will stretch while the other compresses. This differential change results in an observable interference pattern that is indicative of gravitational wave passage.

In the context of LIGO, which stretches across 4 kilometers in each arm, the sensitivity required is astronomical. The goal is to measure fractional changes in distance on the order of one part in 10^{21}—about a thousandth the diameter of a proton. Achieving this remarkable level of precision requires sophisticated technological enhancements, including ultra-stable laser systems, high-quality optical components, and advanced data analysis techniques. The laser's stability is paramount, as any fluctuations could introduce noise that masks genuine signals. This challenge has driven researchers to develop advanced frequency stabilization methods for the lasers and to implement refined optical techniques, ensuring that the instruments can discriminate between gravitational wave signals and environmental noise.

An indispensable component of laser interferometry is the careful calibration and alignment of the system. The mirrors used to reflect the laser beams must be suspended in such a way that they are insulated from external vibrations, thermal expansions, and magnetic interferences. This necessitates the use of pendulum-like suspension systems designed to filter out seismic noise and to maintain the alignment of the optics. These measures enable a highly controlled environment conducive to detecting the faintest signals from the cosmos.

Moreover, the advancement of laser interferometry is intertwined with the challenges posed by thermal noise. The very components of the interferometer generate heat, which in turn can influence measurements. Addressing this has involved maintaining the operational temperature at a specific range, thus minimizing the effects of temperature fluctuations on the system's sensitivity. Creative engineering solutions, like the deployment of cryogenically cooled mirrors and innovative thermal shields, have emerged to combat these challenges.

In addition to these engineering feats, researchers continually innovate by leveraging recent advancements in quantum technologies. Techniques such as squeezed light—manipulating the quantum states of photons to reduce uncertainty in one variable—have emerged as groundbreaking improvements. By employing squeezed light, observatories can amplify their sensitivity and enhance their capability to detect faint gravitational wave signals amidst the background noise. This evolution highlights an ongoing dialogue between theory and experimental design, continuously pushing boundaries and enhancing what is possible.

Laser interferometry's profound success in detecting gravitational waves calls for an international response in building additional observatories to expand this capability further. Future missions will broaden the frequency range of gravitational wave detection, with plans for space-based projects such as the Laser Interferometer Space Antenna (LISA). These forthcoming endeavors will enhance sensitivity beyond terrestrial constraints, opening doors to detecting lower-frequency gravitational waves and bringing the hidden aspects of the universe into clearer focus.

In conclusion, laser interferometry stands as a pivotal technological marvel, intricately designed and meticulously refined, enabling the detection of gravitational waves and the ability to comprehend the universe's most dramatic events. Throughout its development, it has exemplified the relationship between cutting-edge technological innovation and profound scientific inquiry. As researchers continue to refine this method and explore new frontiers, the echoes of gravitational waves will unveil the intricate stories that encapsulate our understanding of the cosmos. Each successful detection serves as an invitation to journey further into the unknown, where the whispers of gravitational waves continue to call for attention, reminding humanity of the beautifully intricate tapestry woven across the vastness of spacetime.

7.3. Super-Sensitive Equipment

In the realm of gravitational wave detection, the development and utilization of super-sensitive equipment have revolutionized how we listen to the whispers of the universe. The precision of our instruments determines our capacity to detect the faint ripples in spacetime caused by catastrophic astrophysical events. An immense range of technological innovations has been harnessed to augment sensitivity and performance, pushing beyond the limitations of human perception and enabling the scientific community to faithfully capture signals that would otherwise be lost in the clamor of the cosmos.

At the forefront of this transformative exploration is laser interferometry, the backbone technique employed by observatories like LIGO and Virgo. The setup involves two long, perpendicular arms where lasers are sent simultaneously. Constructed to detect discrepancies as minuscule as a fraction of the diameter of a proton, this technique epitomizes the quest for unparalleled sensitivity. Each component within the detectors has been meticulously designed and optimized to ensure that the firm's quest for accuracy is unrelenting. For instance, mirrors utilized in these systems are crafted from exceptionally pure glass, polished to a precision that minimizes imperfections, allowing for the reflection of light with near perfection.

Furthermore, the environment in which these sensitive instruments operate is carefully controlled. Vibrations from nearby human activities, seismic activity, and thermal fluctuations can introduce noise —resulting in changes that could impede the detection of gravitational waves. To counter these disturbances, LIGO relies on advanced seismic isolation systems that incorporate pendulum designs crafted to dampen vibrations, shielding the delicate equipment from disruptive forces. Premium building materials, intelligent design, and noise-cancellation techniques synergistically foster an environment conducive to capturing the intricate signals heralding catastrophic cosmic events.

In parallel, attention has been devoted to cooling technologies. The principles of thermodynamics dictate that heat contributes to noise, which in turn could mask the faint signals sought after by scientists. By employing active cooling techniques, researchers manage to mitigate thermal noise during operations. The groundbreaking undertaking involves using advanced cryogenics aimed at lowering the temperature of key components within the apparatus. This creates an optimal environment wherein thermal vibrations are reduced, thus boosting the overall sensitivity and effectiveness of the detection mechanisms.

Moreover, the integration of quantum sensing technology marks a noteworthy landmark in detection capabilities. By exploring the principles of quantum mechanics, scientists are able to experiment with unique lighting techniques, such as squeezed light. This technique is designed to manipulate quantum states, enabling a reduction in the uncertainty of optical measurements, thereby improving sensitivity. QED methodologies encourage the pursuit of previously unattainable thresholds, augmenting the instruments' ability to discern gravitational wave signals from an overwhelming backdrop of noise.

The cumulative effect of this work has led to a remarkable paradigm shift in the field of astrophysics. With advancements in super-sensitive equipment ensuring that even the faintest of signals can be detected, the scientific community has made unprecedented strides in observing the universe's most dynamic events. Detection efforts have not only validated predictions surrounding the existence of gravitational waves but have also opened doors to abundant discoveries about the mechanisms driving the evolution of cosmic bodies.

Crucially, these technological achievements have laid the groundwork for future developments and enhancements in gravitational wave astronomy. Next-generation observatories promise to push further the barriers of detection and sensitivity, capturing an ever-broader spectrum of gravitational wave sources and effects. The global network of gravitational wave observatories aims to implement collaborative methodologies, pooling resources and expertise to maximize capabilities and ensure the continued relevance and effectiveness of the methods employed.

In summary, the innovations reflected in the super-sensitive equipment utilized in gravitational wave detection encapsulate the spirit of exploration that characterizes modern astrophysics. Through ingenuity, collaboration, and relentless inquiry, the quest to understand the cosmic narratives inscribed within gravitational waves has gained momentum, inviting future generations of scientists to continue searching for answers in the echoes resonating through the fabric of spacetime. The meticulous engineering and scientific rigor herald a new era of understanding within the cosmos, allowing humanity to connect with the universe in ways once deemed unimaginable.

7.4. Cooler Temperatures and Quantum Sensing

As we delve into the intricate interplay between cooler temperatures and quantum sensing in the realm of gravitational waves, it becomes evident that advancements in these domains are essential in improving the methodologies we use to detect and analyze gravitational signals from the cosmos. At the heart of this exploration lies a comprehensive understanding of how temperature management can influence measurement sensitivity, along with the innovative applications of quantum mechanics that enhance our observational capabilities.

Temperature control plays a vital role in the operational efficacy of gravitational wave observatories. The rationale behind maintaining cooler temperatures is rooted in the principles of thermodynamics, which dictate that thermal fluctuations contribute to noise within measurement environments. This noise can obscure the faint gravitational wave signals that scientists aim to detect, rendering them nearly imperceptible against a backdrop of thermal vibrations and environmental disturbances.

In response, engineers and physicists have implemented a variety of advanced cooling techniques to mitigate thermal noise. For instance, LIGO and Virgo are equipped with sophisticated thermal management systems designed to maintain the operational temperatures of their critical components. By employing these technologies, which may include cryogenic cooling to preserve the temperature of mirrors and other optical elements, the observatories significantly reduce the vibrational effects of heat. This heightened level of thermal stability allows for the reliable detection of smaller variations in spacetime, hence enhancing sensitivity.

The commitment to cooler operating conditions does not merely stem from an engineering imperative; it embodies a strategic pursuit of clarity in measurements that define gravitational wave events. The collective efforts to control temperature extend to all elements of the observatory, from the interferometer's optics to the suspensions holding reflectors. This meticulous attention to detail ensures that measurements can focus on genuine gravitational wave signals without losing accuracy to unwanted noise.

Alongside cooler temperatures, the field of quantum sensing emerges as a significant frontier, revolutionizing how we approach gravitational wave detection. Quantum mechanics allows for innovations in measurement that transcend classical limitations, opening new pathways for researchers to discern gravitational waves amidst the disturbances of the cosmos. Central to these advancements is the concept of squeezed light, which harnesses quantum properties to reduce uncertainty in one variable—either position or momentum—within a system.

Squeezed light effectively enhances the sensitivity of the measurement apparatus, allowing observatories to amplify the ability to detect faint signals. This innovation is of particular interest in gravitational wave astronomy, where the precise manipulation of light can lead to the differentiation between robust gravitational wave events and background noise. The incorporation of squeezed light into interferometric techniques promises to bolster the capacity of existing observatories and future ones, significantly advancing our overall detection capabilities.

The relevance of quantum sensing extends beyond just squeezed light; the principles of quantum superposition and entanglement galvanize the exploration of novel sensor designs that could enhance performance in gravitational wave detection. By exploiting the myriad peculiarities of quantized systems, researchers continuously push the frontier of how sensitive gravitational observatories can become. As these methods integrate with ongoing advancements in technology and material science, a collaborative ecosystem emerges that juxtaposes cooling technologies, quantum mechanics, and precision engineering.

These advancements in both thermal management and quantum sensing further realize the impact of interdisciplinary collaboration. The seamless integration of physics, engineering, and computing fosters a rich tapestry of learning, enabling researchers to address complex challenges associated with gravitational wave detection. As we unlock the potential inherent in cooler temperatures and quantum mechanics, the unfolding narrative of gravitational wave astronomy transitions toward a horizon brimming with possibilities.

In summary, the nexus between cooler temperatures and quantum sensing represents a pivotal area of exploration within gravitational wave research. The meticulous control of temperature serves to enhance sensitivity by minimizing thermal noise, while innovations in quantum sensing techniques open new avenues for capturing faint signals. Together, these developments promise to amplify our understanding of the universe and its underlying gravitational phenomena, forging pathways into unexplored territories. The journey to decipher the whispers of the cosmos is both a scientific endeavor and a poetic pursuit, urging us to remain attentive to the subtleties that envelop the fabric of reality and invite us to listen ever more closely to the gravitational symphony resonating in the vastness of spacetime.

7.5. Continued Advancements

Gravitational wave astronomy stands at the precipice of unprecedented advancements that promise to reshape our understanding of the universe. The journey from theoretical predictions to tangible detection has been fraught with challenges and triumphs, each phase revealing deeper layers of cosmic mystery. As the field continues to evolve, we witness a confluence of technology, collaboration, and innovation that drives discoveries beyond the boundaries of current knowledge.

In recent years, we have made significant strides in improving the sensitivity of gravitational wave detectors. These advancements have been prompted by a robust scientific inquiry that challenges researchers to refine existing technologies and develop new methodologies. A key area of focus has been the enhancement of laser interferometry techniques—an essential framework for gravitational wave detection. By leveraging cutting-edge laser sources and advanced optical components, observatories like LIGO and Virgo have achieved enhanced precision, allowing them to observe the faintest ripples in spacetime that arise from cataclysmic cosmic events.

In addition to improvements in laser interferometry, the application of quantum sensing techniques has emerged as a transformative frontier. The integration of quantum mechanics into gravitational wave detection has previously unimagined potential, exemplified by techniques such as squeezed light, which reduce noise and improve sensitivity. These innovations are emblematic of a broader trend in the scientific community to embrace interdisciplinary approaches, where ideas from theoretical physics, engineering, and quantum mechanics converge to empower exploration at cosmological scales.

Collaboration has been instrumental in fostering the continued advancement of gravitational wave astronomy, creating a robust network of observatories that spans the globe. The partnerships among LIGO, Virgo, KAGRA, and other emerging facilities exemplify the synergy that arises from collective efforts toward shared scientific goals. By pooling resources, expertise, and data, scientists can more effectively analyze gravitational wave events, correlate observations, and enhance the accuracy of their findings.

Moreover, the expansion of this collaborative landscape lays the groundwork for next-generation facilities that will significantly enhance our ability to detect and interpret gravitational waves. Ambitious initiatives such as the planned space-based observatory LISA

(Laser Interferometer Space Antenna) will provide unprecedented sensitivity over a broader frequency range, enabling the detection of signals from events previously believed to be beyond reach. The potential to observe supermassive black hole mergers and explore early universe phenomena highlights the wealth of discoveries that lie ahead.

Importantly, the advancement of gravitational wave astronomy also has profound implications for our understanding of fundamental physics and cosmology. With each detection, new opportunities arise to probe the nature of gravity, delve into the properties of black holes, and investigate the intricacies of stellar evolution. The application of gravitational wave observations to existing cosmological models challenges preconceived notions and encourages a reevaluation of the cosmic narrative.

As we navigate this era of continued advancements, we must acknowledge the ethical considerations that arise within scientific discovery. The impact of our discoveries extends beyond academia; societal implications, funding priorities, and the ethical obligations of scientists toward public engagement and understanding are all intertwined with the exploration of gravitational waves. Encouraging a more inclusive dialogue about these discoveries will be paramount to ensuring that they resonate within the wider public discourse surrounding science and its role in society.

In summary, the journey of gravitational wave astronomy is characterized by a relentless pursuit of knowledge that inspires future generations of scientists and explorers. The recent advancements in detection techniques, the growth of international collaboration, and the profound implications for our understanding of the universe all signal a bright future. As we eavesdrop on the universe through the delicate echoes of gravitational waves, we open ourselves to a narrative rich with insights about the cosmos and, indeed, our place within it. The mysteries of gravitational waves are far from exhausted; rather, they beckon us to continue listening and learning, to unveil the stories woven into the very fabric of reality, and to engage in the collective exploration of the universe that lies beyond our own horizons.

8. The Saga of Black Holes

8.1. Cosmic Dance Partners

In the grand tapestry of the cosmos, gravitational waves arise from some of the most extraordinary encounters, evoking narratives shaped by the colossal forces at play in the universe. Among these narratives, the cosmic dance of stellar hegemony unfolds, showcasing celestial partners in an intricate ballet—black holes, neutron stars, and accretion disks intertwine and collide, rendering a profound symphony of gravitational disturbances that echo across spacetime. Central to this cosmic choreography are the enigmatic entities called black holes; their unique properties and interactions form the foundation of what we understand as the cosmic dance partners of our universe.

Black holes are phenomenal remnants of stellar evolution, born from the catastrophic collapse of massive stars at the end of their life cycles. This dissolution results in a singularity—an infinitely dense point where the laws of physics as we know them cease to apply—and an event horizon, defining the point of no return. The mesmerizing aspects of black holes arise not only from their mysterious inner workings but also from their gravitational influence on neighboring systems. As these celestial giants maneuver through the cosmic sea, they invite companions into their realm and engage in dynamic interactions that produce gravitational waves—ripples propagating outward, carrying stories of their tumultuous and transformational mergers.

The motion of black holes is a dance in itself, with the gravitational pull they exert compelling surrounding matter into orbits that invoke aspects of classical mechanics. However, as these massive bodies lose energy due to gravitational radiation—especially as two black holes orbit each other before merging—the dynamics transfer from a classical interpretation to one governed by relativistic effects. The intricate choreography becomes more pronounced in events leading up to a merger; the spiraling motion accelerates, causing a crescendo of gravitational waves that culminate in a cataclysmic event signaling the joining of two supermassive entities.

Within the cosmic landscape, neutron stars serve as equally profound partners in this dance, especially in binary systems where they share their orbits with black holes. The interaction between these two types of dense objects produces gravitational waves whose distinctive waveforms tell tales of the violent intricacies of their interactions. When neutron stars collide—often resulting in mergers that yield stellar remnants—the gravitational waves generated shimmy through the fabric of spacetime, narrating the events of catastrophic force, dense matter, and violent release of energy.

The profound implication of these cosmic dance partners extends beyond mere observational intrigue; they present a unique opportunity to unlock insights into the fabric of the universe. As gravitational waves travel through the cosmos, they carry with them a wealth of information about their progenitors—the mass, spin, and distance of these celestial entities can be inferred from the waveforms detected by established observatories. Each detection serves as a window into the past, recounting cosmic events that transpired billions of light-years away, which in turn offers perspectives on how galaxies evolve, the characteristics of matter within extreme conditions, and the fundamental laws governing gravity.

As black holes and neutron stars engage in their cosmic dance, their impacts reverberate far and wide. The gravitational waves emitted not only illuminate the characteristics of the bodies involved but also resonate with the echoes of cosmic history. The occurrences of these waves beg the question: how do these events inform our understanding of gravity, spacetime, and the intricacies of the universe at large? The merger of dance partners enacts a cosmic conversation, continually inviting astronomers to interpret these silent songlines encoded within the waveforms of gravitational radiation.

To further complicate the narrative, as these cosmic partners collide and merge, they interact with the surrounding disks of gas and dust, creating additional gravitational dynamics. The presence of accretion disks fosters an enriched backdrop for studying the interactions between different masses, revealing the origin of heavy elements and shedding light on nucleosynthesis processes that shape the elemental makeup of the universe. As elements forge through these catastrophic stellar encounters, each encounter writes a page in a broader universal history.

The significance of understanding these cosmic dance partners through the lens of gravitational waves is paramount. They offer not only tools for exploring astrophysical phenomena but also, fundamentally, pave the way for theorizing about the nature of spacetime, singularities, and ultimately, the inner workings of the cosmos itself. As we seek to comprehend the elaborate choreography between black holes, neutron stars, and the matter surrounding them, gravitational waves stand as the messengers, urging us to listen closely to the stories they carry, embracing the complex web of connections that define our universe.

In conclusion, the saga of cosmic dance partners is set against a backdrop rich with gravitational interactions, unveiling the stories written in waves of curvature across spacetime. By tuning into these echoes through observatories that capture gravitational waves, we find pathways into celestial narratives long hidden from view. The dance continues, inviting future generations of scientists to partake in this unfolding drama—a story of entity, energy, and the quest for understanding that transcends time and space, underscoring the beauty of our ever-expanding universe where questions beckon and answers linger just beyond the horizon.

8.2. Singularities and Event Horizons

As we delve deeper into the intricacies of black holes and their role in gravitational wave astronomy, we encounter the compelling phenomena of singularities and event horizons. These concepts not only enrich our understanding of black holes but also play a vital role in the generation of gravitational waves. Singularities represent the core of black holes, where matter is believed to be infinitely dense, resulting in unmatched gravitational forces. In contrast, event horizons serve as the demarcation line, beyond which nothing, not even light, can escape the grasp of a black hole's gravity. Understanding these two pivotal elements is crucial for comprehending the cosmic dance that unfolds during black hole mergers and the subsequent gravitational wave emissions.

Singularities exist at the heart of black holes, where our current understanding of physics reaches its limits. According to the framework established by Einstein's General Theory of Relativity, a singularity is a point where the curvature of spacetime becomes infinite—a region where the laws of physics as we know them cease to apply. At this unapproachable interior, gravitational forces become so powerful that matter collapses into an infinitely small volume, leading to extreme densities that boggle the mind. The ideals of classical physics, which govern the behavior of matter and energy, break down in the vicinity of a singularity, challenging our understanding and prompting intense scientific scrutiny into their nature.

Event horizons, on the other hand, shape the external reality surrounding black holes. The event horizon acts as an imaginary boundary, signifying the point of no return. Once an object crosses this threshold, it is inexorably drawn toward the singularity, rendered beyond the reach of any external forces, including light itself. This unique attribute captures the essence of black holes as cosmic entities that challenge our perception of reality; while they consume matter, their presence initiates a wider array of gravitational phenomena that extend beyond themselves.

Accompanying the complex interplay of singularities and event horizons is the gravitational wave production generated during black hole mergers. When two black holes enter a binary system, their motion is not merely predictable; it becomes a choreographed ballet governed by the laws of relativity. As they spiral towards each other, they lose energy in the form of gravitational radiation, which ripples through spacetime. The merging process culminates with their event horizons merging, leading to an explosive release of energy that generates detectable gravitational waves. This transition produces waveforms that carry specific signatures—characteristics linked to the masses, spins, and dynamics of the black holes involved.

The implications of detecting these gravitational waves extend far beyond the confines of black hole physics; they serve as vital probes into the enigmatic processes shaping our universe. Each merger and the resulting waves provide essential empirical evidence, not only validating Einstein's predictions but also deepening our understanding of black hole formation, their variability, and the life cycles of massive stars. Observing black hole mergers through gravitational waves grants astronomers unparalleled insights into the cosmic landscape, illuminating the mysteries surrounding the population of black holes within galaxies.

Event horizons also pose exciting questions about causality and the nature of information in the universe. When information is consumed by a black hole, it raises profound challenges regarding the fundamentals of physics and the preservation of information. Theoretical debates surrounding information paradoxes shed light on contemporary physics, prompting renewed interest in understanding the quantum properties governing black holes.

As this exploration unfolds, the synergy between singularities and event horizons becomes a gateway into the depths of our cosmological inquiries. The unique properties of black holes, paired with the gravitational waves they emit, paint an intricate picture of cosmic evolution. This reinforces the idea that, while black holes may embody ultimate oblivion in the form of singularities, they also serve as powerful conduits of knowledge about gravity, spacetime, and the stylish choreography of celestial dynamics.

In closing, the profound nature of singularities and event horizons illustrates the duality of black holes as both destructive and enlightening components of the universe. As researchers continue to unravel the implications of these celestial phenomena through the observation of gravitational waves, they inevitably challenge broader notions of reality, urging us to rethink our fundamental understandings of the universe. With each wave detected, we are reminded that the mysterious echoes of gravity not only reshape the cosmic landscape but serve as an invitation to join the celebration of discovery, revealing the uncharted territories lying beyond the veil of our current understanding. The continued endeavor to decipher these cosmic whispers iteratively invites us into the vast expanse of knowledge yet to be unveiled, propelled by the gravitational waves emanating from the heart of the universe's most enigmatic entities.

8.3. The Role in Gravitational Waves

The field of gravitational wave astronomy represents a revolutionary leap in our understanding of the universe, driven primarily by the detection of these elusive ripples in spacetime—a phenomenon that can only be perceived through incredibly advanced and sensitive devices. At the heart of this transformative science lies the concept of gravitational waves, which were initially theoretical constructs derived from Albert Einstein's General Theory of Relativity. The role these waves play in our understanding of the universe, particularly in relation to catastrophic events and astronomical interactions, is both profound and multifaceted, as illustrated by several key points.

Gravitational waves serve as cosmic messengers, carrying invaluable information encoded in their waveforms about the most energetic and violent events in the universe—events such as black hole mergers, neutron star collisions, and supernova explosions. Every time a candidate event occurs, gravitational waves ripple through the very fabric of spacetime, and observatories such as LIGO and Virgo detect these tiny fluctuations. Each detection is like tuning into a faint whisper amidst a cacophony, revealing secrets about the workings of the universe long hidden from our observation.

One of the most significant aspects of gravitational waves is that they allow scientists to study astronomical phenomena that are otherwise invisible to electromagnetic observations, such as light. For instance, black holes do not emit light in the way stars or other celestial bodies do; however, their gravitational interactions can be detected through the waves they produce during events such as mergers. When two black holes spiral toward one another, they emit gravitational waves detectable from billions of light-years away, encapsulating information about their masses, spins, and the dynamics of their interaction. This ability to "hear" the universe instead of merely "seeing" it opens a new window into astrophysical phenomena, fundamentally reshaping our understanding of the cosmos.

Additionally, the detection of gravitational waves helps bridge theoretical predictions with empirical evidence. Observations lead to confirmation of astrophysical predictions about the life cycles of massive stars, the formation of black holes, and the behaviors of neutron stars. For example, the observations of binary neutron star mergers marked a significant milestone, not only confirming gravitational wave theory but also providing insight into the origins of heavy elements like gold—a process that had long inferred through astrophysical models but lacked direct evidence. Gravitational waves thus serve as a tool for validating theoretical frameworks and enhancing our understanding of fundamental astrophysical processes.

Moreover, the insights gained from gravitational wave studies extend far beyond isolated events. By observing multiple gravitational wave events, scientists can compile statistical samples that inform models of the populations of black holes and neutron stars across the universe. These data help refine existing cosmological theories and provide a clearer picture of how matter and energy distribute throughout the universe. The ability to derive population statistics directly from gravitational wave detections exemplifies the capacity of this new branch of astronomy to contribute to quantitative analysis in ways that traditional observational methods could not.

The transformative impact of gravitational wave astronomy also underscores the significance of international collaboration and technological innovation in modern science. The diverse network of gravitational wave observatories—ranging from LIGO in the United States to Virgo in Europe—demonstrates how global partnerships facilitate data sharing, analysis, and a more comprehensive understanding of gravitational wave events. The interplay of ideas and resources illuminates the power of scientific community, promoting a culture of cooperation that fosters discovery and innovation.

As the technology and methodologies employed in gravitational wave detection continue to evolve, the potential for future discoveries remains vast. Plans for next-generation observatories, such as the proposed space-based LISA (Laser Interferometer Space Antenna), aim to expand the frequency range of detectable gravitational waves and unveil new cosmic phenomena. Such advancements significantly enhance the depth of inquiry and enrich our understanding of the universe's intricacies.

In summary, the role of gravitational waves extends far beyond their initial theoretical conception. They have emerged as pivotal components in our exploration of the universe, serving as cosmic messengers that convey information about cataclysmic events and providing insights into the essence of gravity and astrophysical processes. The study of these waves transcends mere observation; it deepens our connection to the cosmos and enhances humanity's understanding of reality. As we continue to listen to the whispers of gravity, we remain vigilant in our pursuit of knowledge, recognizing that each wave detected is not merely a scientific achievement but a story told by the universe itself, awaiting interpretation and understanding.

8.4. Collisions and Mergers

In the cosmic arena, not all celestial entities navigate through solitude; a significant part of their existence unfolds in the intricate dynamics of collisions and mergers. These captivating events lie at the heart of gravitational wave phenomena, unveiling mysteries that resonate through both time and space. As massive objects in the universe, such as neutron stars and black holes, collide, they orchestrate dramatic performances that produce gravitational waves —ripples that propagate across the fabric of spacetime, conveying essential information about the astronomical bodies involved and the fundamental laws that govern their interactions.

At the inception of these dramatic cosmic dances are neutron stars, which represent the dense remnants of supernova explosions. Following the collapse of massive stars, their cores may stabilize into an incredibly compact structure composed primarily of neutrons. Neutron stars are immensely dense; a mass similar to that of the Sun is compressed into an object with a radius of less than 12 kilometers. This juxtaposition of mass and size renders neutron stars unique astronomical entities, compellingly involved in binary systems where they may interact with each other or with other massive objects like black holes.

The dynamics surrounding neutron star collisions are profound and richly multifaceted. Neutron stars that occupy binary systems—where two stars orbit a common center of mass—can eventually spiral toward each other due to the emission of gravitational waves, leading to a merger that generates an extraordinary amount of energy. As they orbit, they lose orbital energy through gravitational radiation, progressively accelerating and drawing closer. This inspiral culminates in a rapid coalescence, resulting in an event that emits tremendous gravitational waves.

The gravitational wave signals produced during these neutron star mergers carry distinctive signatures, characterized by a final "chirp" pattern—a sudden increase in frequency and amplitude as the stars approach and merge. Each signal detected serves as a unique fingerprint, decoding the masses, spins, distances, and even the equation of state of the neutron star material, offering glimpses into the fundamental physics characterizing such extreme environments.

Beyond their immediate implications for gravitational wave detection, collisions and mergers of neutron stars have significant consequences for the broader universe, particularly concerning the synthesis of heavy elements. When neutron stars merge, they create conditions conducive to rapid neutron capture processes (r-process nucleosynthesis), leading to the formation of heavy elements such as gold, platinum, and uranium. The remarkable event that took place in August 2017 when gravitational waves from a neutron star merger coincided with electromagnetic observations marked a historic milestone, showcasing the link between gravitational waves and the origin of these elusive elements. The kilonova explosion that followed not only illuminated the aftermath of the merger but also highlighted the importance of multi-messenger astronomy—integrating gravitational wave signals with electromagnetic observations to deepen our understanding of the universe's chemical evolution.

Exploring the ramifications of such mergers also sheds light on the processes that shape the universe at large. The merging of neutron stars or black holes is not just a spectacle; it serves as a basis for uncovering the origins of various cosmic phenomena, including gamma-ray bursts. These high-energy explosions are tied to the catastrophic events of stellar mergers, which emit immense quantities of radiation detectable across vast cosmic distances. Through the lens of gravitational wave observations, scientists glean insights into the characteristics of these astronomical events, contributing to our understanding of how galaxies evolve, the rate of stellar formation, and the chaotic interactions that define the lifecycle of stars.

Moreover, neutron star collisions act as portals that extend our inquiry into the very nature of gravity itself. As scientists observe the unique gravitational wave patterns emitted from these events, they gain opportunities to test general relativity under extreme conditions, probing whether the predictions align with observed phenomena. These endeavors continuously invite further scrutiny into the pillars of theoretical physics, challenging researchers to refine existing models and develop new theoretical frameworks.

As the saga of collisions and mergers unfolds, it becomes evident that these cosmic events transcend mere observations; they are interwoven with narratives that bridge chemistry, physics, and cosmology. The gravitational waves that emanate from these stellar interactions elucidate not only the mechanics of celestial phenomena but also highlight a profound interconnectedness within the universe.

In conclusion, the gravitational waves produced by collisions and mergers are beneficial cosmic phenomena that offer profound insights into the universe's fundamental workings. From the dynamic interplay of neutron stars to the creation of heavy elements and the exploration of cosmic evolution, the role of mergers enriches our understanding of the cosmos. As we tune into these gravitational echoes, we are reminded of the complex and intricate narratives that govern our universe, beckoning us to listen closely and engage with the wonders that lie beyond our reach. Each wave detected resonates not just as a signal but as a story—a story that intertwines the very fabric of reality, illuminating the profound beauty, chaos, and mystery defining our collective journey through the cosmos.

8.5. Mapping the Dark Regions

Mapping the dark regions of the cosmos has become an essential endeavor in gravitational wave astronomy, where the ethereal whispers of gravitational waves guide our understanding of the hidden depths of the universe. As the delicate echoes of cosmic interactions resonate through the fabric of spacetime, they reveal insights into the nature of celestial bodies, the evolution of galaxies, and even the fundamental forces that govern existence. This subchapter seeks to explore the methodologies, discoveries, and implications of mapping these dark regions illuminated by gravitational wave detections.

To understand how mapping these regions unfolds, one must first appreciate the context in which gravitational waves operate. The universe is a vast, complex tapestry where dark matter and dark energy dominate and shape cosmic structures, yet remain invisible to electromagnetic detection methods. Gravitational waves, in contrast, offer a powerful tool to probe these shadowy realms. As they travel through spacetime, they reveal information about cataclysmic events, particularly those occurring near black holes and neutron stars, which often reside in areas that challenge our observational capabilities.

The mapping process begins with detection—observatories like LIGO and Virgo receive the faint signals generated by cosmic events such as black hole mergers or neutron star collisions. Once a gravitational wave signal is detected, the next significant step involves a thorough analysis and characterization of the waveforms, which are influenced by the masses, spins, and distances of the involved bodies. The intricate features of the waveforms serve as fingerprints, granting researchers the ability to infer properties of the event and map its origins in conjunction with electromagnetic observational data.

The remarkable confluence of gravitational wave events and multi-messenger astronomy enriches the mapping process. When a gravitational wave signal coincides with an electromagnetic counterpart, such as gamma-ray bursts or optical signals from a kilonova, it provides crucial positional information. For example, the observation of gravitational waves from the merger of two neutron stars coupled with electromagnetic data allowed astronomers to pinpoint the event's location in space, providing insights into the elemental synthesis occurring during the merger. This convergence enables a more comprehensive understanding of the underlying astrophysical mechanisms at play, enhancing the mapping of darker, less observable regions of the universe.

As scientists delve deeper into analyzing gravitational wave signals, a wealth of knowledge emerges regarding the population of binary systems, including the frequency of neutron star and black hole mergers. By accumulating data from numerous gravitational wave detections, researchers can build statistical models that inform their understanding of the frequency and distribution of these events across the universe. This investigation serves as a critical tool for mapping the cosmos, shedding light on the formation channels and life cycles of these extreme stellar entities.

Moreover, gravitational waves challenge existing cosmological models by unveiling critical insights into phenomena such as the expansion rate of the universe, commonly referred to as the Hubble constant. Maps generated from gravitational wave data reveal discrepancies between direct measurements and those obtained from traditional electromagnetic observations, prompting renewed inquiries into the fabric of space and time. This interplay emphasizes that gravitational wave astronomy not only elucidates dark regions but also invites reconsideration of established theories underpinning the cosmic narrative.

The challenges associated with mapping dark regions are not solely technological; they also engage deeper philosophical considerations about our understanding of the universe. As gravitational waves unveil hidden phenomena, they underscore the limitations of human perception and the importance of embracing uncertainties in scientific inquiry. The notion of darkness—in terms of both cosmic structures and our ignorance—serves as a reminder of the ongoing journey toward understanding our place in the vast cosmos.

Furthermore, mapping the dark regions encourages a spirit of collaboration within the scientific community. As gravitational wave observatories proliferate around the globe and new detection technologies emerge, a unified global network takes form. Scientists from various disciplines come together to decipher the mysteries of the universe, sharing insights and methodologies. This interconnected approach enables a richness of inquiry and fosters an inclusive environment where diverse perspectives enhance our understanding of the cosmos.

As we look to the future of mapping dark regions, we remain poised at the threshold of discovery. Exponential advances in detection technology, data analysis, and international collaboration propel us forward into uncharted territories within gravitational wave astronomy. The genesis of next-generation observatories, including potential space-based initiatives, promises to deepen our knowledge of the universe by expanding our capacity to listen for signals from events previously rendered too faint or too distant for detection.

In summary, mapping the dark regions illuminated by gravitational waves represents a compelling synthesis of technological innovation, collaborative effort, and philosophical inquiry. As we harness the profound insights offered by these cosmic messengers, we are invited into the unfolding saga of the universe—each gravitational wave detected a whisper echoing through the depths of spacetime. The endeavor to understand and map these regions calls for continued exploration, urging scientists and explorers alike to listen closely to the tantalizing narratives woven into the fabric of existence, guiding us closer to a comprehensive understanding of the universe's hidden layers.

9. Collisions in the Cosmos: Neutron Stars and Beyond

9.1. The Dynamics of Neutron Stars

Throughout the universe's vast expanse, neutron stars lie as fascinating and extreme remnants of stellar evolution, serving as both cosmic laboratories and dynamic marvels that fuel our quest for understanding matter, gravity, and the nature of the universe. These dense and compact celestial objects are born from supernova explosions, which occur when massive stars exhaust their nuclear fuel and collapse under their own gravity. The remnants consist predominantly of neutrons, leading to immense densities that can reach over a billion tons per cubic centimeter—conditions found nowhere else in the known universe.

The dynamics of neutron stars are governed by the balance between gravitational forces striving to collapse the star further and the neutron degeneracy pressure that opposes this collapse. This delicate equilibrium allows neutron stars to persist as stable, albeit incredibly dense, objects. The extremely strong gravitational fields surrounding neutron stars significantly influence the behavior of nearby matter, generating fascinating interactions that manifest beyond their immediate vicinity.

When neutron stars find themselves in binary systems, the gravitational dynamics become even more compelling. These binary systems often spiral toward one another over time due to the emission of gravitational waves, which carry away energy and angular momentum, causing the stars to orbit closer. The intense gravitational fields lead to the formation of accretion disks composed of gas and stellar material being drawn toward the neutron stars—a process that enhances the complexity of their interactions. During this inspiral phase, neutron stars exhibit properties such as pulsation and intense electromagnetic radiation, including x-rays.

The gravitational waves produced by binary neutron star mergers herald an exciting area of research. As these stars collide, they generate ripples in spacetime similar to what occurs during black hole mergers, yet with unique waveform signatures that encode rich information about the characteristics of the neutron stars involved. Observations of these mergers have provided critical insights into the population of neutron stars in the universe, revealing details such as their mass distribution and formation mechanisms.

One of the most profound revelations resulting from the collision of neutron stars is the synthesis of heavy elements, a process that stands as a cornerstone for understanding cosmic evolution. When neutron stars merge, they create conditions conducive to rapid neutron capture processes—r-process nucleosynthesis—leading to the production of heavy elements such as gold, platinum, and uranium. The monumental event that occurred in August 2017, when gravitational waves from a neutron star merger coincided with electromagnetic signals recording a kilonova explosion, provided direct evidence of this synthesis. The discovery allowed scientists to link gravitational waves with the production of heavy elements, underscoring the significance of neutron star mergers in cosmic alchemy.

This landmark observation triggered a new chapter in astrophysics, integrating gravitational wave data with electromagnetic observations to unveil a more complete picture of stellar and synthetic phenomena occurring throughout the universe. The newfound understanding of how neutron stars interact with their surroundings and generate heavy elements instilled profound implications for cosmology, enriching theories concerning the formation and distribution of matter within galaxies.

Furthermore, the dynamic interplay of neutron stars in binary and merger scenarios compels researchers to re-evaluate existing models of stellar evolution, gravitational dynamics, and nucleosynthesis. Observing these astrophysical events through gravitational waves provides a means to understand phenomena that are otherwise cloaked in darkness. The waveforms detected offer crucial insights into the intricate dance of matter and energy in the cosmos, reinforcing the idea that neutron stars are pivotal actors in the grand narrative of the universe's evolution.

The embrace of interdisciplinary approaches is essential for fully grasping the dynamics of neutron stars and the implications of their collisions for understanding gravitational waves. Discoveries derived from neutron star interactions not only illuminate specific aspects of stellar evolution, but also echo through the corridors of fundamental physics, inviting tantalizing questions about gravity, quantum mechanics, and the nature of matter itself.

As we continue to explore the mysteries surrounding neutron stars and their violent interactions, we remain poised on the brink of discovery. The future of gravitational wave astronomy holds the promise of unveiling even more secrets, inviting us to listen ever more closely to the celestial symphony woven from the threads of spacetime ripples. In this journey, neutron stars serve as compelling guides, illuminating not only the dark corners of the universe, but also the deeper questions regarding existence, connection, and the intricate workings that shape the cosmos we inhabit. As we delve into the complexities of neutron stars and the gravitational waves they inspire, we find ourselves engaged in a captivating narrative—one that beckons us onward into the depths of cosmic exploration and understanding.

9.2. Gravitational Waves from Star Mergers

Imagine a cosmic rendezvous where two massive stars, their fates intertwined by gravity, spiral toward an inevitable collision. Such dramatic encounters, particularly those involving neutron stars, produce gravitational waves—ripples in the fabric of spacetime that echo across the universe, conveying a wealth of information about their origins and the nature of gravity itself. Gravitational waves from star mergers represent one of the most captivating aspects of astrophysics, merging intricate physics with profound cosmological implications.

Neutron stars, the remnants of supernova explosions of massive stars, are extraordinary celestial objects. They possess densities that dwarf that of ordinary matter, as their cores collapse into a singularity of neutrons held in balance by neutron degeneracy pressure. In binary systems where two neutron stars orbit around each other, an intricate dance unfolds—a spiral motion governed by gravitational interactions results in the gradual loss of orbital energy as they emit gravitational waves. This intricate ballet culminates in cataclysmic mergers, producing some of the most spectacular gravitational wave signatures detectable from Earth.

As two neutron stars draw nearer, the gravitational waves they emit become increasingly intense, creating a distinctive waveform that scientists eagerly observe. These waveforms exhibit characteristic "chirp" patterns—foreshadowing the inevitable merger—a rising frequency and amplitude that signify the stars spiraling together at accelerated rates. By analyzing these waveforms, researchers can glean critical details about the neutron stars involved: their masses, spins, and even the dynamics of the collision event itself.

The implications of these mergers extend beyond gravitational wave detection. They represent a significant avenue for studying the creation of heavy elements through rapid neutron capture processes. When neutron stars collide, they generate extreme conditions that foster nucleosynthesis—an alchemical process that leads to the formation of gold, platinum, and other heavy elements. The 2017 detection of gravitational waves from a neutron star merger, which coincided with electromagnetic signals of a kilonova, provided groundbreaking evidence linking these cosmic events to the synthesis of heavy elements. This remarkable connection not only helped clarify the origins of such elements but also enriched our understanding of cosmic chemical evolution.

Moreover, the gravitational waves produced during neutron star mergers serve as direct probes into the fundamental nature of gravity, providing opportunities to test the predictions of Einstein's general relativity under extreme conditions. Each merger acts as a natural laboratory, allowing astrophysicists to investigate the complexities surrounding gravitational interactions and their ramifications across different scales.

As the field of gravitational wave astronomy develops, the discoveries emanating from these stellar mergers enrich our cosmological narrative. They bolster the conceptual framework linking the life cycles of stars, the origins of heavy elements, and the fundamental forces operating in the universe. The ability to listen to the universe through gravitational waves marks a significant evolution in how we explore and understand the cosmos.

Ultimately, the story of gravitational waves from star mergers beckons us to tune into the cosmic symphony of interactions unfolding in the universe. As we harness the power of advanced detectors to explore these stellar encounters, we deepen our grasp of fundamental physics while engaging with the timeless questions surrounding existence. Each wave detected is not merely a signal—it reflects a profound story of stellar evolution, elemental creation, and the gravitational interplay that governs the grand tapestry of the cosmos. In this way, the echoes of origins inspire us, inviting future generations of scientists and explorers to join in unraveling the mysteries of the universe.

9.3. Discovery of Heavy Elements

The discovery of heavy elements through the lens of gravitational wave astronomy unfolds a multifaceted narrative that transcends mere scientific achievement; it represents a profound intersection of astrophysics, nuclear physics, and cosmology, whereby cataclysmic cosmic events reformulate our understanding of the universe. Hidden within the ripples of gravitational waves lies an extraordinary tale of stellar evolution, elemental creation, and the interconnectedness of celestial phenomena, each revealing significant insights into the genesis of the elements that constitute the very fabric of our existence.

The primary site of heavy element synthesis events occurs during the violent mergers of neutron stars. When these dense remnants collide, they unleash tremendous energy and create extreme conditions conducive to rapid neutron capture processes, termed r-process nucleosynthesis. This stellar alchemy, driven by the intense forces present during the merger, leads to the production of heavy elements such as gold, platinum, and uranium—elements that are not only fundamental to our understanding of chemical evolution but also hold profound significance for human civilization.

Our journey into the discovery of heavy elements begins with the exceptional gravitational wave event detected in August 2017, a momentous merger of two neutron stars that showcased the true power of multi-messenger astronomy. For the first time, gravitational waves detected by the LIGO and Virgo observatories coincided with electromagnetic signals observed across multiple wavelengths, including gamma-ray bursts and optical emissions from the resulting kilonova explosion. The convergence of these observations marked a turning point in astrophysics, allowing scientists to draw direct connections between the gravitational waves produced during the merger and the synthesis of heavy elements.

These observations revealed that mergers not only generate gravitational waves with unique signatures but also create conditions ripe for nucleosynthesis. As neutron stars spiral together and merge, the environment becomes saturated with neutrons, allowing for rapid neutron capture processes to unfold. This process leads to the formation of heavy, stable isotopes that can then be ejected into the cosmos, enriching the interstellar medium and seeding future generations of stars and planets. Thus, the very fabric of the universe is shaped by these stellar events, as heavy elements coalescing from the ashes of neutron star mergers contribute to the cosmic chemical evolution, reaffirming the connection between cosmic phenomena and the building blocks of life itself.

Furthermore, the implications of discovering heavy elements through gravitational wave observations extend to our understanding of galactic structures and star formation as well. The material expelled during these mergers enriches the gas clouds that serve as the birthplaces of new stars. This transformative process influences galactic dynamics—affecting the formation rates of stars and the types of celestial bodies that emerge. The very existence of heavy elements in the universe, enabling the formation of planets and organic molecules, is rooted in these cataclysmic events, accentuating the intricate relationship between cosmic events and the emergence of life.

As gravitational wave astronomy continues to evolve, the discovery of heavy elements serves as a catalyst for interdisciplinary dialogue among various scientific fields, uniting physicists, chemists, and astronomers. The collaborative spirit fosters a deeper understanding of the mechanisms that lead to the synthesis of elements across different environments in the universe, encouraging researchers to examine the interplay of stellar life cycles, supernova explosions, and neutron star mergers as they confront fundamental questions about the origins of matter.

The techniques developed for investigating gravitational waves not only enhance our grasp of neutron star mergers and their associated synthesis of heavy elements but also open new pathways for studying cosmic events. Future advancements in observational technology and international collaboration will further fortify the framework through which we explore these phenomena. As next-generation observatories come online and enhance our ability to detect gravitational waves, the potential to unveil further complexities about the universe's elemental makeup and the processes driving cosmic evolution expands exponentially.

In conclusion, the discovery of heavy elements through gravitational wave astronomy encapsulates a remarkable journey of inquiry, transcending disciplines and enriching our understanding of the universe. As we tap into the echoes of neutron star mergers, we learn not only of the dramatic events that birthed these elements but also reflect on their role in shaping the cosmos as we know it today. The gravitational waves serve as an invitation to splendid exploration, guiding us to an unfolding narrative interwoven with the very threads of existence—one that connects stellar births and deaths with the elemental foundation of life and our place in the vast expanse of the universe. Through this discovery, we are reminded that the cosmos is an interconnected system, continuously evolving, waiting for us to listen closely and uncover the stories hidden within the whispers of gravitational waves.

9.4. Building Blocks of the Universe

In the universe's grand design, our understanding is constructed upon diverse building blocks—fundamental elements and forces that shape the dynamics of cosmic interactions, weaving the very fabric of reality. These building blocks are not just limited to atomic structures; they extend into the realms of fundamental forces, stellar evolution, and, crucially, the relationships between massive celestial bodies. At the heart of this narrative is gravity, a force that regulates the motions of planets, stars, galaxies, and even the cosmos at large. To unveil the profound whispers of gravitational waves, we must delve into the intricate composition of these building blocks that underpin our universe.

From the perspective of particle physics, the universe is composed of elementary particles—quarks and leptons are the building blocks of matter, while bosons mediate the fundamental forces. These particles interact under various forces governed by the laws of quantum mechanics, allowing us to explore interactions at microscopic scales. However, when we zoom out to a cosmic scale, the dynamics shift toward gravitational influences governed by Einstein's General Theory of Relativity, which provides insight into how mass and energy warp spacetime itself, leading to the formation of gravitational waves.

As massive celestial bodies such as stars and black holes form, they give rise to complex interactions that define their existence. The lifecycle of a star—from its formation in dense molecular clouds to its eventual collapse into a neutron star or black hole—embodies the interplay between nuclear processes and gravitational forces. Each phase in this evolution contributes to the building blocks of the universe, with the fusion of elements within stars forging the very materials that populate galaxies, planets, and, ultimately, life itself.

Furthermore, when massive stars reach their endpoints and undergo supernova explosions, they give rise to neutron stars and black holes —elements driving some of the most dynamic interactions observable in the universe. Binary systems, composed of these dense remnants, engage in intricate gravitational dynamics, leading to the emission of gravitational waves. The collisions and mergers of these stellar masses are iconic events, serving as monumental reminders of the celestial mechanics that govern our universe.

Understanding the building blocks of the cosmos also requires addressing the concept of dark matter and dark energy—elusive constituents that dominate modern cosmological inquiries. Though not yet fully understood, these components appear to exert gravitational influences on visible matter and the universe's expansion, intricately intertwining with our understanding of gravitational waves. As gravitational wave astronomy emerges as a robust scientific field, probing these dark regions provides pathways to unlock many cosmic secrets that have long remained hidden from observation.

As we venture deeper into the narratives surrounding our universe, we uncover that the building blocks reflect the interplay of forces, particles, and celestial bodies, all of which converge to create a tapestry of interactions that define cosmic landscapes. The gravitational waves detected from cataclysmic events encapsulate stories forged from these building blocks, revealing fundamental truths about the nature of matter and energy while reshaping our celestial narrative.

In this context, it becomes clear that the impulse to explore the universe is interwoven with a profound curiosity to understand the forces that govern it. Each gravitational wave detected serves not merely as a result of a cosmic event, but as a key that unlocks the mechanisms behind gravity, mass, and the intricate structures that make up our universe.

As we embrace the journey through these building blocks, the intricate web connecting particles, forces, cosmic bodies, and phenomena heightens our appreciation for the interconnectedness of all aspects of existence. While we may only catch fleeting glimpses of the immense complexity of the universe, each gravitational wave detection invites us to listen closely, delve deeper, and continue our boundless pursuit of knowledge about the magnificent cosmos we inhabit—a cosmos intricately woven from the very building blocks of reality itself.

9.5. A New Chapter in Astronomy

The discovery of gravitational waves has heralded a new era in astronomy, framing a narrative of profound implications and exciting prospects. As we transition into this transformative chapter, we find ourselves at the convergence of advanced observational techniques, interdisciplinary collaboration, and theoretical speculation. The echoes of collisions between massive cosmic entities—neutron stars, black holes, and their interactions—provide window-like glimpses into the deeper fabric of the cosmos, revealing secrets that have remained concealed for millennia.

At the heart of this understanding are gravitational waves—the ripples in spacetime generated by the acceleration and merging of massive objects. Initially a theoretical construct, the detection of these waves has propelled gravitational wave astronomy into the forefront of scientific exploration. Each event captured by observatories like LIGO and Virgo serves as a key, unlocking extraordinary celestial narratives written in the language of gravity. These waves carry with them fingerprints of their dynamic origins, revealing details about the masses, spins, and distances of their progenitors.

The implications of gravitational wave discoveries extend beyond the boundaries of astrophysics and challenge our understanding of fundamental truths—not just about gravity, but about cosmic evolution, stellar life cycles, and the very elements that compose our universe. For example, the 2017 detection of gravitational waves from a neutron star merger provided ground-breaking confirmation of the association between such astronomical events and the origin of heavy elements like gold and platinum. As these neutron stars collided and merged, they created conditions ripe for nucleosynthesis, enriching the cosmos and contributing to the elemental diversity that forms our world.

Moreover, the establishment of a global gravitational wave network exemplifies the spirit of international collaboration that characterizes contemporary science. With the interconnectivity of observatories in various parts of the world—each equipped with sophisticated technology designed for heightened sensitivity and precision—researchers can share vital data and insights. This cohesive effort promotes a culture of openness, fostering a sense of unity among scientists working toward a shared understanding of the universe.

The innovative technologies employed for gravitational wave detection have transformed our observational strategies. Laser interferometry—the cornerstone technique underpinning facilities like LIGO —relies on measuring minute changes in distance caused by passing gravitational waves. Through advancements in laser sources, optical components, and noise mitigation techniques, gravitational wave observatories can reach unparalleled sensitivity, paving the way for the exploration of previously hidden cosmic phenomena. Indeed, as these detection methods continue to evolve, the potential for new discoveries expands exponentially.

With each wave detected, we delve deeper into the uncharted territories of the universe. The journey through gravitational wave astronomy invites scholars from diverse fields—physics, engineering, and computer science—to converge towards a common goal of understanding the cosmos. It challenges conventional paradigms and pushes the boundaries of scientific inquiry, encouraging interdisciplinary collaboration that propels us forward. As we engage with each gravitational event, we illuminate not only the origins of matter but the very nature of reality itself.

In essence, the saga of gravitational waves represents more than just the detection of faint cosmic signals; it is a compelling narrative characterized by the resilience of human curiosity, the triumph of collaborative effort, and the drive to unveil the mysteries woven into the cosmos. As we continue to listen closely to the commands of gravity's whispers, we cultivate a collective consciousness that inspires future generations of explorers, inviting them into a shared journey of discovery that transcends time and space.

As we conclude this chapter and reflect upon the progress made, we recognize that versatility and adaptive thinking will define the future of gravitational wave astronomy. Exciting prospects await, as next-generation observatories promise enhanced detection capabilities and broader scopes of inquiry. The quest for understanding the universe continues, and gravitational waves stand at the forefront, guiding us into the depths of cosmic exploration, drawing us ever closer to unveiling the exceptional stories crafted among the stars. With ears attuned to this celestial symphony, we are poised to decipher the exciting mysteries of the universe, welcoming the engagement of future explorers who will continue probing the boundless realms of gravitational waves and their cosmic implications.

10. The Global Gravitational Network

10.1. International Collaboration

International collaboration in the realm of gravitational wave astronomy has emerged as a cornerstone of modern astrophysics, representing the collective efforts of scientists, engineers, and researchers from diverse geographic and cultural backgrounds. This cooperation is vital for the advancement of gravitational wave detection, interpretation, and the broader cosmic inquiry that such phenomena initiate. As we venture into this subchapter, we will explore the significance of international collaboration, its impact on gravitational wave astronomy, and the ethos of unity it fosters among the scientific community.

At the forefront of this collaborative effort is the remarkable network of gravitational wave observatories that span the globe. Pioneering facilities like LIGO in the United States, Virgo in Italy, and KAGRA in Japan epitomize the principle of global cooperation in scientific discovery. Each observatory contributes unique strengths, advanced technologies, and varying observational capabilities—collectively enhancing the capacity for detecting and analyzing gravitational waves. When a significant event occurs, such as the merger of neutron stars or black holes, each observatory can independently analyze the waves that traverse through spacetime, leading to more robust and comprehensive understandings of the events.

The historical context of these collaborations is essential to appreciate their profound implications. LIGO made the groundbreaking detection of gravitational waves in 2015 when it observed the merger of two black holes. This success opened the door for intercontinental collaboration, as other existing observatories and new partners initiated synergies to enhance the collective datasets available to researchers. The collaboration with Virgo was particularly significant, as its geographic proximity to LIGO allowed for triangulation and improved source localization. The ability to combine signals from multiple detectors provides vital corroborative data, ensuring that false positives are minimized and enabling richer insights into the dynamics at play.

The ethos of international collaboration extends beyond mere operational efficiency; it represents a philosophical commitment to advancing knowledge for the greater good of humanity. This spirit fosters organized science meeting meaningful inquiry. It cultivates an inclusive community of diverse voices, perspectives, and ideas, enriching the processes of discovery and interpretation. The open exchange of ideas and findings encourages stronger methodologies informed by the collective wisdom of scientists dedicated to unraveling the mysteries of the cosmos.

One tangible expression of this collaborative spirit can be seen in the ongoing efforts to share data and research across borders. The establishment of platforms for real-time data sharing allows for seamless collaboration when gravitational wave events are detected. Scientists across the globe can engage in immediate discussions, analyzing the implications of the data generated and refining their understanding collectively. This collaborative platform is critical for the future of gravitational wave astronomy, as it fosters a culture of shared inquiry where every contribution adds to the broader knowledge pool.

Furthermore, international collaboration helps to expand educational opportunities and the public's engagement with science. Global investment into gravitational wave astronomy translates into educational outreach initiatives that foster interest in the field among budding scientists and students. These efforts aim to inspire curiosity, cultivate talent, and encourage future generations to participate actively in scientific endeavors. Public engagement serves to demystify gravitational wave science, inviting the public to share in the excitement of discovery and understand its ramifications.

Looking ahead, the continuation and expansion of international collaboration are poised to shape the future of gravitational wave astronomy. Plans for next-generation observatories and novel detection techniques necessitate robust partnerships among institutions and countries. Future advancements, such as space-based observatories like the Laser Interferometer Space Antenna (LISA), will require unprecedented levels of cooperation and resource-sharing to realize their full potential. The iterative process of refinement and adaptation of existing methodologies will benefit profoundly from the contributions of a global scientific community united by purpose.

In summary, international collaboration remains a linchpin for the progress and vitality of gravitational wave astronomy. The collective efforts across countries and cultures not only fortify the pursuit of knowledge but also enrich our understanding of the universe by fostering a spirit of unity and shared discovery. As we continue to listen to the gravitational echoes resonating within the cosmos and work towards unveiling its mysteries, this collaborative ethos reminds us of the strength that emerges when humanity gathers together in pursuit of a common goal—understanding our universe and, in turn, ourselves. The gravitational wave landscape is but a reflection of our collective aspirations—a testament to the capacity for collaboration, innovation, and exploration that lies inherent in the human spirit.

10.2. The Role of KAGRA

The Role of KAGRA

In the intricate tapestry of gravitational wave astronomy, KAGRA stands as a crucial thread, adding depth and complexity to the quest for understanding cosmic phenomena. Located in Japan, KAGRA (Kamioka Gravitational Wave Detector) represents a significant leap forward in gravitational wave detection, implementing advanced technologies and methodologies to probe the universe's most profound whispers. Its role is defined not only by its technical innovations but also by its contribution to international cooperation and the scientific community's collective pursuit of knowledge.

KAGRA's design is unique, integrating several key advancements that enhance its sensitivity and measurement capabilities. Unlike its counterparts LIGO and Virgo, which operate on the Earth's surface, KAGRA is situated underground, which helps to minimize various sources of noise, such as seismic vibrations and thermal fluctuations. This innovative choice amplifies the detector's ability to discern faint gravitational signals from the cacophony of background disturbances that often obfuscate observations. By employing such meticulous engineering and thoughtful design, KAGRA positions itself as a leader in the field, pushing the boundaries of what is achievable in gravitational wave astronomy.

One of the defining features of KAGRA is its use of cryogenic technology. The mirrors utilized in KAGRA's interferometer are cooled to a fraction of a Kelvin, significantly reducing thermal noise—an important step that enhances the precision required for gravitational wave detection. This approach allows KAGRA to tune into the delicate signals emitted by cosmic events with an unprecedented level of sensitivity. The incorporation of cryogenics sets KAGRA apart from other observatories, showcasing the ingenuity and innovative spirit that characterizes modern observational astronomy.

Collaborative endeavors underpin KAGRA's operational philosophy. As part of the global gravitational wave network, KAGRA contributes crucial data that enhance the collective effort to understand the universe. When KAGRA detects a gravitational wave event, its data can be shared with neighboring observatories such as LIGO and Virgo, creating a comprehensive picture of cosmic phenomena. This collaboration not only bolsters the validity of observations but also allows for advanced analysis techniques that capitalize on contributions from multiple observatories, ultimately leading to a deeper understanding of the underlying astrophysical processes.

The significance of KAGRA extends beyond its advanced technological capabilities; it also serves as a focal point for international engagement in gravitational wave research. Through collaborative projects, workshops, and conferences, KAGRA fosters communication and connectivity within the scientific community, bridging researchers from different countries and disciplines. This cooperative spirit strengthens institutional ties and paves the way for groundbreaking discoveries, demonstrating the power of united inquiry in the pursuit of knowledge.

As gravitational wave astronomy continues to evolve, KAGRA's ongoing contributions promise to play an indispensable role. Future advancements in technology, including potential upgrades to KAGRA's detection capabilities, herald a bright horizon for gravitational wave studies. The anticipated collaboration with next-generation observatories aims to deepen the exploration of the cosmos, enhancing the prospect of discovering new sources of gravitational waves and uncovering the enigma of cosmic events that shape our universe.

The insights gleaned from KAGRA extend across numerous realms within astrophysics. By observing various merging events and interactions, KAGRA contributes to the statistical understanding of black holes and neutron stars, enriching our knowledge of their population and distribution within the galaxy. This empirical data directly informs models of stellar evolution and the enigmatic processes that govern the lifecycle of celestial bodies.

Ultimately, the role of KAGRA in gravitational wave astronomy transcends its operational capabilities; it embodies the spirit of exploration, collaboration, and scientific inquiry that characterizes this bold and transformative field of study. As we continue to listen to the gravitational waves emanating from the cosmos, KAGRA invites the scientific community and the public alike to engage with the broader narrative—a story defined by interconnectedness, profound discovery, and the relentless pursuit of knowledge that reverberates through the universe itself. The journey through gravitational wave astronomy is enriched by KAGRA's contributions, urging us onward as we seek to unravel the mysteries woven into the fabric of reality.

10.3. Future Observatories

Future observatories represent the next frontier in our quest to understand the cosmos through the lens of gravitational wave astronomy. With the success of existing facilities like LIGO, Virgo, and KAGRA, the scientific community is poised to build upon these achievements, advancing both technology and methodologies to delve deeper into the mysteries of the universe. The advent of next-generation observatories promises unprecedented sensitivity and a broader frequency range, allowing researchers to capture gravitational waves from a wider array of cosmic events and enhance our understanding of the fundamental aspects of astrophysics.

One of the most exciting developments in this arena is the proposed construction of observatories designed to operate in space, such as the Laser Interferometer Space Antenna (LISA). By positioning detectors beyond the interference of Earth's atmosphere, space-based observatories will circumvent many environmental noise factors that limit ground-based facilities. This strategic positioning will enable the detection of lower-frequency gravitational waves—signals generated by enormous astronomical phenomena, including supermassive black hole mergers and the early universe's dynamics. Such observations could reveal unparalleled insights into the nature of gravity, dark matter, and the fluctuations of spacetime.

The commitment to advancing gravitational wave observatories also extends to improvements in technology and instrumentation. Innovations in laser sources, photodetection techniques, and gravitational wave signal processing will enhance the detectors' sensitivity manifold, enabling them to observe even fainter signals that interplay in the cosmic dance of celestial bodies. Cutting-edge methods, such as employing squeezed light in interferometers or utilizing advanced seismic isolation techniques, are currently being researched to further bolster the ability to capture these elusive waves. As we pursue such endeavors, each technological advancement paves the way for deeper inquiries and richer interpretations of the observed phenomena.

Global collaboration will play an essential role in the evolution of future observatories. The international gravitational wave network exemplifies a spirit of unity and cooperation that can only serve to strengthen our collective ability to probe the cosmos. Partnerships among institutions across continents ensure the sharing of insights, technology, and resources, fostering an environment where diverse perspectives converge to tackle scientific challenges. This collaborative framework will be crucial as new observatories come online, allowing researchers to combine their datasets and analyze events from multiple vantage points, ultimately producing a more comprehensive understanding of the cosmos.

Future observatories will also provide fertile grounds for interdisciplinary collaboration. Fields such as cosmology, particle physics, and even philosophy stand to benefit from the influx of data and insights generated by gravitational wave observations. As science progresses toward a more holistic understanding of the universe, the ability to interpret gravitational wave signals in the context of broader astrophysical questions will unlock new avenues of research and inquiry.

In addition, the philosophy of experimental science will move beyond the traditional boundaries of theoretical and observational paradigms, prompting an exploration of the ethics surrounding repository data sharing, public engagement, and the implications of new discoveries. Future observatories may not only unravel cosmic mysteries but also inform discussions about humanity's role within a broader cosmic narrative.

As we reflect on the potential of future observatories, we are reminded that each advancement in detection capabilities heralds a new chapter in our journey to listen to the whispers of the universe. The cumulative findings from these facilities will redefine our understanding of dark matter, dark energy, and the underlying laws governing cosmic behavior, transforming our comprehension of the universe's intricate nature. With a wealth of discoveries on the horizon, future observatories invite the next generations of scientists, dreamers, and explorers to engage in this remarkable journey, ultimately reshaping the narrative of our existence in the grand cosmic tapestry.

As we stand at the cusp of this exhilarating new era, excitement fills the air. The future of gravitational wave astronomy awaits, and with it, a world of uncharted mysteries beckons—an invitation to embrace the unknown, capture the echoes of the cosmos, and uncover the astonishing stories woven into the very fabric of reality. The stage is set, and the journey is just beginning.

10.4. Data Sharing and Analysis

In the rapidly evolving field of gravitational wave astronomy, data sharing and analysis play a pivotal role in transforming fleeting cosmic echoes into robust scientific insights. The ability to listen to these whispers from the universe hinges upon not just the detection of gravitational waves but also the meticulous work that follows—an intricate dance of collaboration, interpretation, and validation. As we delve into this crucial subchapter, we explore how data sharing and analysis stimulate advancements in our understanding of the cosmos, foster international collaboration, and shape the future of astronomical research.

At the outset, it is important to appreciate the sheer volume of data generated by gravitational wave observatories. Instruments like LIGO and Virgo capture signals at an astounding rate, producing petabytes of data that encompass a wide array of gravitational wave events—everything from black hole mergers to neutron star collisions. This avalanche of information, however, presents both a tremendous opportunity and a formidable challenge. To extract meaningful insights, teams of scientists must navigate through layers of noise, interference, and uncertainty, filtering through complex datasets to identify genuine signals that indicate the occurrence of significant cosmic events.

Data sharing serves as an essential mechanism for enhancing the quality and reliability of analyses. Interoperability among gravitational wave observatories fosters a collaborative environment where independent institutions can pool their resources and expertise to develop cumulative datasets that inform their understanding of cosmic phenomena. The sharing of raw gravitational wave data not only strengthens the mutual validation of experimental findings but also facilitates cross-contamination of methodologies, leading to improved detection techniques and better theoretical models.

The collaborative effort extends well beyond the realm of gravitational waves; it encompasses a vast network of interdisciplinary cooperation among astronomers, physicists, computational scientists, and engineers. As researchers analyze data, they draw upon expertise from diverse fields to construct comprehensive models that help decode the intricate signals encapsulated within the gravitational waves. The integration of various scientific approaches enables researchers to tackle the multifaceted challenges intrinsic to analyzing these waveforms, fostering an environment of ingenuity that ultimately expands our glimpse into the universe.

As the international gravitational wave community thrives, the spirit of collaboration resonates through platforms that promote data sharing, open access, and transparency in research. Initiatives such as the Gravitational Wave Open Science Center (GWOSC) empower researchers and enthusiasts alike, offering datasets and tools to facilitate exploration and understanding of gravitational wave events. This democratization of data serves to inspire new avenues of research and inquiry. Citizen scientists and amateur astronomers can engage with the material, contributing to the broader conversation surrounding gravitational waves and calling attention to the communal nature of scientific inquiry.

Moreover, the advent of sophisticated data analysis techniques—augmented by developments in machine learning and artificial intelligence—has revolutionized the methodology of interpreting gravitational wave signals. These technologies can identify patterns and anomalies in vast datasets with remarkable efficiency, unveiling signals previously obscured by noise. By harnessing the computational power of machine learning algorithms, researchers can improve their ability to distinguish between genuine gravitational wave events and irrelevant signals, enhancing the fidelity of the analyses conducted across the network of observatories.

A critical aspect of data analysis in gravitational wave astronomy also involves developing theoretical models that align with observational findings. Researchers actively incorporate the inferred properties of the detected signals—such as mass ratios, spins, and distances—into models that elucidate the behaviors of black holes and neutron stars. Each gravitational wave event contributes to a growing compendium of knowledge about the population of compact objects in the universe and their evolution over cosmic timescales.

The dynamic interplay between data sharing, analysis, and theoretical modeling not only enhances our understanding of specific gravitational wave events but also catalyzes transformative questions about the fundamental laws of physics. Every detection encourages a re-examination of existing models, fostering discussions about the nature of gravity, the connections between general relativity and quantum mechanics, and the implications for deep cosmic mysteries such as dark matter and dark energy.

As we look towards the future, the importance of robust data collection, sharing, and analysis in gravitational wave astronomy cannot be overstated. The anticipated growth of next-generation observatories will generate increasingly large datasets, necessitating further advancements in data management, filtering, and interpretation techniques. The collaborative frameworks established now will pave the way for deeper engagement in cosmic inquiry and produce an enhanced understanding of the universe that lies just beyond our current grasp.

In conclusion, data sharing and analysis are the lifeblood of gravitational wave astronomy, shaping the trajectory of our exploration of the cosmos. The interconnectedness fostered by collaboration, the integration of diverse scientific disciplines, and the innovative use of technology within this realm lead us toward profound discoveries that redefine our understanding of existence. As we continue to listen attentively to the whispers of the universe conveyed through gravitational waves, we stand united in our quest for knowledge, poised to unravel the intricate narratives woven into the fabric of reality itself.

10.5. The Spirit of Scientific Unity

The global effort to uncover the mysteries of gravitational waves exemplifies the spirit of scientific unity and collaboration that transcends borders, disciplines, and cultures. This paradigm shift in astronomy, enabled by technological innovations and the concerted efforts of a diverse international community, has redefined our understanding of the cosmos. The intricate interplay of individual contributions, institutional partnerships, and global observatories showcases a harmonious pursuit of knowledge, echoing the very essence of scientific exploration.

At the heart of this unity lies the realization that gravitational wave phenomena cannot be fully understood in isolation. The complex nature of cosmic events, such as black hole mergers and neutron star collisions, necessitates multi-faceted approaches that draw from a broad spectrum of expertise. The interconnectedness of astrophysics, engineering, computer science, and even fields like philosophy and ethics forms a rich tapestry of inquiry, where insights gleaned from one discipline inform and enhance the understanding in another.

The establishment of a global network of observatories—most famously, LIGO, Virgo, and KAGRA—acts as the backbone of this collaboration, allowing for coordinated research efforts aimed at detecting and analyzing gravitational waves. These institutions serve as a physical manifestation of the scientific unity that characterizes modern inquiry. Each observatory contributes its unique advantages —LIGO's sensitivity, Virgo's location, and KAGRA's innovative cryogenic systems—harmonizing efforts that amplify the capacity to probe the unknown.

This cooperative spirit extends to data sharing and analysis, where open access to gravitational wave datasets fosters an atmosphere of transparency and inclusivity. Initiatives like the Gravitational Wave Open Science Center encourage scientists, students, and even citizen scientists to engage with the data, spawning curiosity and facilitating discoveries that would remain hidden if confined to exclusive circles. This comprehensive approach invites broader participation in the scientific endeavor, a crucial factor in advancing gravitational wave astronomy.

The sense of unity in this endeavor is accentuated by the recognition that the implications of gravitational wave discoveries extend beyond the purely academic. Each detection serves not only as a validation of a unique event but also as a catalyst for interdisciplinary dialogue —prompting discussions among physicists, chemists, cosmologists, and even philosophers about the nature of reality, the origins of the universe, and humanity's place within it. Gravitational waves become a bridge, linking diverse avenues of inquiry in pursuit of the same ultimate goal: understanding the intricacies of our cosmos.

Moreover, the ethical considerations surrounding the exploration of the universe are amplified within this collaborative framework. As we gain insights that reshape our understanding of fundamental forces and elements, we must also engage in discussions about the impact of such knowledge on society, the environment, and even our concept of existence. The engagement of scientists in these conversations emphasizes that our quest for knowledge is not merely a pursuit of information but carries profound responsibilities toward the broader implications of our discoveries.

As we look toward the future, the spirit of scientific unity will remain paramount. The next generation of gravitational wave observatories promises remarkable advancements in detection capabilities and a continued commitment to collaboration. By nurturing this ethos of togetherness, we pave the way for deeper explorations into the unknown, harnessing the collective spirit of humanity in unveiling the universe's most profound mysteries.

In conclusion, the journey ahead in gravitational wave astronomy embodies the spirit of scientific unity—an unwavering collaboration between individuals and institutions dedicated to understanding the cosmos. This collaborative symphony encourages inquiry, fosters innovation, and reflects our collective responsibility to explore and interpret the wonders of existence. Each gravitational wave detected is a testament to this spirit, an echo of the interconnectedness that defines our pursuit of knowledge and the remarkable narrative of humanity striving to comprehend the universe's grand tapestry. As we continue to listen to the whispers of gravitational waves, we affirm our shared commitment to exploration, discovery, and the beauty of scientific unity that binds us together in this endeavor.

11. Revolutionizing Cosmology

11.1. Impacts on Cosmological Models

The discovery of gravitational waves has brought about a paradigm shift in our understanding of the universe and drastically impacted existing cosmological models. The implications of these enigmatic ripples, resulting from the most violent and energetic events in the cosmos, stretch far beyond what was previously conceivable, unraveling threads woven deep into the fabric of space and time. This section delves into the profound impacts gravitational waves have on cosmological frameworks, shedding light on how they shape our interpretations of universal functions and phenomena.

Traditionally, cosmological models have relied heavily on electromagnetic observations—light in its various forms emanating from stars, galaxies, and other cosmic bodies. However, the advent of gravitational wave astronomy broadens the sensory toolkit available to astrophysicists, allowing them to perceive and analyze events that are otherwise invisible to conventional observational methods. This transition not only validates existing theories but also challenges long-held assumptions about the nature of astronomical phenomena.

Gravitational waves hold a unique position in enhancing our understanding of stellar interactions and cosmic events. They provide direct evidence of systems involving black holes and neutron stars, confirming theoretical predictions such as those concerning black hole mergers. This newfound empirical data offers astronomers a deeper comprehension of the dynamics involved in such extreme processes, leading to refinements in the models that characterize the life cycles of stars and their ultimate fates. For example, gravitational wave observations have revealed unexpected populations of massive black holes, prompting researchers to re-evaluate theories regarding their formation, growth, and coalescence.

Moreover, the gravitational waves generated by neutron star mergers serve as a conduit for connecting cosmic mysteries to heavy element synthesis. The observation that these mergers lead to the creation of heavy elements through rapid neutron capture processes introduces a new layer of complexity to our understanding of nucleosynthesis. Previously attributed primarily to supernovae, the confirmation that gravitational waves provide insights into the origins of gold, platinum, and other heavy elements compels cosmologists to rethink galactic chemical evolution models.

One of the most significant challenges facing modern cosmology is the understanding of dark energy and dark matter—both elusive entities dominating the universe's composition. The study of gravitational waves offers fresh avenues for investigating these phenomena. For instance, insights gleaned from binary neutron star mergers can provide constraints on the nature of dark matter, as the precise understanding of neutron star masses helps to refine the calculations surrounding their interactions.

Additionally, as gravitational wave detectors continue to enhance their sensitivity, they could potentially probe the early universe's conditions. This includes examining the remnants of the rapid expansion during cosmic inflation—a pivotal moment in the universe's history. Gravitational waves may encode information about this epoch and offer a new way to investigate the mechanisms responsible for cosmic inflation, thus impacting the models that frame our understanding of how the universe evolved from its initial configuration.

The discoveries stemming from gravitational wave observations have sparked a reassessment of the expansion rate of the universe—a phenomenon commonly referred to as the Hubble constant. The discrepancies apparent between measurements from gravitational waves and those derived from traditional methods pose significant questions about how data is interpreted and how cosmological models account for variations across observational paradigms.

As we witness the interplay between observations and theoretical frameworks evolve, the impact of gravitational waves resonates across every corner of modern cosmology. They represent a monumental leap in our journey to understand the universe, illuminating dark regions previously opaque to our inquiries. The insight they provide serves not only to enrich our comprehension of the cosmos but also cultivates an environment ripe for broader scientific discourse, bridging disciplines that connect gravitational physics with the very foundations of cosmology.

In conclusion, the incorporation of gravitational waves into the realm of cosmological models signifies a transformative movement— a departure from traditional observational methodologies ushering in a new chapter in our exploration of the universe. The waves serve as cosmic signifiers, directing researchers' gaze toward an enriched tapestry of existence filled with dynamic interactions, elemental creation, and mysteries pertinent to humanity's understanding of its place within the cosmos. As gravitational wave detection technology advances, the promises of continuous refinement of cosmological models bring us closer to grasping the fundamental truths of the universe, carving pathways into the unknown for generations to come. Every wave detected is a whisper from the cosmos itself, urging us to listen, learn, and explore.

11.2. Dark Energy and Dark Matter Revelations

In the field of cosmic observation, the revelation of dark energy and dark matter driven by gravitational wave detections has profound consequences for our understanding of the universe. Historically, the cosmos was thought to be largely composed of matter we could detect through light-based observations, such as stars and galaxies; however, the discovery of gravitational waves opened entirely new dimensions of inquiry. They illuminate the complex interplay between visible and invisible forces that shape the framework of our universe.

Dark energy, an enigmatic force believed to drive the accelerated expansion of the universe, has emerged from various lines of thought and observational evidence. Until the arrival of gravitational wave astronomy, our insights into dark energy largely relied upon redshift measurements of distant supernovae and cosmic microwave background radiation. However, the ability to detect the merger of compact objects like black holes and neutron stars introduces new observational avenues, reinforcing and challenging existing cosmological models. Gravitational wave detections act as invaluable tools that further inform our understanding of not only the distribution and dynamics of dark matter but also the evolution and fate of the cosmos itself.

Moreover, the merging of celestial bodies generates gravitational waves that carry information encoded in their waveforms—characteristics linked to the masses and velocities of the objects involved, and their associated gravitational effects. Decoding these signatures offers vital insights into how dark matter influences the formation of structures within the universe. Each detection helps astronomers refine the parameters surrounding the mass, density, and spatial distribution of dark matter, revealing its role in cosmic architecture.

In tandem, the exploration of gravitational waves elucidates the nature of dark energy through its effects on cosmic expansion. As gravitational waves carry data about the acceleration of mergers, they intersect with discussions about the origins of dark energy. The correlation of these observations with cosmic evolution muscle against conventional models that inadequately describe the universe's acceleration. Through this intersection, scientists endeavor to grasp the interplay between gravitational waves and the fundamental cosmic forces that govern the universe's fate.

The revelations garnered from gravitational wave observations not only challenge prior assumptions about dark energy and dark matter but also spark philosophical inquiries that provoke deeper questions about existence and reality. The intricate relationship between gravitational waves and cosmological components indicates that our understanding of the universe remains incomplete—and reinforces the notion that much lies beyond the observable spectrum still to be unraveled.

As we look forward, the future of gravitational wave astronomy promises even more insights into dark energy and dark matter. The potential development of next-generation observatories, enhanced sensitivity, and improved data collection techniques will yield an unprecedented wealth of information. By illuminating the interactions and influences of these enigmatic components, gravitational waves will serve as crucial elements within the vast puzzle of cosmology.

In conclusion, the exploration of dark energy and dark matter through the revelations provided by gravitational waves redefines our understanding of fundamental cosmic mechanics. Each detection acts as a stepping stone toward elucidating the perplexities that have long puzzled astronomers and physicists alike. As we continue to listen to the echoes of the universe, we delve into the profound mysteries surrounding dark energy and dark matter, each breakthrough anchoring our journey toward a more robust grasp of the universe's grand narrative—an invitation to explore the depths of existence and the ever-evolving fabric of reality.

11.3. Probing the Early Universe

The early universe, a realm shrouded in mystery and defined by extreme conditions, stands as a pivotal area of study in modern cosmology. Probing this extraordinary epoch has become possible through the insights gained from gravitational wave astronomy. These ripples in spacetime, originating from some of the most cataclysmic events in cosmic history, offer a unique perspective into the birth and evolution of our universe, shedding light on phenomena that have long eluded direct observation.

At the beginning of the universe, shortly after the Big Bang, temperatures soared, and the fundamental forces as we understand them today were not yet differentiated. During this period, known as the Planck epoch, gravity was unified with the other fundamental forces, existing in a state of profound significance. The subsequent moments of cosmic inflation rapidly expanded the universe, smoothing out any irregularities and setting the stage for the structures that would form later. Gravitational waves produced during this early period, though enigmatic and difficult to detect, are believed to carry crucial information about the conditions present at this time.

Observing gravitational waves provides a new gateway into understanding the dynamics of the early universe. For instance, if the gravitational waves from inflationary events could be detected, they would serve as a direct remnant of the rapid expansion phase, allowing scientists to test theories of inflation and gain insight into the initial conditions of the universe. These potential discoveries herald the possibility of connecting cosmic events directly to the evolution of the universe's structure and character.

As gravitational wave detectors improve in sensitivity, they offer the prospect of revealing signals from the early universe that are not buried by the background noise of other astrophysical events. Comprehensive data from a variety of sources, including cosmic microwave background radiation, electromagnetic observations, and now, gravitational wave detections, collectively inform our understanding of cosmological models, advancing the dialogue about the most fundamental aspects of reality.

Events that occur in this early era include those that lead to the formation of black holes, the genesis of neutron stars, and the condensing of matter into galaxies. Through the analysis of gravitational wave signals from more recent mergers of black holes or neutron stars, astrophysicists make connections back to these early events, piecing together the sequence of stellar and cosmic evolution.

The implications of these findings extend beyond mere observations; they hold profound consequences for the founding theories of cosmology, challenging and refining existing models. For instance, understanding how primordial black holes formed could reshape theories about the growth of structure in the universe and lead to new insights regarding dark matter. Each gravitational wave signal detected acts as a piece of evidence unraveling the tapestry of cosmic history.

Furthermore, probing the early universe through gravitational waves may also offer insights into the nature of dark energy, an enigmatic force driving the universe's accelerated expansion. By studying the characteristics of gravitational waves across different epochs, researchers strive to unlock secrets related to the dynamics of cosmic expansion and explore whether modifications to existing cosmological models are necessary.

As we delve deeper into gravitational wave observations, the early universe serves as an exhilarating frontier for exploration and discovery. The potential to uncover the mysteries shrouded in the dawn of time ignites imaginations, inviting scientists, philosophers, and curious minds alike to engage in this grand endeavor.

In conclusion, probing the early universe through gravitational waves represents a transformative chapter in cosmic exploration—one that unravels the narratives of creation, evolution, and existence itself. Each wave detected echoes the profound questions that resonate through time and space, sparking curiosity and urging humanity to delve deeper into the awe-inspiring mysteries of the cosmos. As we continue this journey, we move closer to understanding the effects of the universe's conditions on its trajectory, revealing an intricate relationship between gravitational waves and the evolutionary story that shapes the cosmos. The whispers of the early universe call to us, inviting exploration, challenge, and insight as we endeavor to cover the infinite complexities of existence itself.

11.4. New Insights into the Big Bang

In the realm of astrophysics, the exploration of gravitational waves is intimately intertwined with our understanding of the Big Bang—the monumental expansion that marked the inception of our universe. As scientists have gradually begun to decode the whispers of gravitational waves, new insights into the nature and aftermath of the Big Bang have emerged, reshaping our comprehension of cosmic evolution. This chapter elucidates these remarkable discoveries, reflecting on the ways in which gravitational waves are rewriting the narrative of our understanding of the universe's early moments.

The conventional view of the Big Bang posits that the universe began as an incredibly hot and dense singularity that subsequently underwent rapid expansion. Traditional observations—such as redshift measurements and the cosmic microwave background (CMB) radiation—have played significant roles in corroborating this theory, providing essential clues about the universe's evolution over billions of years. However, the advent of gravitational wave astronomy introduces a new layer of complexity and intrigue, as it offers researchers the opportunity to explore cosmic events that occurred during the universe's infancy.

Gravitational waves serve as a unique probe into the very conditions that defined the early universe. The theory of inflation—an exponential expansion of space during the first moments after the Big Bang—was initially speculative, yet gravitational waves produced during this phase could carry critical evidence of these primordial conditions. Mathematical models suggest that the violent fluctuations and chaotic events associated with inflation would have generated gravitational waves with specific characteristics, potentially illuminating the mechanisms underlying the very birth of our universe.

One possibility that arises from this line of inquiry is that detecting primordial gravitational waves may provide evidence regarding the shapes and dynamics of the early universe, ultimately lending credence to inflationary models. As research regarding gravitational wave frequencies and amplitudes advances, we could begin to capture signals originating from this epoch, marking a significant breakthrough in our understanding of cosmic origins.

As gravitational wave observations continue to accumulate, their potential implications for the Big Bang scenario expand. Each wave detected from later cosmic events can serve as a foundation for estimating the rate of expansion, shedding light on the interplay between dark energy, dark matter, and visible matter. For example, insights gained from the merger of neutron stars not only inform stellar evolution but also help researchers refine parameters linked to cosmic density and the energy dynamics of the universe, thus having a direct influence on our understanding of the universe's expansion rate.

The discoveries stemming from these gravitational wave observations represent an invitation to reconsider traditional cosmological models, expand our theories, and challenge longstanding assumptions about the universe. The congruence of gravitational wave data with electromagnetic observations provides an enriched narrative that contributes to our quest for understanding how the universe evolved from its tumultuous beginnings to its present state.

Moreover, the interconnection of gravitational wave astronomy with the Big Bang relates directly to the dance of gravitational interactions that govern cosmic evolution. Each gravitational wave detection impacts our understanding of the dynamics within galaxies and the formation of cosmic structures, tracing narratives that connect the universe's infant size to its grand, intricate tapestry today.

In conclusion, the insights gleaned from gravitational waves illuminate a new chapter in our understanding of the Big Bang—a chapter that expands upon the existing framework built by traditional observations. Gravitational waves invite us to engage with questions regarding the early universe and the processes that birthed it, serving as cosmic signposts illuminating the path forward in our exploration of existence. As we continue to listen to the universe and interpret the gravitational waves it emits, we embrace the excitement of discovery, finding ourselves enriched by a tapestry interwoven with stories that transcend time and space—stories that beckon us ever closer to unveiling the mysteries of our cosmos.

11.5. Exploring Cosmic Expansion

As we embark on our journey to explore cosmic expansion, we are delving into one of the most profound concepts inherent in cosmology. The universe is not static; it is a veritable ocean of change, forever expanding, drifting apart as galaxies move away from each other. This notion is central not only to our understanding of the universe's structure but also to the dynamics of the very fabric of spacetime, a concept initiated by the groundbreaking theories of gravitational waves.

The idea of cosmic expansion is rooted in the work of Edwin Hubble in the 1920s, who demonstrated that distant galaxies are moving away from us, and the farther they are, the faster they recede. This observation gave birth to what we now call Hubble's Law, which provides the foundation for our contemporary understanding of an expanding universe. However, the implications of an expanding cosmos deepen significantly when we introduce the framework of gravitational waves, which are borne from the dynamics of massive moving bodies throughout this cosmic expanse.

To comprehend cosmic expansion, we first must revisit the principles of General Relativity, which describes gravity as the bending of space-time by mass. As cosmologists analyze data from gravitational waves, they gain valuable insights into the behavior of massive celestial bodies—such as binary black holes or neutron stars—within an expanding universe. The characteristics of gravitational waves emitted during these events encapsulate vital information about their sources and can highlight how those sources interact with the expanding fabric of the cosmos.

Recent gravitational wave detections have revealed the critical role that merging black holes and neutron stars play in understanding cosmic evolution. As these cosmic entities collide, they not only emit gravitational waves, but they also serve as tactors for broader cosmological questions. For instance, the mergers can shed light on the formation rates of black holes and provide insights into their distribution across different epochs in the universe's history. This understanding is crucial in disentangling the effects of cosmic expansion over time.

Moreover, gravitational wave observations can help refine measurements of the Hubble constant, which defines the rate at which the universe is expanding. Discrepancies in measuring the Hubble constant using different observational methods have led to a contentious "Hubble tension" within the scientific community. By triangulating data from gravitational waves and correlating them with measurements of cosmic distances, researchers can improve the precision with which we estimate this expansion rate, providing a more coherent narrative for the universe's growth.

The interplay between gravitational waves and cosmic expansion also invites us to explore the nature of dark energy—a mysterious form of energy believed to be driving the accelerated expansion of the universe. The capture of gravitational waves emanating from mergers allows scientists to gain deeper insights into how dark energy interacts with and shapes cosmic structures. As we probe the ramifications of gravitational waves within this broader context, we unlock potential pathways to answer fundamental questions about dark energy's properties and behavior.

The discovery of gravitational waves further embeds the significance of cosmic inflation—a critical phase theorized to have occurred microseconds after the Big Bang, leading to the universe's rapid expansion. The signatures produced in waveforms may harbor clues regarding the stability of inflationary models and the conditions present in the universe's infancy. This aspect not only enhances our comprehension of the cosmos but opens discussions related to the fundamental mechanisms governing the universe.

As we explore these relationships, we also recognize the importance of evolving observational technologies. As next-generation observatories come into focus and the sensitivity of detectors improves, the ability to capture faint gravitational wave signals from various epochs across cosmic time will continue to grow. This anticipated advancement will enable researchers to glean insights from previously unreachable sources, enhancing our understanding of cosmic expansion further.

In summary, exploring cosmic expansion through the lens of gravitational waves signifies a transformative chapter within astrophysical research. The ability to observe cosmic events, ascertain their implications, and categorize their properties provides insights that tie the universe's expansion to the mechanisms governing its structure. With each gravitational wave detected, we engage in a deeper dialogue with the cosmos—each ripple serving as a reminder that we occupy a dynamic system shaped by forces much larger than ourselves. The journey into the mechanics of cosmic expansion beckons us as we listen closely to gravitational waves, inviting us to comprehend the intricate dance of the universe, continuing to evolve, expand, and reveal its hidden mysteries.

12. The Art of Data: Interpreting the Signals

12.1. Data Collection Techniques

In the exploration of gravitational wave astronomy, the techniques of data collection play a pivotal role, shaping our understanding of the universe through meticulous observation and analysis. These methods have evolved significantly, mirroring advancements in technology and the growing complexity of the inquiries we seek to address. Within this context, we delve into the techniques by which researchers capture the elusive signatures of gravitational waves— those faint ripples in spacetime that promise to unlock profound mysteries about cosmic events and the fundamental principles governing the universe.

The foremost method employed in gravitational wave detection is laser interferometry, which forms the foundation of observatories like LIGO, Virgo, and KAGRA. In this technique, coherent laser beams are split and directed down two long, perpendicular arms, each extending kilometers. When a gravitational wave passes through the detector, it causes minute changes in the distances to the mirrors at the ends of each arm, leading to a measurable alteration in the interference pattern of the combined light. This interference pattern is central to detecting the subtle changes produced by passing gravitational waves.

The sensitivity required for these instruments is staggering, capable of measuring changes on the order of one-thousandth the width of a proton. Achieving such precision necessitates an extraordinary level of engineering, as the observatories must be insulated from various sources of noise—everything from seismic vibrations and thermal fluctuations to human activity. As a result, careful design considerations come into play, including the use of pendulum-like suspensions that help shield sensitive components from external vibrations. Additionally, noise reduction techniques such as seismic isolation systems play a critical role in ensuring that only the gravitational wave signals are captured.

In contemporary research, advanced techniques complement traditional data collection methods. The vast amount of data generated in gravitational wave observations requires innovative strategies for filtering and analysis. Machine learning and artificial intelligence are increasingly utilized to sift through extensive datasets, identifying patterns that discern genuine gravitational wave signals from background noise. By training algorithms to recognize the unique characteristics of gravitational waveforms, researchers enhance their capacity to detect fainter signals earlier, paving the way for rapid response in analyzing significant cosmic events.

Furthermore, data collection techniques now foster interdisciplinary collaboration, encouraging scientists from astrophysics, engineering, computer science, and beyond to work collaboratively. This synergy enables the pooling of diverse expertise to enhance the quality and comprehensiveness of the observations. The integration of different scientific disciplines allows for a richer interpretation of the data collected, effectively bridging gaps between theory and observation.

Once detected, the gravitational wave signals are subjected to rigorous analysis to extract meaningful information. This involves evaluating the characteristics of the waveforms—such as amplitude, frequency, and duration, each of which encodes valuable data about the astrophysical event. The analysis helps to infer the properties of the astronomical sources, giving insight into parameters like the masses, spins, and distances of the involved celestial bodies.

Additionally, the visualization of collected data takes center stage in interpreting gravitational waves. Researchers often employ sophisticated tools for visualizing the signals, allowing them to compare and contrast different waveforms in relation to theoretical predictions. These visualizations are essential for communicating findings, highlighting the importance of effectively conveying complex scientific information to the broader community and fostering public engagement in gravitational wave astronomy.

The interplay of data collection techniques in gravitational wave astronomy highlights the transformative potential of observational science. Each advancement—not just in technology, but in methodologies, collaboration, and interdisciplinary approaches—serves to amplify our understanding of the universe. As we enhance our capability to detect and analyze gravitational waves, we open windows to the untold stories of the cosmos, peeling back layers that reveal the intricate dynamics of celestial events and the fundamental truths underlying existence itself.

In summary, the techniques of data collection in gravitational wave research embody a synthesis of precision engineering, collaborative efforts, and innovative methodologies that empower our quests for understanding the cosmos. With each wave detected, we move closer to unraveling the mysteries embedded within the celestial fabric, illustrating the power of scientific inquiry as we endeavor to listen to the whispers of the universe. Through these techniques, we not only seek knowledge but embrace the beauty of scientific exploration, furthering humanity's journey toward comprehending the vast complexities of existence.

12.2. Filtering the Cosmic Noise

The cosmos is a noisy place, resonating with a variety of signals and vibrations from distant celestial bodies. Within this symphony of cosmic sounds, gravitational waves emerge as subtle ripples, often obscured by the cacophony of other cosmic events and terrestrial influences. The task of distinguishing these delicate waves from the background noise is a fundamental challenge in gravitational wave astronomy, necessitating innovative filtering techniques and a thorough understanding of the various sources of interference. This subchapter delves into the methods employed to filter cosmic noise, allowing astronomers to listen closely to the whispers of the universe.

Understanding the nature of noise in gravitational wave detectors begins with acknowledging the complexities of the environments in which these instruments operate. Every gravitational wave observatory, whether it be LIGO, Virgo, or KAGRA, faces a multitude of noise sources that can impede the detection of faint signals. These sources can be broadly categorized into two types: instrumental noise and environmental noise. Instrumental noise arises from the components of the detector, such as laser fluctuations, thermal noise, and mechanical vibrations from the equipment itself. Environmental noise, on the other hand, encompasses vibrations from seismic activity, the movement of vehicles, human activities, and even atmospheric effects.

A multitude of advanced techniques has been developed to filter out this noise, allowing researchers to isolate the signals of interest. One such technique is the implementation of noise reduction algorithms that analyze the data in real time. These algorithms can detect patterns characteristic of noise and effectively subtract these disturbances from the observational data, thereby revealing the underlying gravitational wave signals. The efficacy of these algorithms relies on a thorough understanding of both the expected characteristics of gravitational waves and the types of noise present in the detector system.

Seismic isolation systems are critical components employed to mitigate the influence of ground vibrations on gravitational wave detection. These sophisticated devices use a combination of weighted pendulums and active feedback systems to create a robust shielding mechanism against environmental disturbances. By suspending sensitive components, such as optical mirrors, from the ground and placing them in a controlled environment, seismic isolation systems significantly reduce the impact of noise transmitted through the ground. This careful engineering creates a stable and quiet environment conducive to detecting the elusive gravitational waves that ripple through spacetime.

Furthermore, researchers actively implement various environmental monitoring systems that track potential noise sources in real time. By correlating the detection of gravitational waves with events like earthquakes, heavy machinery operation, or even local atmospheric conditions, scientists can establish a deeper understanding of the effects of environmental noise on data integrity. This comprehensive approach to noise management not only helps identify sources of interference but also informs adaptive strategies to minimize their impact during detection runs.

In tandem with sophisticated filtering techniques, the role of data collection cannot be overstated. Gravitational wave observatories generate vast amounts of data, compiling signals over time to improve the reliability of the results. By gathering long-term datasets, researchers can analyze trends, establish noise profiles specific to different environments, and refine their algorithms for distinguishing between noise and gravitational wave signals. This iterative analysis process ensures continuous improvements in detection capabilities, fostering an ongoing dialogue among scientists about best practices in data processing.

Moreover, the very nature of gravitational waves provides unique opportunities to study and understand cosmic events elusive to traditional electromagnetic observations. As these waves propagate through the universe, they can carry information about the chaotic dances of massive celestial bodies, such as the merging of neutron stars or black holes. Filtering the noise surrounding these signals is, therefore, not merely an issue of signal-to-noise ratio; it is a means to decipher the rich stories encoded in the gravitational waveforms, revealing new insights into stellar formation, black hole population dynamics, and the evolution of galaxies.

The ongoing advancement of technology plays an essential role in enhancing filtering techniques. Continuous investments in new sensor designs, algorithm development, and noise-cancellation technologies contribute directly to the refinement of observational capabilities. The collaborative network of gravitational wave observatories allows for shared learning, as researchers exchange methods and insights that have proven effective in different contexts.

In conclusion, filtering cosmic noise is a critical aspect of gravitational wave astronomy that enables researchers to distinguish faint signals from the myriad of disturbances permeating the universe. Through sophisticated noise reduction algorithms, seismic isolation systems, and robust data analysis techniques, scientists enhance their ability to listen closely to gravitational waves and unravel the profound stories embedded within them. In doing so, they embark on a journey to unveil the mysteries of the cosmos—an invitation for future generations to continue exploring and experiencing the echoes of the universe through the lens of gravitational waves. As our understanding evolves and technology progresses, the art of filtering cosmic noise will remain a cornerstone in the pursuit of knowledge about the universe and its fundamental workings.

12.3. Signal Characteristics

Signal Characteristics in gravitational wave astronomy represent a critical aspect of our understanding since they encapsulate the intricate stories of some of the universe's most extreme events, such as collisions between black holes and neutron stars. The detection and analysis of these signals allow scientists to glean vital information about the very fabric of spacetime and the properties of the astronomical objects producing these waves.

At its core, understanding signal characteristics begins with recognizing the unique waveform patterns produced by various astronomical phenomena. Each cosmic event generates a distinct gravitational waveform, providing a key to unlock details about the system involved. Gravitational wave signals are often represented as time-frequency plots, which visualize how the amplitude and frequency of the wave change over time. The distinguishing features of these waveforms can reveal critical properties, such as the masses, spins, and distances of the merging bodies.

For example, signals from binary black hole mergers are characterized by a clear "chirp" pattern—an increase in frequency and amplitude as the two black holes spiral closer before merging. The highest frequencies in the waveform occur just before the merger, representing the peak gravitational wave emission during this cataclysmic event. The unique shape of this "chirp" serves as an inferential tool for astrophysicists, allowing them to extract quantitative parameters about the black holes involved.

In contrast, the waveforms produced by neutron star mergers can show differences that encapsulate additional dynamics, such as the interactions between dense neutron matter and the relativistic jets associated with astronomical explosions. The resulting signals not only encompass information about the neutron stars' masses and spins but also hint at the rich astrophysical processes that occur during and after the merger, including element synthesis.

Moreover, understanding signal characteristics transcends merely identifying the fundamental shapes of the waves. Advanced numerical relativity simulations play a vital role in modeling the expected waveforms emitted from gravitational wave events, allowing scientists to generate template banks for matching observed data. These models—crafted from the principles of general relativity—offer a comprehensive framework that accounts for various factors, such as the eccentricity of orbits and the directional dynamics of spins, producing realistic gravitational waveforms that are compared against the data collected by observatories.

The ability to visualize and analyze these signals profoundly impacts our understanding of stellar populations and the cosmic landscape. By cataloging different types of waveforms and their associated parameters, researchers can infer the occurrence rates of black hole and neutron star mergers across the universe. This statistical approach aids in refining models of galaxy formation and evolution, as the population dynamics derived from gravitational waves deepen our comprehension of how massive stars are created, evolve, and ultimately succumb to gravitational collapse.

In addition to these characteristics, the interplay between gravitational waves and electromagnetic signals further enriches our understanding. The simultaneous observation of gamma-ray bursts from neutron star mergers with gravitational wave signals exemplifies the burgeoning field of multi-messenger astronomy. This collaborative approach allows researchers to elucidate the relationships between gravitational waves and other forms of radiation, developing a more comprehensive picture of cosmic phenomena.

Furthermore, signal characteristics inform theoretical discussions about fundamental physics. By analyzing deviations from expected waveforms, scientists explore potential modifications to general relativity or consider new physics that could influence gravitational interactions. Each detection and its subsequent analysis contribute to an ongoing dialogue, prompting questions and contemplations about the nature of gravity, spacetime, and their implications for our understanding of the universe.

In summary, signal characteristics are foundational to gravitational wave astronomy, encapsulating the essence of cosmic events that ripple through spacetime. The analysis of these signals informs a rich narrative that expands our understanding of stellar evolution, reveals the intricate dynamics of collisions between celestial bodies, and informs discussions about fundamental physics. As we continue to enhance our capabilities in detecting and interpreting signals, we are poised to unveil the stories woven into the cosmos, echoing across the vast expanses of time and space. Each signal detected represents not merely an event but an invitation to explore the profound mysteries of the universe, urging us to listen closely and embrace the complexity that lies within.

12.4. Visualizing the Cosmos

In the grand narrative of our universe, visualization is a critical component that enables us to interpret and appreciate the profound phenomena occurring at cosmic scales. To truly understand the significance of gravitational waves, we must embark on an imaginative journey—a mental voyage that allows us to visualize the fabric of spacetime and the events encapsulated within it. This visualization extends beyond mere representations; it fosters our abilities to form connections between abstract theoretical frameworks and the tangible realities of celestial interactions.

At the foundation of this visualization lies the conceptual framework of spacetime itself, which amalgamates the familiar three dimensions of space with the dimension of time. Picture spacetime as an elastic sheet, stretched taut, where massive objects like stars and black holes indent the surface, creating warps that influence the trajectory of nearby objects. This intuitive model provides a tangible means to comprehend the gravitational effects that arise from mass, facilitating insights into phenomena such as gravitational waves. As massive celestial bodies accelerate or collide, they disturb the surrounding spacetime, producing ripples that propagate outward—these are the gravitational waves we now strive to detect and analyze.

Visualizing the cosmos necessitates considering the timescale of cosmic events. Gravitational waves serve as messengers transporting information from billions of light-years across the expanse of space, linking us to events that occurred long before their signals reached Earth. The waves travel at the speed of light, and this leads to an appreciation for the vast distances involved and the evolving nature of the events themselves. Each observed wave provides a snapshot of a moment in the universe's history, allowing researchers to piece together the celestial puzzle and chart the dynamics of cosmic evolution.

With the emergence of gravitational wave detectors such as LIGO and Virgo, our conceptual toolbox has expanded to include sophisticated algorithms and analytical techniques that allow us to visualize complex waveforms. Each gravitational wave event is captured as a time-series signal, revealing unique patterns indicative of specific astrophysical interactions. The ability to convert these time-series data into frequency domain representations enables scientists to analyze the components of gravitational waves effectively. Tools such as spectrograms visually display these waveforms, allowing researchers to dissect the intricacies of the signals and gain a more nuanced understanding of celestial dynamics.

Additionally, the benefits of data visualization extend to public communication and outreach. Engaging the general audience through captivating visual representations of gravitational wave events fosters a sense of connection and curiosity about the broader universe. Infographics, immersive simulations, and captivating illustrations serve as accessible means by which the public can grasp abstract concepts, sparking interests and inspiring future generations to delve into the mysteries of astrophysics.

Visualizing cosmic events prompts not just an analytical mindset, but also an emotional response—a sense of wonder and awe. As we develop mental imagery of black hole mergers or neutron star collisions, we are reminded of the intricate forces shaping our universe. We come to recognize that gravitational waves represent the echoes of cataclysmic events, weaving a narrative that transcends time and space—a dance of mass and energy that continues to unfold throughout the cosmos.

The capacity to visualize the cosmos, enriched by technological innovations and gravitational wave discoveries, moves us closer to comprehending the interconnectedness of celestial phenomena. It encourages us to recognize that we are participants in this grand narrative, engaging with the universe as stewards of knowledge. As we continue our foray into the future of gravitational wave astronomy, we will undoubtedly encounter new discoveries, rich insights, and refined conceptual frameworks that will further enhance our abilities to visualize and understand the magnificent tapestry of existence.

In summary, visualizing the cosmos serves as an indispensable tool for interpreting gravitational waves and bridging the realms of theory and observation. By employing intuitive models, analytical techniques, and engaging visuals, we cultivate a deeper understanding of the universe's workings. This ongoing exploration is an invitation— to listen closely, to connect with the echoes of the universe, and to embrace the extraordinary journey of discovery that lies before us. The whispers of gravitational waves beckon us to continue exploring, illuminating the path toward understanding the enigmatic forces that govern the grand interplay of our cosmic landscape.

12.5. The Role of Artificial Intelligence

In the fascinating and rapidly advancing field of gravitational wave astronomy, artificial intelligence (AI) plays a pivotal role in revolutionizing our understanding and interpretation of the signals emitted by some of the universe's most dynamic celestial events. The ability to listen to gravitational waves offers unprecedented insights into cosmic phenomena, such as mergers of black holes and neutron stars, but the vast amount of data generated and the inherent noise associated with observational methods pose significant challenges. Thus, harnessing the capabilities of AI has become essential for efficiently processing and analyzing this data, enabling scientists to draw meaningful conclusions while enhancing the overall accuracy and efficiency of gravitational wave detection.

One of the most critical applications of AI in gravitational wave astronomy lies in the analysis of waveforms. Each detection produces a vast and intricate dataset characterized by unique patterns corresponding to specific events. Traditional data analysis techniques can be time-consuming, relying on human experts to sift through data and identify gravitational wave signals amidst the noise. However, AI algorithms, particularly machine learning models, have been developed to expedite this process. These algorithms can effectively identify and classify waveforms by training on vast collections of simulated data, discerning signals that may be too faint for human analysis alone. The development of these techniques accelerates the pace of discovery, allowing researchers to explore a broader range of cosmic phenomena.

Moreover, AI facilitates real-time data processing, a crucial factor in gravitational wave detection. As gravitational wave observatories operate in "live" mode, they continuously monitor for incoming signals. In this context, AI can act as an intelligent filtering system, identifying potential gravitational wave events as they occur. The speed at which AI can analyze data enables researchers to respond swiftly to significant detections, coordinating follow-up observations across a range of electromagnetic wavelengths. This level of agility is vital in the era of multi-messenger astronomy, where the combination of gravitational wave signals with electromagnetic observations illuminates the global narrative of cosmic events.

The effectiveness of AI does not merely dwell in its ability to process data efficiently; it is also pivotal in enhancing the accuracy of gravitational wave models. By leveraging advanced algorithms, scientists can refine the templates used to match observed waveforms with theoretical predictions. These machine learning approaches can explore the parameter space more comprehensively, elucidating the masses, spins, and distances of the involved celestial bodies. As AI continues to evolve, it opens doors to new opportunities to investigate previously unseen or obscured phenomena, offering insights into the evolution of astrophysical processes over time.

In addition to waveform analysis, AI contributes to other facets of gravitational wave research, including noise reduction and anomaly detection. By deploying machine learning techniques, researchers can develop systems capable of differentiating between noise patterns and genuine waveforms. This automatic filtering helps improve detection rates and can potentially unearth new astrophysical signals that might otherwise be overlooked. Over time, these trained models will refine their accuracy, evolving alongside advancements in observational technology.

While the integration of AI in gravitational wave astronomy is transformative, it comes with its own set of challenges and ethical considerations. As algorithms take on more significant roles in data processing and interpretation, researchers must ensure that AI systems are transparent, the decision-making processes adequately explained, and biases minimized. Rigorous validation of the algorithms is also critical, as scientists must remain vigilant about assessing the accuracy of predictions generated by AI systems.

Moreover, as AI capabilities expand, the potential for public engagement in gravitational wave research grows. Citizen scientists—enthusiasts eager to contribute—can harness AI tools developed by research teams to participate in the analysis, interpretation, and visualization of data. This democratization of science enhances public interest and appreciation for astrophysical phenomena, inviting diverse perspectives to enrich the community's collective understanding.

In summary, the role of artificial intelligence in gravitational wave astronomy represents a transformative leap forward. By enhancing data processing, analysis, and modeling techniques, AI empowers scientists to extract meaningful insights from the universe's whispers, accelerating the pace of discovery and deepening our comprehension of cosmic events. As this technology continues to evolve, the intertwining of AI and gravitational wave astronomy stands as a beacon of possibility for the future—a clear invitation to explore the myriad mysteries of the cosmos while ensuring that the collective endeavor remains grounded in transparency, ethics, and an appreciation for the intricacy of the universe we inhabit. Through this technology, we take steps closer to deciphering the profound stories echoing through the fabric of spacetime, seeking to understand the cosmic narrative that has shaped the universe from its very inception.

13. Astrophysical Conundrums Solved

13.1. Solving the Hubble Tension

In the realm of modern astrophysics, "Solving the Hubble Tension" represents a significant scientific challenge that encapsulates the ongoing discourse surrounding our understanding of the universe's expansion. The Hubble Tension refers to the persistent discrepancy between two methods of measuring the Hubble constant, which describes the rate at which the universe is expanding. On one hand, measurements derived from the cosmic microwave background (CMB) radiation, as observed through satellites like Planck, yield a lower value for the Hubble constant. In contrast, measurements derived from local distance ladder methods, which involve observing supernovae and analyzing the redshift of galaxies, produce a higher value. This conundrum raises profound implications for cosmological models and our grasp of fundamental physics.

Addressing the Hubble Tension begins by acknowledging that it is intricately linked to concepts such as dark energy and the overall composition of the universe. The cosmological model built upon general relativity predicts how the universe should behave based on parameters including matter density, energy density, and dark energy. Discerning the nature of dark energy and its density is pivotal to understanding cosmic expansion, and any discrepancies in the Hubble constant prompt a reevaluation of how these components operate and interact on cosmic scales.

In seeking to resolve the Hubble Tension, researchers have begun to explore potential solutions that may arise from refining observational data or proposing alternative models. One avenue of exploration has been the improvement of distance measurements, utilizing gravitational wave detectors like LIGO and Virgo to assist in precisely calculating cosmic distances to merging events. The capability of gravitational waves to serve as "standard sirens" allows scientists to bypass traditional luminosity distances and attain direct measurements of distance based solely on gravitational wave signals. As more gravitational wave events are observed, the potential to calibrate the distance ladder with newfound accuracy could shed light on the discrepancies observed in the Hubble constant.

Further investigation also involves scrutinizing the potential effects of systematic errors in the datasets used to determine the Hubble constant. Researchers are rigorously assessing methodologies across different observatories to identify and mitigate any biases in measuring distances or redshifts. By developing a more unified approach that encompasses data from CMB measurements, supernova observations, and gravitational wave signals, astrophysicists hope to reconcile these values and arrive at a consensus.

An innovative consideration involves exploring the consequences of modifications to general relativity itself. Some scientists have proposed alternative theories to account for gravitational effects that may influence cosmic expansion. These theoretical explorations yield fascinating prospects for rethinking the underlying mathematics that govern cosmological dynamics, encouraging a revaluation of established paradigms surrounding gravity and expanding universe models.

The implications of solving the Hubble Tension extend beyond mere measurement; they resonate throughout our understanding of the universe's evolution. Resolving this discrepancy holds the potential to reinvigorate discussions concerning the role of dark energy in cosmic inflation, the formation of structure in the universe, and the fundamental principles that govern gravitational interactions across cosmic scales.

As gravitational wave astronomy continues to mature, there is hope that the collective efforts of the scientific community can address and ultimately solve the Hubble Tension. This endeavor reflects the broader aspiration to deepen our understanding of the cosmos, where listening to the echoes of distant events may provide crucial insights into the mechanisms that govern the very fabric of reality.

In conclusion, solving the Hubble Tension represents a formidable challenge encapsulating profound implications for cosmology and fundamental physics. As researchers engage in collaborative efforts to reconcile discrepancies between measurements, they carve pathways toward greater understanding of the universe's expansion, dark energy, and the very principles that govern existence. Ultimately, this exploration serves as an invitation to continue listening closely to the gravitational whispers that illuminate the cosmos, urging us onward as we unravel the intricacies of our universe and the truths concealed beneath the surface.

13.2. Mysteries of Black Hole Birth

The formation of black holes is a captivating cosmic mystery, entwined with gravitational waves—a hidden language of the universe that speaks to the cataclysmic events giving birth to these enigmatic entities. The study of black hole birth delves into the intricate processes involved in stellar evolution, mass collapse, and the extraordinary phenomena that result from the merging of massive stars. Gravitational waves serve as direct evidence of these birth events, encapsulating critical information about the nature of black holes and their role in the cosmic narrative.

To understand the genesis of black holes, one must first explore the lifecycle of massive stars. Stars like our Sun have relatively predictable fates; they swell into red giants and ultimately expel their outer layers, leaving behind a dense white dwarf. However, massive stars—those with initial masses over about 20 times that of the Sun—experience a far more dramatic end. As these massive stars exhaust their nuclear fuel, gravitational forces govern their fate, triggering core collapse under immense pressure. This process culminates in an explosive supernova event, which not only marks the death throes of the star but also an opportunity for black hole formation.

When the core collapses, if the remaining mass exceeds a certain limit, known as the Tolman-Oppenheimer-Volkoff (TOV) limit, nothing can halt the gravitational implosion, and a black hole emerges. It is at this juncture that black holes begin to exert their influence on the universe, warping spacetime and initiating the emission of gravitational waves. When massive stars undergo supernova explosions, the asymmetry in their collapse generates bursts of gravitational waves that travel across the cosmos, eventually reaching Earth and enabling scientists to extract vital information about the collapse process.

These gravitational wave signals serve as invaluable probes into the inner workings of black hole formation. Each detected signal carries unique characteristics that reveal the masses, spins, and dynamics of the forming black holes. The detection of gravitational waves resulting from core-collapse supernovae or the mergers of stellar binaries offers insights into the population of black holes and their mass distributions, contributing to our understanding of black hole demographics.

Intriguingly, recent observations have exposed the presence of black holes that do not align with traditional models of stellar evolution. For instance, the existence of black holes with masses greater than expected poses challenges to our understanding of the dynamics driving supernova explosions and the mergers of compact objects. Gravitational wave observations have revealed a diverse array of black hole masses, suggesting that multiple formation pathways may exist—including interactions within dense stellar clusters that enable black holes to merge and grow before supernova progenitor events.

Moreover, black hole mergers present an exciting opportunity for understanding the birth of black holes and the dynamics of their formation. When two black holes spiral toward one another and ultimately collide, they emit gravitational waves characterized by distinctive waveforms that provide insights into their origins, including their respective mass configurations and the mechanisms behind their collision. This process exemplifies how black holes interact gravitationally, lending credence to the idea that black holes often form in binary systems, undergo inspiral, and eventually lead to mergers that propel new waves through the fabric of spacetime.

This narrative of black hole birth and the subsequent release of gravitational waves introduces a deeper inquiry into the complexities surrounding the nature of black holes themselves. Questions surrounding the existence of intermediate-mass black holes, potentially forming through distinct pathways, prompt further exploration into the dynamics of stellar interactions, the properties of matter under extreme conditions, and the interplay of gravity that has formed the colossal structures we observe today.

As we continue to grapple with these fascinating phenomena, the probing of black hole birth transitions from theoretical inquiry to observational reality. Each gravitational wave detection tantalizes researchers with the opportunity to refine existing models, develop new frameworks, and unlock new secrets about the early universe. The stories etched in gravitational waves beckon us to listen in awe and appreciation, revealing narratives that extend far beyond the boundaries of our current understanding.

In conclusion, the mysteries surrounding the birth of black holes unfold gracefully along the flowing strands of gravitational waves, intertwining cosmic events that shape the universe. As we delve into the nature of these enigmatic entities, we continue to uncover the intricate dance of mass and energy, engaging in a dialogue with the cosmos that spans time and distance. The gravitational waves serve not only as messengers of cosmic events but as invitations to explore the depths of our universe and the forces that govern its existence. With every wave detected, we inch closer to comprehending the profound stories hidden within the fabric of reality, guided by the voices of gravity that call us onward into the great unknown.

13.3. Understanding Gamma-ray Bursts

Understanding Gamma-ray bursts (GRBs) presents one of the most fascinating puzzles within modern astrophysics, linking the realms of high-energy phenomena and gravitational wave astronomy. GRBs are intense bursts of gamma-rays, the most energetic form of electromagnetic radiation, and they can last from milliseconds to several minutes. These events are believed to be associated with the death throes of massive stars or the mergers of binary compact objects, such as neutron stars or black holes, and they offer a tantalizing glimpse into some of the most extreme conditions in the universe.

A gamma-ray burst can release more energy in a few seconds than the Sun will emit over its entire lifetime—an extraordinary display of power that draws scientists' attention from across the globe. The mechanisms behind these bursts remain an area of active research and debate, but the prevailing theories point to two primary types: long and short GRBs. Long GRBs, lasting more than two seconds, are typically associated with the collapse of massive stars into black holes during supernova events. This can occur when a massive star exhausts its nuclear fuel and implodes, leading to the creation of a rapidly rotating black hole that emits jets of radiation along its poles. When these jets are pointed toward Earth, they manifest as gamma-ray bursts.

On the other hand, short GRBs, lasting less than two seconds, are hypothesized to result from the merger of binary neutron stars or black holes. When these compact objects spiral together and eventually collide, they generate remarkable gravitational waves while simultaneously releasing intense bursts of gamma radiation. This connection to gravitational wave events provides a unique opportunity to study the interplay between these high-energy astrophysical phenomena.

The significance of GRBs is further amplified by their role as cosmic markers. Observing GRBs can provide astronomers with critical distance measurements, thanks to their immense brightness. Because GRBs are visible across vast cosmic distances, they allow scientists to probe the early universe, shedding light on the properties of galaxy formation and the presence of star-forming regions. The study of GRBs thus serves as a window into the evolution of the universe itself, offering insights into the cosmic structures that existed shortly after the Big Bang.

The association between GRBs and gravitational waves is of particular interest. The detection of gravitational waves from binary mergers, coupled with GRB alerts, represents a significant advance in multi-messenger astronomy. When the merger of two neutron stars produces gravitational waves, simultaneous observations of the emitted gamma-ray burst can provide unparalleled insights into the characteristics of these dynamic events. The confluence of gravitational wave signals and electromagnetic radiation enhances our understanding of the mechanisms underlying such catastrophic mergers, revealing details about the neutron star equations of state and yielding insights into the processes of element formation.

Despite the advances made in understanding GRBs, significant questions remain unresolved. The precise mechanisms driving these intense emissions, along with the details of their progenitor systems, continue to challenge scientists. Current observational efforts, including the coordination of gravitational wave networks with gamma-ray observing satellites, aim to enrich the understanding of these extraordinary bursts and their origins.

In conclusion, understanding gamma-ray bursts serves as a crucial nexus within modern astrophysics, bridging studies of high-energy phenomena with gravitational wave astronomy. By investigating these extreme cosmic events and their relationship with gravitational wave detections, researchers can unlock vital information about the universe's most violent processes. As observational techniques and collaborative efforts continue to evolve, the mysteries surrounding GRBs will undoubtedly inspire scientific inquiry while reshaping our understanding of the foundational aspects of the cosmos. Each burst of energy echoes the rhythms of the universe, inviting us to listen closely and embrace the stories they carry about celestial dynamics, cosmic evolution, and the grandeur of existence itself.

13.4. Puzzles of Galactic Formation

In the vast expanse of the universe, the process of galactic formation remains one of the profound puzzles that scientists strive to unravel. For decades, researchers have sought to understand how galaxies— the grand structures that house stars, gas, dust, and dark matter—are created, evolve, and interact across cosmic time. Gravitational waves, the subtle ripples in spacetime resulting from cataclysmic cosmic events, play a pivotal role in this narrative, offering scientists new insights into the dynamics of galactic formation and providing tangible evidence of the interactions between massive celestial bodies.

Understanding galaxy formation begins with examining the fundamental processes at play in the early universe. Shortly after the Big Bang, matter began to coalesce under the influence of gravitational forces. Over time, pockets of gas and dark matter accumulated, creating primordial structures that would become the seeds of future galaxies. The expansion and cooling of the universe permitted atomic structures to form, leading to the creation of hydrogen and helium, the foundational building blocks that would fuel future star formation.

An increasingly empowered view of cosmic evolution begins to take shape when gravitational waves enter the narrative. These waves, generated during the mergers of black holes, neutron stars, and other massive structures, offer a novel method of probing the dynamics of galaxy formation. When two black holes collide, they produce gravitational waves that convey crucial information about their properties —like mass, spin, and trajectory. Observing the patterns of these waves helps scientists decipher the evolutionary pathways taken by the merging bodies and their role within larger galactic structures.

For instance, the merger of two black holes within a galaxy reveals facets of gravitational interactions that are crucial to understanding how supermassive black holes form at galactic centers. The dominant theories posit that supermassive black holes arise from the mergers of stellar black holes or gas clouds in dense environments. By analyzing the gravitational wave signals emitted during these mergers, researchers can estimate the mass distribution within a galaxy and probe the complex relationships between black holes and their host galaxies.

Moreover, the observation of gravitational waves contributes to the context in which galaxies form and evolve. By providing evidence of dynamic processes—particularly the mergers and interactions among massive bodies—these gravitational signals help forge connections between individual astronomical events and the larger tapestry of cosmic evolution. They serve as markers for understanding how galaxies interact, merging and colliding, leading to the restructuring, growth, and even eventual demise of these cosmic giants.

Another challenging aspect of galactic formation involves the role of dark matter, which constitutes a significant fraction of the universe's mass. Although invisible, dark matter significantly influences the gravitational forces experienced by galaxies. The gravitational waves produced during merger events provide insights into the distribution and dynamics of dark matter surrounding galaxies. This information is crucial for piecing together the galactic puzzle and understanding how dark matter shapes the formation and stability of various galactic structures over time.

However, along with the advances gravitational waves bring, they also present their own set of challenges and questions. The intricate interplay between gravitational waves and galactic formation processes invites researchers to reconsider theoretical models and interpretations of the cosmic landscape. Tensions between observations of galactic structures and the predictions of dark matter dynamics prompt ongoing dialogue on the origins, fate, and distribution of galaxies throughout the universe.

Educational initiatives centered around these discoveries emphasize the importance of making these complexities accessible—not just to scientists but to the public. Engaging the broader community in discussions surrounding galactic formation and gravitational waves fosters curiosity and interest while encouraging future generations to explore scientific inquiry.

As technological advancements continue to propel gravitational wave astronomy, resonating signals from galactic formation processes shall be mapped out more comprehensively. Ongoing contributions from next-generation observatories promise opportunities to detect more remote wave events, enabling researchers to probe deeper into the mysteries of galaxy formation. For each ripple in spacetime, we witness echoes from the past—an invitation to listen closely as we strive to comprehend our universe's evolution through the intricate lens of gravitational waves.

In conclusion, the puzzles of galactic formation represent an exciting frontier in the realm of astrophysics, intricately woven together with the phenomena of gravitational waves. By integrating observations of gravitational waves into the broader cosmological narrative, we gain invaluable insights into the dynamics that shape galaxies, fostering a richer understanding of our universe's intricate design. This ongoing inquiry beckons liberation from established constraints, inviting a cooperative spirit of exploration to illuminate the mysteries of existence dwelling in the cosmic dance of formation, interaction, and evolution. As we strive to untangle these cosmic enigmas, we grow ever closer to understanding the delicate harmonies interwoven within the grand orchestra of galactic formation and evolution.

13.5. Challenges Ahead

The journey ahead in the study of gravitational waves and their implications in our understanding of the universe is filled with challenges that will demand the continued ingenuity and collaborative spirit of scientists around the globe. As we look to the future, it is clear that the complexities of gravitational wave astronomy will engender significant questions about the underlying principles of astrophysics, the dynamics of cosmic objects, and the nature of reality itself.

One of the most pressing challenges involves the ongoing quest for improved sensitivity in gravitational wave detectors. While current observatories like LIGO and Virgo have made remarkable strides in detecting gravitational waves, the signals from many cosmic events are still faint and difficult to distinguish from background noise. To capture the full spectrum of gravitational wave sources, including those from the early universe or from the merger of supermassive black holes, researchers must develop next-generation observatories equipped with cutting-edge technology capable of unprecedented sensitivity. This includes innovations in laser sources, mirror technology, and seismic isolation systems, all essential for enhancing the precision required to discern the faintest cosmic echoes.

As gravitational wave astronomy evolves, the challenge of effectively sharing and analyzing vast datasets will also loom large. The amount of information generated by observatories is immense, and efficient data analysis techniques must keep pace with advancements in sensitivity. Incorporating artificial intelligence and machine learning techniques into data processing offers promising solutions, allowing for real-time analysis and the ability to identify transient gravitational wave signals amid the ever-present noise. However, ensuring that these machine learning algorithms are accurate, unbiased, and effectively vetted remains a critical component of this process, necessitating careful validation and continuous oversight.

International collaboration will be more crucial than ever to address the challenges that lie ahead. The nature of gravitational wave astronomy calls for pooling resources, expertise, and knowledge to tackle the shared goals of understanding the cosmos. This spirit of teamwork and cooperation will enhance the robustness of observations and interpretations, allowing scientists to answer some of the universe's most profound questions. Not only will this cooperation facilitate data sharing among existing observatories, but it will also prepare the groundwork for future projects that might leverage cutting-edge technology and theoretical advancements.

As the scientific community delves deeper into the implications of gravitational wave discoveries, it must also confront ethical considerations and societal ramifications. With newfound capabilities to probe the mysteries of existence, researchers are called upon to reflect on the impact of their understanding—how it shapes our perceptions of the universe, influences public discourse about science, and even informs education. Engaging the public in the narrative of gravitational wave discoveries will be essential, fostering widespread scientific curiosity and a collective appreciation for the wonders of the cosmos.

Among the philosophical conundrums emerging from gravitational wave research, questions surrounding black hole formation, cosmic expansion, and the nature of dark matter and dark energy will continue to captivate scientists. As gravitational waves shine a light on these enigmas, they serve as catalysts for further inquiry, challenging traditional models of cosmology and prompting deeper investigations into the fundamental forces that govern the universe.

Furthermore, as we probe the far reaches of the universe, we will enhance our understanding of phenomena such as gamma-ray bursts, the birth of neutron stars, and collisions between massive structures. Each new gravitational wave detection can illuminate an aspect of cosmic evolution, culminating in a richer, more nuanced comprehension of galactic dynamics and the origins of heavy elements.

In reflection, the challenges ahead in gravitational wave astronomy encompass a multitude of scientific, technical, ethical, and philosophical dimensions. This moment invites eager minds to embark upon explorations into uncharted territories, where the whispers of gravitational waves echo stories waiting to be uncovered. With advancements in technology, continued collaboration, and a commitment to democratizing science through public engagement, we are on the precipice of new discoveries that will redefine our understanding of the universe—a realm beyond our current comprehension, yet tantalizingly within reach.

As we advance into this new chapter, we find ourselves compelled to listen intently to the cosmic narratives that gravitational waves present, remaining vigilant and persistent in the pursuit of knowledge. Each challenge met and each mystery resolved becomes an invitation to deeper inquiry—a promise of exploration that stretches far beyond our horizon, beckoning us onward into the vastness of the cosmos.

14. In the Mind of a Scientist

14.1. Pioneers and Innovators

The quest for understanding gravitational waves represents a confluence of pioneering intellect and innovative spirit. Within the expansive cosmic landscape, countless individuals and teams have devoted their lives to unveiling the mysteries behind these ethereal whispers in spacetime. This chapter, "Pioneers and Innovators," delves into the personal stories of those who have contributed not only their expertise but also their passion and tenacity.

The journey into the realm of gravitational wave astronomy began with groundbreaking theoretical insights from figures like Albert Einstein, whose General Theory of Relativity laid the groundwork for understanding how massive bodies influence the very fabric of spacetime. However, the realization of his vision required subsequent pioneers who dedicated themselves to bridging theory with empirical evidence. In the decades that followed Einstein, scientists embraced the challenge of detecting gravitational waves—a task deemed nearly impossible by many.

Among these pioneers was Kip Thorne, a gravitational physicist whose profound curiosity and insights guided the development of LIGO. He envisioned a future where gravitational waves were not just theoretical constructs but observable phenomena. Thorne's leadership and collaboration with other scientists and engineers, such as Rainer Weiss and Barry Barish, galvanized the immense challenge of constructing the first gravitational wave observatory. Their dedication to addressing complex engineering issues and their relentless pursuit of sensitivity standards propelled LIGO from concept to reality.

Yet it was not solely the tools and techniques that defined this journey; human stories positioned at the heart of the mission fueled the collective passion. Teams faced setbacks and frustrations, grappling with the intricacies of noise reduction and precision measurements. Their stories became interwoven narratives of resilience—a tribute to the notion that scientific inquiry is often met with obstacles that demand not just knowledge but also creativity and collaboration.

As LIGO transitioned into its operational phase, excitement surged within the scientific community. The first detection of gravitational waves in 2015 marked not just a technical achievement but a culmination of decades of effort and determination—a victory for the entire community. Within these celebrations were voices of diverse backgrounds, each contributing unique perspectives that enriched the collective endeavor. Scientists, engineers, and students joined forces, underscoring the artistry inherent in scientific discovery—a profound interplay of intellect and imagination.

The pursuit of gravitational waves also brought forth the emergence of young innovators, eager to contribute to humanity's understanding of the cosmos. As gravitational wave astronomy evolved, so too did educational outreach initiatives aimed at fostering curiosity among the next generation. The stories of progress became stories of mentorship and inspiration—illuminating paths for aspiring scientists and inviting them to partake in the exploration of this magnificent universe.

The journey into gravitational waves has inspired broader conversations about the nature of science and the wider appreciation for the human stories intertwined within scientific exploration. It has prompted reflections on the shared responsibility of the scientific community not only to advance knowledge but also to engage the public in this narrative, fostering a sense of ownership over cosmic discoveries.

In the culmination of "Pioneers and Innovators," we recognize that the journey into gravitational waves is not merely a scientific endeavor, but a testament to humanity's capacity for curiosity and discovery. As we continue to celebrate the contributions of cohorts of researchers, engineers, and aspiring scientists, we reaffirm our commitment to the pursuit of knowledge—a testament that ultimately invites each of us to listen closely, to ponder the vast cosmos, and to embrace the artistry of exploration that unifies us all.

This chapter is a heartening reminder that every whisper of gravitational waves carries the potent stories of passion, perseverance, and ingenuity. It depicts the dynamic interplay of voices that advance our understanding of the universe, beckoning new explorers to engage in the adventure of discovery and contributing to a legacy of knowledge in our quest to comprehend the boundless wonders that lie beyond our own horizons.

14.2. Human Stories of Discovery

In the pursuit of understanding the cosmos, human stories of discovery emerge as the heartbeat of scientific progress, illuminating the trajectories that shape our quest for knowledge about gravitational waves. Behind every significant advancement in this field lies the dedication, curiosity, and collaborative spirit of scientists who have pushed boundaries and redefined our comprehension of the universe. The trajectory of gravitational wave research is filled with moments of triumph, unprecedented challenges, and profound implications, and these human stories are as essential as the technological innovations themselves.

The path toward the detection of gravitational waves was initiated by the visionary theories of Albert Einstein, whose General Theory of Relativity radically reshaped our conception of gravity and its relationship with spacetime. However, it was the subsequent generations of scientists and researchers who translated this theoretical insight into pursuit-driven endeavors. It began in the early 20th century, when pioneers grappled with the implications of Einstein's theories and sought methods to test the existence of gravitational waves. Skepticism loomed amid technological constraints, yet the seeds of curiosity were planted and nurtured by the minds of early astrophysicists.

The narrative takes a pivotal turn with the emergence of researchers who turned Einstein's radical ideas into a tangible quest. Kip Thorne,

Barry Barish, and Rainer Weiss exemplify the drive and perseverance behind the construction of LIGO—the Laser Interferometer Gravitational-Wave Observatory. Their stories exemplify unwavering commitment; it was not merely about detecting waves, but also about building a community and fostering collaborative efforts that would transcend traditional divisions. Each challenge faced—from funding to engineering hurdles—became a shared endeavor that unified researchers across disciplines and institutions.

As LIGO transitioned from concept to reality, anticipation built within the scientific community. The first successful detection of gravitational waves on September 14, 2015, marked a historic milestone, not only for LIGO but for the entire field of astrophysics. The joy that surged through the community was palpable—a celebration that echoed the contributions of countless scientists who had come together on a shared mission. This moment served as a testament to the cumulative effort of the global scientific family, each voice contributing its unique perspective, labor, and insight.

However, the story does not conclude with the triumph of detection; it serves as a springboard for further exploration. In the years that followed, the field of gravitational wave astronomy rapidly evolved, broadening its scope as research findings reverberated throughout the scientific community. Researchers began to recognize the vital narratives encoded within the waveforms of gravitational waves, unlocking secrets about the mergers of black holes and neutron stars, the synthesis of heavy elements, and the dynamics of stellar evolution.

These narratives extend beyond the laboratory. As gravitational wave observations captured the attention of the public, the result was an awakening of interest and curiosity about astrophysics. Scientists took to outreach programs, engaging with various demographics and sharing the excitement of discovery. Citizen science projects emerged, inviting people to delve into the universe's mysteries, bridging the gap between academia and the public.

The spirit of collaboration continued to flourish, culminating in an international network of gravitational wave observatories for data analysis and interpretation. Researchers across the globe united to share knowledge and insights, blurring the lines between institutions and reifying the idea that scientific inquiry is a collective endeavor—one shaped by diverse voices and perspectives. This shared curiosity fosters an unrelenting dedication to unraveling the complex stories woven into the fabric of gravitational waves.

Yet, challenges persist. As new discoveries arise, so do profound questions and ethical considerations surrounding the implications of our findings. Scientists must confront not only the mysteries of black hole formation and the essence of dark energy but also the consequences of their work—in terms of societal impact, funding, and the evolution of scientific philosophy. The dialogue surrounding these issues invites all members of the scientific community to reflect on their responsibilities to the broader society and the ongoing journey of exploration.

In summary, the human stories of discovery embedded within gravitational wave astronomy illuminate the relentless quest that defines our understanding of the cosmos. From the visionary theories of Einstein to the collaborative efforts of contemporary researchers, each individual contributes to the collective narrative that strengthens our understanding of the universe. The excitement of discovery, the collaboration across disciplines, and the engagement with the public represent not only milestones in scientific inquiry but a call to action for future generations—an invitation to listen closely to the whispers of the cosmos and immerse themselves in the compelling, interconnected stories that define our cosmic narrative. As we reflect on these stories of discovery, we are reminded that we are all part of a larger tapestry, united in our pursuit of knowledge that seeks to comprehend the universe's vast complexities.

14.3. Facing Scientific Paradigms

In today's scientific landscape, the phrase "Facing Scientific Paradigms" encompasses a myriad of challenges and opportunities that shape our understanding of gravitational waves and their broader implications for physics and cosmology. As the field of gravitational wave astronomy gains momentum, it brings to light the complex interplay between innovative discoveries and the established frameworks of scientific thought. This section explores the significance of confronting scientific paradigms, the transformative power of emerging data, and the ways in which this evolution influences prevailing notions within both astrophysical research and the wider scientific community.

Historically, scientific progress has often involved a confrontation with established paradigms, where new ideas either build upon or disrupt existing theories. The trajectory of gravitational wave astronomy exemplifies this pattern, as it challenges traditional observational approaches rooted in electromagnetic radiation. Until recently, most astronomical phenomena were studied primarily through the lens of light—visible, infrared, and radio observations provided critical insights into the cosmos. However, the advent of gravitational wave astronomy has introduced an entirely new form of observation that complements and, in some cases, reshapes these existing frameworks.

At the core of this transformation lies the realization that some of the universe's most significant events—such as black hole mergers and neutron star collisions—emit gravitational waves, which are often undetectable by traditional means. The successful detection of these waves by observatories like LIGO has ushered in a fundamental shift in astrophysics, revealing that our understanding of cosmic structures is incomplete without accounting for the dynamic processes that generate gravitational waves. Dare we say, we are now tasked with turning our attention to what lies beyond light and beginning to listen more closely to the gravitational echoes that permeate the cosmos.

The impact of this shift extends well beyond mere observation; it provokes broader philosophical introspection within the scientific community. As researchers face these new paradigms, they must grapple with questions surrounding the nature of knowledge, the interplay between theory and observation, and the boundaries of human comprehension. In doing so, they navigate a terrain that often challenges established beliefs, affirming the need for adaptability and openness in scientific inquiry.

Moreover, the interpretation of gravitational wave data presents unique challenges. Each signal carries intricate details reflective of complex astrophysical processes, demanding not just precision in measurement but also rigorous analytical frameworks that are subject to constant reevaluation. Models rooted in general relativity have survived the test of time, but they may not be sufficient to capture the nuances of discoveries yet to come. Researchers are encouraged to innovate, refine their theoretical models, and embrace a mindset that welcomes dissent and contrasting perspectives—a hallmark of scientific progress.

Another critical aspect of facing scientific paradigms centers on the collaborative spirit that has emerged through gravitational wave astronomy. The global network of observatories and researchers exemplifies how shared knowledge and expertise can reshape our understanding of the universe. By facilitating collaboration across institutions and nations, this community has fostered an environment where new paradigms can be explored, critiqued, and refined under the scrutiny of the larger scientific discourse.

Looking ahead, the frontier of gravitational wave research is brimming with potential discoveries that may challenge our current understanding of the universe. The deployment of next-generation observatories and advancements in data collection and analysis methodologies will likely unveil new cosmic phenomena that test existing models and frame future inquiries. The paradigm shifts prompted by these revelations will be both profound and exhilarating.

In conclusion, "Facing Scientific Paradigms" signifies the evolution of gravitational wave astronomy from its nascent stages to a transformative field that continues to reshape our understanding of the universe. The implications of this journey transcend the observational realm, inviting researchers to reevaluate fundamental scientific principles, collaborate across disciplines, and embrace a spirit of curiosity and openness. As we advance into this exciting new chapter, we remain engaged in the age-old quest for knowledge—one that impels us to listen closely to the universe's whispers and daringly confront the paradigms that define our grasp of reality. It is in this pursuit that we inch closer to unveiling the mysteries of gravity, space, and the vast cosmos that envelops us.

14.4. The State of Modern Cosmological Thought

The evolution of modern cosmological thought has undergone transformative changes, significantly influenced by the advent of gravitational wave astronomy. These ripples in spacetime, once theoretical constructs, now stand as vibrant beacons of our understanding of the universe's mechanics and evolution. Gravitational waves have not only validated longstanding theoretical predictions but have also challenged existing paradigms, prompting a re-evaluation of our cosmic narratives.

Central to the modern state of cosmological thought is the interplay between theory and observation. Prior to the detection of gravitational waves, cosmology relied heavily on electromagnetic observations—data captured through optical telescopes, radio waves, and more. This electromagnetic approach provided critical insights into the structure and behavior of galaxies, stellar populations, and other celestial phenomena. However, the realization that observable events in the universe often produce gravitational waves has expanded the horizon of cosmic inquiry, highlighting phenomena that lie beyond the reach of electromagnetic radiation.

The implications of gravitational wave observations are far-reaching. For instance, the discovery of binary black hole mergers has provided essential data about the population of black holes, particularly their masses and spin characteristics. These findings not only inform our understanding of black hole evolution but also challenge traditional models of stellar mass distribution and the dynamics of stellar populations. Exploring the gravitational waves emitted during such mergers brings into sharper focus the fundamental processes that govern stellar evolution, birthing new avenues of inquiry concerning the lifecycle of stars and the formation of compact objects.

Moreover, the study of gravitational waves has proven instrumental in addressing questions surrounding dark matter and dark energy —two critical components of the universe whose nature remains elusive. Insights gained from gravitational wave observations enhance our understanding of these mysterious forces, shedding light on how dark matter influences cosmic structures and potentially revealing the nature of dark energy's role in the accelerated expansion of the universe. This connection underscores the importance of gravitational waves as tools for piecing together the larger cosmic puzzle.

As cosmological thought continues to evolve, the intersection of gravitational wave astronomy with other fields will shape future trajectories of research. The merging of gravitational waves with electromagnetic counterparts through multi-messenger astronomy is paving the way for a broader understanding of cosmic phenomena. This collaboration cultivates an interdisciplinary approach, bridging insights from physics, astronomy, and even computer science to refine our analytical techniques and enhance our capacity for cosmic interpretation.

The modern state of cosmological thought is not without its challenges, however. The complexity of data collected from gravitational wave observatories necessitates sophisticated analysis and filtering techniques to distinguish genuine signals from terrestrial noise. Furthermore, grappling with the implications of discoveries prompts philosophical inquiries into our understanding of existence, the nature of time, and the universe's destiny.

As we navigate these complexities, the vibrant tapestry of cosmological thought possesses an essential narrative—one that invites future generations to engage in the ongoing exploration of the universe. Each gravitational wave detected is a storytelling tool, weaving connections between events that occur across vast distances and timescales. The narratives emerging from these discoveries bring together disparate pieces of knowledge, painting a more comprehensive picture of the universe we inhabit.

In this era of gravitational wave astronomy, the state of modern cosmological thought exemplifies the beauty and intricacy of scientific inquiry. As cosmology continues to grapple with the mysteries of gravitational waves, the evolution of our understanding reveals the interplay between discovery and interpretation, propelling us forward into uncharted territories of knowledge. The universe beckons us to listen closer, challenging us to remain curious and inspired as we uncover the secrets that lie beyond our own galaxy, ultimately reshaping our perception of existence itself.

14.5. The Future of Scientific Inquiry

Scientific inquiry has taken a significant leap forward with the advent of gravitational wave astronomy, revealing profound insights about the cosmos and reshaping our understanding of fundamental physics. As we explore the future of scientific inquiry, we confront numerous possibilities and challenges that will define not just our approach to gravitational waves but the broader landscape of knowledge in astrophysics and related disciplines.

The journey that brought us to this turning point began with theoretical audacity, as the foundational principles articulated by Albert Einstein challenged stagnant ideas about gravity and the nature of the universe. This radical shift paved the way for scientific exploration into realms once thought unattainable. As gravitational wave detectors like LIGO and Virgo moved from concept to reality, they prompted a surge in research activity aimed at uncovering the mysteries hidden within the cosmos.

At the heart of this exploration is the promise of multi-messenger astronomy—the synergy between gravitational waves and electromagnetic signals. As we improve our observational capabilities, we will increasingly be able to correlate gravitational wave detections with traditional astronomical observations, leading to richer interpretations of cosmic events. The potential for simultaneous observations of gravitational waves and electromagnetic radiation from events such as supernovae or gamma-ray bursts will deepen our understanding of the underlying physics of these phenomena, fostering new questions and lines of inquiry about the universe.

The next generation of gravitational wave observatories, including potential space-based missions like the Laser Interferometer Space Antenna (LISA), is poised to unlock even more secrets from the cosmos. These upcoming initiatives will extend the search into lower frequencies, allowing us to probe supermassive black hole mergers and other processes that remain presently elusive. As technological advancements in detection and data analysis continue to evolve, researchers will uncover more about the birth and death of stars, the genesis of heavy elements, and the dynamics driving cosmic expansion.

However, along with opportunities lie challenges. The vast amount of data generated by gravitational wave observations will require innovative approaches for data management and analysis. Advances in machine learning and artificial intelligence, already gaining traction in gravitational wave astronomy, will further transform how we process and interpret the data collected. Such methods will enhance our capacity for real-time detection and identification of signals, while also serving to filter out noise and enhance systematic analyses.

Equally important is the role of international collaboration in addressing the challenges and harnessing the opportunities that lie ahead. As gravitational wave observatories expand their reach globally, fostering collaborative networks among institutions across countries becomes ever more critical. This spirit of unity not only facilitates data-sharing and cross-validation of findings but also enhances knowledge transmission, allowing for multicultural insights that inform scientific discovery.

The ethical implications of gravitational wave research will also demand attention. As we delve deeper into cosmic phenomena, questions about the consequences of our discoveries—not just in terms of knowledge but also in terms of societal impact—arise. The ongoing dialogue about the responsibilities of scientists and the public's engagement in scientific endeavors is essential to ensure that advancements benefit humanity and deepen our appreciation of the universe.

Ultimately, the future of scientific inquiry in the realm of gravitational waves beckons a vibrant and inclusive landscape. Building upon the successes of today, future generations of scientists will embark upon an exhilarating expedition into the unknown, guided by the gravitational waves that ripple through spacetime. As each signal detected conveys its unique narrative, we are continuously reminded of our place in the grand cosmic tapestry—a reminder that beneath each wave lies a story, and each story presents an invitation to listen, seek, and understand.

As we stand on the cusp of these new discoveries and developments, we are encouraged to remain curious, daring, and engaged. The future of gravitational wave astronomy is bright, filled with prospects for unveiling the universe's most intimate secrets, pressing the boundaries of knowledge ever wider, and inviting new explorers into this magnificent journey of cosmic discovery. In this spirit, the spirit of inquiry shall persist, guiding us as we endeavor to decipher the grand tale of existence that unfolds across the galaxies.

15. The Public's Role in Discovery

15.1. Encouraging Scientific Curiosity

Encouraging scientific curiosity is a central theme in the journey through gravitational wave astronomy and beyond. It represents not only a catalyst for discoveries within the scientific community, but also a vital engagement with the public as we navigate the inherent complexities of the universe. This engagement encourages individuals—particularly the younger generations—to embrace a mindset of inquiry, wonder, and exploration. By fostering scientific curiosity, we empower individuals to actively participate in the scientific discourse, paving pathways toward a more enlightened society.

At the root of encouraging scientific curiosity lies the intrinsic human desire to explore the unknown. The study of gravitational waves embodies this pursuit, as it invites questions about the universe's origins, its evolution, and the fundamental laws governing reality. Scientific curiosity flourishes in environments where questions are celebrated, fostering an atmosphere that encourages inquiry as a means of connecting with the marvels of nature.

Engaging students in scientific inquiry from an early age is critical to cultivating a lifelong love for science. Educational programs that highlight the significance of gravitational wave detection can spark inspiration and invoke passion among budding scientists. Through hands-on experiments, interactive demonstrations, and workshops, educators can illuminate the profoundly personal nature of exploration. Students who can engage with tangible aspects of science, asking questions and seeking answers, will ultimately foster their curiosity and drive discovery.

In this technological age, the digital landscape offers new avenues for sustaining scientific interest. Online platforms provide access to a wealth of information, resources, and opportunities for students and enthusiasts alike to engage with current research. Social media channels serve as conduits for sharing discoveries and promoting dialogue, allowing scientists to connect directly with members of the public.

By making complex scientific concepts accessible and relatable, these platforms can ignite curiosity and inspire a diverse audience to grasp the importance of gravitational wave astronomy.

Citizen science initiatives have emerged as powerful tools in this context, enabling members of the public to actively participate in the scientific process. Projects that enlist volunteers to analyze data, help identify gravitational wave signals, or even contribute to simulations foster a sense of ownership and empowerment. This engagement highlights that science is not limited to researchers in laboratories; it is a collective endeavor driven by curiosity that unites communities across various demographics.

Furthermore, the portrayal of science in popular culture acts as a conduit for wider engagement. Films, books, documentaries, and educational programs that highlight gravitational wave discoveries can resonate deeply with audiences, sparking enthusiasm for science in ways that traditional education may not. When people encounter themes of cosmic exploration and the mysteries of existence portrayed in familiar media, they are often inspired to seek deeper understanding and engagement with such concepts.

Ultimately, encouraging scientific curiosity requires a deliberate effort to create environments rich in questions, wonder, and exploration. This endeavor is a shared responsibility among educators, scientists, and communicators, all united by the goal of conveying the mysteries of the universe to a broader audience.

In conclusion, the encouragement of scientific curiosity is a vital undertaking that propels the journey of discovery within gravitational wave astronomy and far beyond. By instilling a sense of wonder and fostering a culture of inquiry, we can ignite passions that lead to extraordinary explorations of the cosmos. As we invite the public into the dialogue surrounding gravitational waves, we empower individuals to embrace a lifelong quest for knowledge, unlocking new dimensions of understanding while nurturing the next generation of explorers. Through collective effort, we can ensure that curiosity remains a guiding force in unveiling the stunning complexities woven into the fabric of our universe.

15.2. Public Engagement in Science

Public engagement in science has emerged as an integral element in the continuum of gravitational wave astronomy, facilitating not only the dissemination of knowledge but also inspiring curiosity and enthusiasm among diverse audiences. The journey of discovery in this field extends beyond the confines of research laboratories and academic discourse; it beckons the public to explore the mysteries of the universe alongside scientists, creating a shared narrative woven through the threads of inquiry, enthusiasm, and wonder.

The dynamics of public engagement begin with the recognition that science is a communal enterprise, one that thrives on the exchange of ideas, perspectives, and experiences. Gravitational wave astronomy presents a compelling narrative that transcends technical details, inviting participation from individuals eager to learn about the cosmos. As significant discoveries continue to unfold—such as the first detection of gravitational waves from merging black holes—the excitement surrounding these events captures public attention, creating opportunities for meaningful engagement.

A key aspect of fostering public interest lies in effectively communicating the importance and implications of gravitational wave research. Researchers, educators, and communicators must work together to craft accessible narratives that resonate with various audiences. By employing relatable analogies and vivid storytelling, they can connect complex scientific concepts to everyday experiences, instilling a sense of wonder. Outreach initiatives—ranging from public lectures and community workshops to engaging digital content—serve as conduits for conveying the excitement of gravitational waves, urging the public to ponder their significance and embrace the joy of discovery.

Citizen science projects have emerged as pivotal mechanisms for engaging the public in scientific endeavors. By inviting enthusiasts to actively participate in the analysis of gravitational wave data, researchers empower individuals to contribute meaningfully to the exploration of the cosmos. These projects foster a spirit of collaboration, blurring the line between scientists and citizens while reinforcing the notion that science is accessible and inviting. When everyday people are equipped with the tools to contribute to the search for gravitational waves, they become integral players in the scientific narrative, nurturing a greater appreciation for the complexities of the universe.

Fostering science education from an early age also plays a critical role in public engagement. Integrating gravitational wave research into curricula stimulates curiosity and excitement in young minds, allowing students to explore the fundamental concepts of physics, space, and time. Hands-on activities—such as simulations that model gravitational waves, demonstrations showcasing the principles of interferometry, or interactive workshops that engage students in the discovery process—cultivate a sense of wonder. By instilling a love for inquiry, these educational initiatives nurture future generations of scientists and explorers.

Moreover, the role of popular culture in enriching public engagement cannot be overlooked. Gravitational waves have captured imaginations through literature, film, and television, leading to representations that weave astronomy into captivating narratives. Scientists can leverage these cultural touchstones, partnering with creators to bring gravitational waves to wider audiences, tempting curiosity and sparking interest. The integration of science and culture serves to bridge knowledge gaps and inspire a collective sense of wonder about the universe.

Finally, public engagement in science extends to fostering discussions about the ethical implications of astronomical discoveries and how they impact our understanding of existence. As scientists unlock the secrets of the universe, they must consider the broader ramifications of their findings on society, the environment, and the ethical frameworks within which they operate. Engaging the public in these nuanced conversations reinforces transparency in scientific pursuits and fosters a sense of shared responsibility.

In conclusion, public engagement in gravitational wave astronomy represents a vibrant tapestry of exploration, outreach, collaboration, and curiosity. By creating inviting spaces for dialogue, participation, and exploration, scientists can bridge the gap between research and everyday experiences, inspiring individuals to delve into the beauty of the cosmos. Each gravitational wave detection becomes an opportunity to celebrate shared discovery, inviting the public to embark on a journey of understanding together. In essence, through public engagement, we pave the way for a deeper comprehension of the universe—a universe where echoes of the cosmos resonate far beyond the confines of the observatory, uniting us all in our quest to unveil the mysteries of existence.

15.3. Citizen Science Projects

Citizen science projects represent a transformative intersection between professional scientific inquiry and public engagement, encouraging participants from all walks of life to partake actively in the exploration of gravitational waves and the larger cosmos. Through these initiatives, the once esoteric field of astrophysics becomes more accessible, inviting curious minds to contribute to our understanding of the universe. This collaborative spirit not only enhances data collection efforts but nurtures a sense of ownership and excitement about scientific discovery among participants.

At the core of many citizen science projects related to gravitational waves is the need for volunteers to assist in analyzing the vast datasets generated by observatories like LIGO and Virgo. The deluge of information these sophisticated detectors produce each time a gravitational wave event is captured is staggering. Various techniques are deployed to sift through this data, but the sheer volume can easily overwhelm even the most robust computational systems. Citizen scientists can step in to help—analyzing gravitational wave signals, identifying patterns, and even classifying the types of events observed, such as mergers of black holes or neutron stars.

One notable example of a citizen science initiative within this realm is the Gravity Spy project. Launched as part of the LIGO collaboration, Gravity Spy invites volunteers to engage with data from LIGO's detections, training them to identify and classify various noise sources present in the gravitational wave data. Participants examine spectrograms—visual representations of frequency over time—and help distinguish between potential gravitational wave signals and instrumental noise. By harnessing the collective efforts of citizen scientists, researchers accelerate their ability to refine analyses and improve the accuracy of detected gravitational wave signals.

The value of these projects extends beyond merely crunching numbers; they help nurture scientific literacy and curiosity among participants. By engaging in the scientific process, individuals develop a better understanding of gravitational waves, astrophysics, and the broader context of cosmic phenomena. Citizen scientists become ambassadors of science, sharing their experiences and insights within their communities and sparking curiosity among peers and family members, which can ultimately foster a more science-friendly culture in society.

Moreover, citizen science projects empower participants with a sense of agency, prompting them to contribute meaningfully to the scientific enterprise. The realization that anyone, regardless of their background, can contribute to our knowledge of gravitational waves instills a sense of connection between individuals and the cosmic narrative. This democratization of science cultivates a community of passionate individuals eager to engage with the universe's profound mysteries.

The integration of citizen science projects with the professional scientific community also encourages diverse perspectives in research. Participants approach gravitational wave phenomena with unique viewpoints, often questioning established paradigms and providing novel insights that can challenge conventional wisdom. This dynamic interplay fosters a vibrant scientific dialogue that enhances the collective understanding of gravitational waves and their implications for cosmic exploration.

Looking to the future, the role of citizen science is set to expand further, especially as advancements in data collection technology continue to evolve. With the prospect of next-generation gravitational wave observatories on the horizon, such as space-based initiatives like LISA, the potential for larger datasets will only increase. Citizen science projects will evolve to meet these challenges, ensuring that public engagement remains at the forefront of scientific progress.

In closing, citizen science projects mark a significant milestone in gravitational wave astronomy, weaving a fabric of collaboration, engagement, and exploration that transcends traditional boundaries in science. By enabling participation in the scientific process, these initiatives encourage curiosity, foster understanding, and empower individuals to contribute meaningfully to the quest for knowledge. The role of citizen scientists is a testament to the idea that when we come together to listen to the symphonies of gravitational waves, we not only unravel the universe's secrets but also foster a shared narrative—one that invites everyone to play a part in the grand exploration of our cosmos.

15.4. Fostering Science Education

Fostering science education is integral to the expansion of our understanding of the universe, particularly in the rapidly evolving field of gravitational wave astronomy. With the recent advancements in technology, educational initiatives have made it possible to engage new generations and cultivate curiosity about the cosmos like never before. This subchapter will explore the importance of science education in fostering interest in astrophysics and gravitational waves, the methods employed to engage students and the public, and the potential impact on the future of scientific inquiry.

At the heart of fostering science education lies the recognition that curiosity is innate within us all. From an early age, children are drawn to the mysteries of the natural world—be it the stars in the night sky or the forces that shape their everyday lives. Gravitational waves embody a captivating narrative that connects fundamental physics with the cosmos, presenting an exceptional opportunity to inspire students. Educational initiatives tailored to the subject of gravitational waves can instill an enduring sense of wonder, guiding young minds toward a future in science and exploration.

To effectively foster science education in this realm, innovative teaching methods are essential. Educators are increasingly incorporating hands-on experiments, interactive simulations, and engaging multimedia resources into the curriculum. For instance, activities that simulate the effects of gravitational waves on spacetime—using rubber sheets to demonstrate the principles of curvature—help students visualize and grasp complex concepts more intuitively. This active learning approach facilitates an immersive experience, allowing students to connect scientific principles with observable phenomena.

Collaborative projects, such as citizen science initiatives, have also emerged as powerful vehicles for education. Through participatory research opportunities, students and members of the public can engage with the scientific process on a fundamental level. For instance, a project that involves analyzing gravitational wave data enables participants to be directly involved in ongoing research, yielding a sense of ownership and excitement about their contributions. Such experiences empower individuals to act as ambassadors of science within their communities, promoting appreciation and understanding of astrophysics.

Moreover, outreach programs designed to connect scientists with schools, museums, and community centers further enhance science education. These initiatives allow budding scientists to interact directly with researchers and experts, fostering mentorship relationships that inspire enthusiasm for scientific inquiry. Events such as public lectures, workshops, and stargazing nights create opportunities for face-to-face dialogue, igniting curiosity and drawing individuals into the world of astrophysics.

In addition to local outreach, leveraging digital platforms serves to expand the reach of science education. Social media, online courses, and educational websites offer resources for individuals who wish to learn more about gravitational waves and related concepts. The accessibility of these platforms democratizes knowledge and enhances engagement with a broader audience, removing traditional barriers to education. As a result, individuals from varied backgrounds can cultivate an interest in scientific inquiry, regardless of their geographic location or institutional affiliation.

Another vital dimension of fostering science education is the role of popular culture in shaping public perceptions and interest in science. Films, documentaries, and literature highlighting concepts related to gravitational waves can capture the imagination of a diverse audience. This interplay between art and science invites discussion and encourages a culture in which scientific concepts are woven into broader narratives, fostering curiosity and engagement.

As we foster science education in the context of gravitational wave astronomy, we also must consider the ethical ramifications of our discoveries. Conversations surrounding the nature of knowledge, responsibility in research, and the societal impacts of scientific advancements are crucial. Educating future generations about these considerations will instill a sense of accountability and ethical grounding, ensuring that advancements in astrophysics contribute positively to humanity.

In conclusion, fostering science education is paramount in expanding our understanding of gravitational waves and the universe at large. By employing innovative teaching methodologies, promoting collaborative projects, leveraging digital platforms, and fostering dialogue, we instill curiosity, creativity, and a sense of responsibility among future generations. This ongoing endeavor will ensure that the excitement and wonder surrounding gravitational wave astronomy continue to inspire those who seek answers to the profound questions of the cosmos. As we journey forward into the unknown, encouraging scientific curiosity and education will be essential in unlocking the mysteries woven within the fabric of reality, inviting all to participate in the exploration of our universe.

15.5. Science in Popular Culture

In the modern landscape of scientific inquiry, "Science in Popular Culture" assumes a multifaceted importance, particularly within the domain of gravitational wave astronomy. The engagement of popular culture with scientific concepts and discoveries enriches public understanding and fosters a deep-seated appreciation for the mysteries of the universe. As gravitational wave astronomy takes center stage in the quest for knowledge about our cosmos, its portrayal in popular culture invites audiences to explore profound questions about existence and humanity's connection to the universe.

One of the compelling aspects of gravitational wave research is its ability to intertwine with narratives that capture the imagination of the public. Science fiction films, novels, and documentaries have increasingly incorporated themes related to gravitational waves, presenting audiences with glimpses of cosmic phenomena that were previously only theoretical. Cinematic portrayals of black holes, neutron stars, and cosmic mergers resonate with viewers, providing both entertainment and a foundation for understanding gravitational waves. These narratives invite broader conversations about the reality of such phenomena, encouraging viewers to engage with the intricacies of the universe beyond the confines of traditional scientific discourse.

The portrayal of gravitational waves in popular media transcends mere representation; it serves as a bridge that connects scientific advancements to the consciousness of society. Documentaries exploring the construction of gravitational wave observatories and the significance of their discoveries provide meaningful insights into the ongoing dialogue between scientific exploration and public engagement. By demystifying complex concepts, these films and programs offer accessible frames of reference for audiences, cultivating curiosity and appreciation for the phenomenal intricacies of gravitational wave detection.

Moreover, popular culture plays a critical role in showcasing the careers and contributions of scientists involved in gravitational wave research. Through portrayals of key figures like Kip Thorne, Rainer Weiss, and other pioneers, the human element of science becomes fully realized, highlighting the diverse paths that lead individuals to contribute to breakthroughs in gravitational wave astronomy. Such narratives serve to inspire aspiring scientists and offer relatable models for young viewers who may be contemplating their future in science and exploration. Celebrating the accomplishments of scientists fosters connection and empowers individuals to pursue paths of inquiry within the scientific community.

Also significant is the potential for public engagement provided by popular culture to stimulate discussions about the implications of gravitational wave discoveries. As awareness of the gravitational waves phenomenon spreads, conversations about their significance can expand to ethical considerations—prompting audiences to think critically about how these discoveries influence our understanding of existence and our place within the cosmos. Engaging with these contemplations serves not only to enrich public discourse about science but also empowers individuals to reflect on their relationship with the universe and the responsibilities that accompany scientific advancement.

At the same time, the integration of gravitational wave astronomy into popular culture offers opportunities for collaboration between scientists and artists—illustrators, writers, and filmmakers can work alongside researchers to create narratives that enrich our collective understanding. Propelling creativity and scientific dialogue into new domains, these partnerships manifest a commitment to celebrating knowledge and the wonders it reveals, bridging the gap between hard science and imaginative storytelling.

As gravitational wave research continues to flourish, the integration of science into popular culture will remain integral to both public engagement and scientific inquiry. The narratives that emerge from this union echo the complexity of the universe while inviting audiences to participate in a shared journey of exploration. Every gravitational wave detected is not just a data point; it represents stories of cosmic creation, evolution, and collisions—the events that shape our universe.

In conclusion, "Science in Popular Culture" serves as a vital conduit for transforming abstract scientific ideas into relatable narratives that engage, inspire, and challenge public perception. Through the lens of popular media, gravitational wave discoveries inspire curiosity, foster dialogue, and cultivate a deeper appreciation for the cosmos. As we continue to explore the gravitational waves that ripple through space-time, we are urged to listen closely—to engage with the wonders of the universe—as we navigate the uncharted waters of discovery together. This synergy furthers our understanding, invites exploration, and rekindles the human curiosity that has defined our journey through the realms of science and existence.

16. Beyond Our Own Galaxy

16.1. Studying Distant Galaxies

Studying distant galaxies is a multifaceted endeavor that not only widens our understanding of the cosmos but also serves as a testament to the evolution of observational techniques, theoretical frameworks, and human curiosity. Gravitational waves, the ripples in spacetime produced by cataclysmic cosmic events, now serve as invaluable tools in probing the enigmatic realms of distant galaxies. The marriage of gravitational wave astronomy with observations of extragalactic signals leads us into a realm where the insights gained extend our cosmic horizon, revealing secrets about galaxy formation, dark matter, and the very nature of the universe.

As we embark on this journey of studying distant galaxies, it is essential to first contemplate the nature of galaxies themselves. Galaxies, the fundamental building blocks of the universe, are vast collections of stars, gas, dust, and dark matter bound together by gravity. Each galaxy possesses a unique history, characterized by its formation processes, interactions with neighboring systems, and evolutionary patterns spanning millions to billions of years. Our understanding of distant galaxies has primarily relied on electromagnetic observations —light of various wavelengths emitted by stars and other celestial bodies—but the advent of gravitational wave astronomy has ushered in a new approach for studying the cosmos.

Gravitational waves have the potential to provide insights into events occurring in galaxies across vast distances—mergers of black holes or neutron stars that may take place within these galaxies serve as unique opportunities to capture the violent dynamics occurring in some of the universe's most extreme environments. The detection of gravitational waves from such events can help construct a more complete picture of the surrounding galaxy, illuminating the interactions between significant cosmic forces and providing data about the distance and mass of the entities involved.

When we analyze the gravitational wave signals produced by merging binaries, researchers can infer not only the properties of the objects involved but also relevant details about their host galaxies. The extraction of such information is facilitated by the additional data gathered through electromagnetic observations of those same galaxies. This multi-messenger approach fosters a richer dialogue between gravitational wave signals and the electromagnetic observations, enhancing our understanding of the life cycles and interactions of celestial phenomena.

Moreover, gravitational wave observations from distant galaxies also open an avenue to investigate the nature of dark matter. Galaxies are believed to harbor significant quantities of dark matter—an invisible substance that exerts gravitational influence without emitting light. Understanding the distribution of dark matter is critical for piecing together the evolution of galaxies, and observations of gravitational waves emerging from merger events provide exquisite insights into the environments in which these cosmic interactions unfold. The correlation of gravitational wave events and their host galaxies offers an unprecedented means to probe the presence and characteristics of dark matter in cosmic structures.

An intriguing possibility lies in the potential to analyze gravitational waves as proxies for studying the early universe. As we delve into the gravitational wave signals associated with early merging events, we can glean insights into the processes that shaped the formation of galaxies during the universe's infancy. By connecting these signals with electromagnetic observations of distant galaxies, we attain greater cosmic context, enriching our comprehension of galaxy formation and evolution in the early stages of the universe.

However, the study of distant galaxies through gravitational waves is not without challenges. The faint signals, which become more diluted by cosmic expansion, lead to difficulties in identifying precise sources. As gravitational wave observatories continue to enhance their detection capabilities, the accuracy of source localization must improve, and researchers must work collaboratively to refine methodologies that bridge the gap between gravitational waves and electromagnetic observations.

In summary, the study of distant galaxies, now paired with the insights derived from gravitational wave observations, expands our cosmic narrative. By uncovering the intricate dynamics of galaxy formation, dark matter distribution, and the early universe's processes, we can collectively deepen our understanding of the universe that surrounds us. As we listen attentively to the gravitational echoes emanating from distant galaxies, we embrace the collaborative spirit of discovery, enriching our perception of the grand tapestry of existence woven throughout the cosmic expanse. Each wave detected becomes a glimpse into our distant past, revealing the symphonic dance of stars, galaxies, and the fabric of reality itself.

16.2. Understanding Extragalactic Signals

Understanding signals from extragalactic sources forms a pivotal aspect of modern astrophysics, intricately connecting gravitational wave research to the larger narrative of cosmic discovery. These signals, emanating from regions well beyond our Milky Way galaxy, provide crucial information about the fundamental processes that shape the universe. The insights garnered from observing these distant phenomena not only expand our knowledge of gravitational waves but also enhance our comprehension of the universe's evolution, structure, and the cosmic interactions occurring across vast distances.

Extragalactic signals encompass a range of astrophysical phenomena, from the merging of black holes and neutron stars in distant galaxies to the emission of gamma-ray bursts associated with catastrophic stellar collapses. Gravitational waves resulting from these events serve as unique messengers, carrying information about their origins over billions of light-years and allowing researchers to probe environments previously thought to be unreachable. Through the combined efforts of gravitational wave observatories like LIGO and Virgo, astronomers have access to a wealth of data that offers profound insights into the behaviors of galaxies, the population of stellar remnants, and the cosmic evolution that has unfolded across time.

A crucial characteristic of gravitational wave observations is their ability to access phenomena that remain obscured by factors such as distance, brightness, and cosmic dust. Unlike electromagnetic observations, which can be hindered by the interstellar medium, gravitational waves can traverse through the vast emptiness of space with remarkable fidelity. This unique quality enables scientists to study events hidden from traditional telescopes, thus bridging gaps in our understanding of extragalactic structures and dynamics.

For instance, through gravitational wave detections, researchers can glean the properties of black hole populations in distant galaxies. By analyzing the waveforms from binary black hole mergers, scientists can identify mass distributions and spins, offering insights into how these black holes formed and evolved over time. This precise information can illuminate the underlying processes governing black hole formation, such as the role of mass transfer in binary systems and the characteristics of progenitor stars.

Furthermore, the interplay between gravitational waves and electromagnetic signals creates a rich tapestry for future exploration. Observing additional channels—such as multi-messenger signals that accompany gravitational waves—provides holistic insights into cosmic events and their ramifications for galactic evolution. This synergy enables researchers to refine models of star and galaxy formation while investigating the pathways that lead to significant astrophysical phenomena, such as the creation of heavy elements through the mergers of neutron stars.

The challenge of extracting meaningful data from distant extragalactic signals lies in the inherent complexities of analyzing gravitational waveforms. Scientists must collaborate to develop sophisticated modeling techniques to accurately match observed signals with the predicted waveforms generated during specific astrophysical events. The need for robust theoretical frameworks that integrate observations from gravitational wave detectors with traditional electromagnetic measurement techniques underscores the interdisciplinary nature of this research.

As we consider the implications of these extragalactic signals, one must also acknowledge the ethical responsibilities tied to the discoveries we make. As gravitational waves unveil the profound dynamics of cosmic activities, researchers must contemplate the implications of such knowledge and the responsibilities it entails. Public engagement and transparency become increasingly important as new findings challenge and broaden public understanding of our place within the cosmos.

In conclusion, the quest to understand extragalactic signals represents a dynamic avenue of inquiry in the field of gravitational wave astronomy. By elucidating the processes that govern the formation and evolution of galaxies, researchers can piece together the larger narrative of cosmic history that stretches across vast distances. As we continue to listen to the gravitational echoes emanating from these distant regions, we uncover stories that deepen our understanding of the universe, weaving an intricate picture of stellar interactions, galactic structure, and the fundamental questions that lie at the heart of existence itself. The allure of these distant signals beckons us onward, inviting future generations of scientists to engage in the ongoing exploration of the cosmos and the remarkable narratives that await discovery beyond our own galaxy.

16.3. The Quest for Extraterrestrial Waves

The quest for extraterrestrial waves is an integral and exciting journey within the broader landscape of gravitational wave astronomy, culminating at the very edges of current scientific understanding. This ongoing endeavor is not merely about detecting fleeting signals from far-off cosmic events; it encompasses the ambition to explore the potential existence of gravitational waves produced by phenomena beyond our immediate observations, including the tantalizing prospect of signals from extraterrestrial civilizations. The implications of such discoveries invite remarkable questions about our place in the universe and the relationship between humanity and the cosmos.

At the forefront of this quest lies the realization that gravitational waves offer a unique window through which scientists can scrutinize the most violent and energetic events in the universe. Beyond binary black hole mergers and neutron star collisions, there exists the possibility that the mechanics of celestial bodies may offer hints of extraterrestrial activity, including advanced technologies and astrophysical signatures indicative of intelligent life. While the primary focus has been on understanding cataclysmic cosmic events, the quest for extraterrestrial waves pushes the frontier into uncharted areas of exploration.

The notion of extraterrestrial waves suggests a marriage of gravitational wave detection with the search for extraterrestrial intelligence (SETI). As we learn to dissect the intricate patterns of gravitational waveforms from known astronomical sources, there exists the tantalizing potential for distinguishing signals that may not conform to established natural processes. Speculating on the possible gravitational signatures of extraterrestrial technologies evokes a broader cosmic dialogue, illuminating the quest for life beyond our planet.

Understanding and identifying extraterrestrial waves necessitate not only the advancements in detector sensitivity but also a robust theoretical framework that accommodates novel possibilities. By developing models to predict the characteristics of gravitational wave signals from hypothetical extraterrestrial sources, scientists can establish a baseline for comparison against natural cosmic phenomena. Such models would explore scenarios involving large-scale engineering constructs, such as Dyson spheres or other speculative astronomical infrastructure that could generate detectable gravitational waves.

To enhance the credibility of these pursuits, an interdisciplinary approach will prove vital. Marrying astrophysics with insights from sociology, philosophy, and cognitive science provides a comprehensive framework for understanding the broader implications of extraterrestrial waves. This collaborative spirit invites researchers from various fields to contribute their expertise, bolstering the collective endeavors to unravel the mysteries of the cosmos and assess the implications of discovering extraterrestrial signatures.

Furthermore, the quest for extraterrestrial waves capitalizes on the ethos of transparency and engagement with the public. As interest in cosmic phenomena peaks, fostering communal curiosity and involvement becomes paramount. Citizen science initiatives focused on gravitational wave detection can deepen the connections between researchers and the public—sparking sense of ownership and agency in the journey of discovery. Through inclusive programs that invite participation and insight, interest in exploring the potential of extraterrestrial waves cultivates an environment where curiosity flourishes.

Looking forward, ongoing advancements in gravitational wave technology will play a significant role in refining the quest for extraterrestrial waves. The development of next-generation observatories and space-based initiatives, such as the proposed Laser Interferometer Space Antenna (LISA), will extend detection capabilities, paving the way for exploring unknown realms of the cosmos. These endeavors allow researchers to probe distant regions of space, examining gravitational waves generated from various sources—both natural and potentially artificial.

In conclusion, the quest for extraterrestrial waves represents an exhilarating chapter within gravitational wave astronomy—a quest that transcends conventional boundaries while seeking to uncover the profound mysteries of the universe. As we enhance our detectors, refine our expectations, and engage with the public, we inch closer to unearthing potential signals that could revolutionize our understanding of life beyond Earth. Gravitational waves not only resonate through the annals of cosmic history; they beckon all of us to listen closely and embrace the expansive possibilities that lie ahead. The stories encoded in these waves extend far beyond our world, inviting exploration into the realms of connection, existence, and our place within the magnificent universe we inhabit.

16.4. Lessons from the Cosmic Frontier

Lessons from the Cosmic Frontier provides profound insights into the lessons learned through the exploration of gravitational wave astronomy and the broader context of its implications within the scientific community. As we stand at the intersection of theory, observation, and interpretation, we find ourselves compelled to reflect on the transformative impacts that the study of gravitational waves has had on our understanding of the universe.

One of the paramount lessons derived from this journey is the power of collaboration. Gravitational wave astronomy exemplifies the global effort made by scientists, engineers, and researchers from diverse backgrounds, unified by the common ambition to unlock the secrets of the cosmos. The synergy between observatories such as LIGO, Virgo, and KAGRA has not only enhanced our ability to detect and analyze gravitational waves but has also fostered an ethos of cooperation that transcends national borders. This collaborative spirit stands as a testament to the capacity for human ingenuity when diverse perspectives come together to tackle complex challenges and inquiries.

Moreover, the discoveries gleaned from gravitational wave detections challenge preconceived notions and long-standing paradigms in astrophysics. Each observed event—from the merger of binary black holes to the collision of neutron stars—provides a new perspective on the lifecycle of cosmic bodies, expanding our understanding of stellar evolution and the forces that shape the universe. The insights garnered from these events serve as an invitation to reevaluate our theoretical frameworks, prompting continuous refinement and adaptation as new data emerge.

As we delve further into the implications of gravitational wave astronomy, we recognize the significant philosophical questions that arise. The intersection of observational findings with the fundamental concepts of existence, time, and gravity invites us to ponder our place within the cosmic tapestry. The exploration of the universe through gravitational waves leads to deeper inquiries about the nature of reality and the interconnectedness of all entities, ultimately fostering a more holistic understanding of our existence in the grand narrative of the cosmos.

In addition, the contributions of gravitational wave astronomy under-score the importance of science education and public engagement. As we share the stories of our discoveries, we invite society to journey alongside us—fostering curiosity, breaking down perceived barriers, and inspiring future generations to explore the realm of astrophysics. The continuous engagement with diverse audiences enhances soci-etal appreciation for science and proves vital in cultivating a more science-literate future.

As we explore challenges still ahead, including refining detection techniques and addressing ethical implications tied to our discoveries, the spirit of scientific inquiry remains steadfast. Gravitational wave astronomy serves as a clarion call for researchers to embrace uncer-tainty, triumph over obstacles, and promote an inclusive environment where collaborative exploration thrives.

In this ongoing venture into the cosmic frontier, the lessons we draw from gravitational wave astronomy elucidate not just scientific progress but also human connections, societal responsibilities, and philosophical reflections. The journey underscores a shared commit-ment to understanding the universe, echoing through the very fabric of spacetime as we listen closely to the gravitational whispers that beckon us onward.

As we continue to thrive in this inspiring pursuit, the lessons learned from the cosmic frontier promise richer understanding and deeper connections—reminding us that the adventure of discovery is not only about unveiling the universe's mysteries but also about fostering unity and curiosity within humanity itself. In this spirit, the echoes of gravitational waves beckon future explorers to engage, question, and immerse themselves in the exquisite complexities gleaned from the cosmos, leading us toward a horizon filled with promise and possibility.

16.5. The Broader Cosmic Context

The cosmos, a vast expanse filled with mysteries, beckons humanity to unravel its secrets through the enigmatic whispers of gravitational waves. These ephemeral ripples in spacetime provide insights into cataclysmic events that occur in the depths of the universe, from the colliding remnants of stars to the merger of black holes. As we venture into the broader cosmic context of gravitational waves, it becomes apparent that these observations do not merely illuminate isolated phenomena; they reshuffle our understanding of fundamental astrophysics, our universe's structure, and the very nature of existence.

The significance of gravitational waves extends beyond astronomy; they challenge and refine our cosmological models, reshaping foundational theories established through traditional observations of light. Each event captured provides a unique glimpse into the processes driving the universe's evolution, allowing researchers to piece together the intricacies that define cosmic structures and their dynamics. For instance, the gravitational waves detected from neutron star mergers have revealed crucial information about the synthesis of heavy elements, offering unprecedented insights into the complex dance of matter that fuels the creation of stars and planets.

The broader cosmic context encapsulates the interconnectedness of phenomena, showcasing how black holes, neutron stars, and galaxies engage in a continuous dialogue across time and space. Gravitational waves not only serve as messengers of dynamic events but also offer thematic narratives about the processes that govern cosmic interactions. As we analyze these signals, we navigate new frontiers in the field of astrophysics, leading to fresh inquiries about dark matter and dark energy—two elusive components that dominate the universe yet remain poorly understood.

Moreover, the discovery that gravitational waves originate from events across vast distances places humanity's existence within a more expansive narrative—one that evokes fundamental philosophical explorations about our place in the cosmos. As we confront the implications of observing gravitational waves from the distant past, our understanding of time, existence, and interconnectedness deepens, prompting reevaluations of humanity's relationship with the universe at large.

This quest also necessitates international collaboration, weaving together the expertise of scientists and engineers across the globe. The cooperative efforts among LIGO, Virgo, KAGRA, and future observatories exemplify the spirit of unity in exploration. As researchers pool resources and knowledge, the gravitational wave community functions as an interconnected web, fostering innovations that challenge traditional paradigms while driving forward our collective understanding of the cosmos.

Looking to the horizon, the future prospects of gravitational wave astronomy are ignited by the potential development of next-generation observatories—whether terrestrial or space-based. These advancements will enhance sensitivity, expand observational capabilities, and delve deeper into the secrets woven into the fabric of the universe. As we position ourselves for the ongoing quest, the essence of scientific inquiry reiterates that the journey is as vital as the discoveries it yields.

Each gravitational wave detected presents an invitation for all who are curious to engage with the broader cosmic narrative. The quest for knowledge embodies the timeless spirit of discovery, evoking an enthusiasm that draws in individuals from all walks of life. As we strive to listen closely to the echoes of the universe, we embrace the profound mysteries within—an ongoing conversation with the cosmos that requires humility, creativity, and collaboration.

In conclusion, the broader cosmic context of gravitational waves provides an intricate landscape for inquiry, reflection, and connection. By illuminating the interconnections between cosmic events, our under-standing of gravity, and humanity's deeper philosophical inquiries, we create a foundation upon which future explorations can build. As we tune into the whispers of the cosmos, we embark on a journey rich with meaning, unlocking the gates to understanding as we engage with the breathtaking complexities and the beautifully woven narratives that define our universe.

17. Beyond the Horizon: Future Prospects

17.1. Next-Generation Observatories

The exploration of next-generation observatories represents an exciting frontier in the field of gravitational wave astronomy, promising to expand our understanding of the universe significantly. As technological advancements and innovative methodologies converge, scientists are set to embark on a journey that will transform how we perceive cosmic events and their implications on a grand scale. The evolution from initial gravitational wave detection to the operationalization of advanced observatories marks a pivotal chapter in our quest to listen closely to the whispers of the cosmos.

Next-generation observatories aim to enhance detection capabilities dramatically, enabling astronomers to capture gravitational waves with unprecedented sensitivity and resolve signals from a wider range of sources. The vision for these observatories encompasses several key advancements in technology, reflective of the collaborative spirit propelling the field forward. For instance, plans for projects such as the Laser Interferometer Space Antenna (LISA) highlight the potential for deploying gravitational wave detectors in space. This strategic placement circumvents many terrestrial limitations, enabling researchers to detect low-frequency gravitational waves emanating from distant cosmic events, such as supermassive black hole mergers—a domain previously beyond reach.

The road to space-based detection involves intricate planning and the seamless integration of complex technologies. LISA, for example, will feature three spacecraft positioned in a triangular formation millions of kilometers apart, utilizing laser beams to measure changes in distances caused by passing gravitational waves. The technical challenges inherent in launching and operating such a large-scale project are considerable, but the potential insights gained from observations made in this way are nothing short of revolutionary. This evolution not only promises novel observations but also invigorates discussions about how to structure space-based astronomy in a way that maximizes international collaboration and scientific progress.

As we project into the future of gravitational wave astronomy, the potential of these next-generation observatories heralds a new era of scientific inquiry marked by ethereal discoveries and unforeseen revelations. Together with terrestrial observatories, these facilities will form a comprehensive network capable of monitoring gravitational waves across a spectrum of frequencies, allowing researchers to piece together a more complete narrative of the cosmos.

The challenges that lie ahead are multifaceted, spanning technical, ethical, and philosophical dimensions. The quest for improved sensitivity and accuracy will require ongoing innovation, rigorous validation of detection techniques, and careful consideration of the impact of these advancements on broader astrophysical theories. Additionally, as we deepen our understanding of cosmic events through gravitational waves, we must also engage with the ethical implications of our discoveries, considering how they shape our understanding of the universe and humanity's place within it.

Throughout this process, the quest for knowledge and the passion for exploration must remain at the forefront. Each gravitational wave event detected is not merely a measurement; it is an invitation to delve deeper into the mysteries of existence. By framing our discoveries within the context of philosophical inquiry and ethical deliberation, we ensure that the pursuit of knowledge enhances not only our comprehension of the cosmos but also our responsibility to engage with it meaningfully.

Ultimately, the unveiling of the universe illuminated by gravitational waves represents a journey full of promise and possibility. As we embark on the path toward next-generation observatories, we are reminded that each wave detected serves as a testament to the boundless curiosity and determination that defines the human spirit. It is a celebration of exploration that transcends individual endeavors, uniting scientists, communities, and future explorers in a shared quest to understand the universe's whispers and the stories they tell about the fundamental nature of reality. This exhilarating journey beckons us onward, inviting us to continue listening intently to the cosmic symphony unfolding before our eyes, shaping a richer narrative for generations to come.

17.2. The Road to Space-Based Detection

The exploration of gravitational wave astronomy has opened new horizons in our understanding of the universe, marking a key transition from theory to empirical reality. The capacity to detect and analyze gravitational waves fundamentally alters our cosmic narrative, reshaping our interpretations of celestial dynamics and interactions. This journey encapsulates how scientific inquiry, technological innovation, and philosophical exploration converge to enrich our comprehension of existence.

As we reflect on the journey of discovery encapsulated in "Gravity's Ghosts: Unveiling Gravitational Waves," we recognize the profound implications of this research. From Albert Einstein's revolutionary theories that laid the groundwork for understanding gravity to contemporary advancements made at observatories like LIGO and Virgo, the path forward is paved with insights that connect diverse threads of knowledge, inviting us to challenge established paradigms and embrace the unknown.

Looking to the future, we see the promise of next-generation observatories that will enhance detection capabilities, allowing us to probe deeper into the cosmos. Space-based initiatives like the Laser Interferometer Space Antenna (LISA) will elevate our ability to capture low-frequency gravitational waves generated by massive cosmic events, expanding our understanding of processes such as black hole formation and the origins of heavy elements.

However, this journey is not without its challenges, as we navigate complex questions surrounding dark matter, dark energy, and the very foundations of scientific thought. The integration of artificial intelligence and machine learning into data collection and analysis represents an innovative direction that enhances our capability to interpret gravitational wave signals, while also highlighting the need for ethical considerations as discoveries unfold.

As we move beyond mere observation to deeper understanding, the interconnectedness of interdisciplinary collaboration emerges as a vital theme, bridging physics, astrophysics, and engineering. This synergy fosters an environment where diverse perspectives create richer insights into cosmic phenomena, reinforcing that scientific exploration transcends individual endeavors.

In addition, the call for public engagement and fostering scientific curiosity underscores our responsibility to bridge the gap between advanced research and societal understanding. By inviting the public into the realm of scientific inquiry, we stimulate a culture of curiosity that will inspire future generations to embark on their own journeys of discovery.

As we conclude this exploration and reflect on the themes presented, we understand that the path forward remains illuminated by a spirit of wonder. Each gravitational wave detected calls upon us to listen closely, as we strive to decipher the mysteries hidden within the fabric of spacetime. This cosmic inquiry not only enriches our understanding of the universe but also invites us to contemplate our place within it—an open invitation for all explorers, current and future, to join in the pursuit of knowledge and the everlasting journey toward understanding the grand tapestry of existence.

In summary, "Gravity's Ghosts: Unveiling Gravitational Waves" not only chronicles the remarkable journey of gravitational wave astronomy; it serves as a testament to human curiosity, collaboration, and the boundless quest for understanding that defines our human experience. As we step forward into the future, let us embrace the cosmic echoes, engage with the mysteries, and carve out a path of discovery that resonates for generations to come.

17.3. Vision for 21st-Century Science

In the 21st century, the scientific landscape is evolving rapidly, driven by unprecedented advancements in technology and a deeper understanding of the universe. As we reflect on the vision for 21st-century science, it is imperative to recognize the revolutionary implications that gravitational waves and their study propose for our understanding of cosmology, astrophysics, and the nature of reality itself.

The detection and analysis of gravitational waves symbolize not just a triumph of human ingenuity, but also mark the opening of new avenues of inquiry into the workings of the cosmos. For centuries, the scientific community has relied predominantly on electromagnetic observations—light and other forms of radiation—to study astronomical phenomena. However, gravitational waves have introduced a completely new facet of the cosmic narrative, allowing us to "listen" to the universe in ways previously unimaginable. This paradigm shift emphasizes the importance of developing multifaceted approaches to science, combining observational techniques with theoretical frameworks from physics, mathematics, and computer science.

At the core of this vision lies the potential to deepen our understanding of fundamental cosmological principles. The gravitational waves emitted by cataclysmic events—such as mergers of black holes and neutron stars—carry critical information about the masses, spins, and dynamics of these celestial bodies. This data can help refine existing models of stellar evolution and provide insights into the distribution and formation of cosmic structures. For example, the mergers observed thus far have revealed unexpected populations of black holes, prompting astrophysicists to interrogate existing theories about how these objects form and evolve within galaxies.

The vision for 21st-century science also encompasses a robust commitment to international collaboration, emphasizing that the pursuit of knowledge is not confined to specific borders or institutions. The successful establishment of a global network of gravitational wave observatories exemplifies this collaborative ethos. By pooling resources, expertise, and data, the scientific community is better positioned to achieve the common goal of understanding the universe more comprehensively. International partnerships not only enhance our capacity to detect gravitational waves but also respond to fascinating questions about the universe's origins, structure, and composition.

Additionally, the interplay of technological advancements and scientific inquiry reflects ongoing engagement with ethical considerations. As we probe deeper into the universe through gravitational waves, navigating the moral ramifications of our discoveries becomes increasingly important. Understanding how these revelations might influence public perceptions, inform policy decisions, and shape society is essential as we engage with cosmic phenomena. Scientists must strive to maintain transparency and foster dialogues with the public, recognizing our collective responsibility to ensure that advancements in science continue to benefit humanity and align with ethical principles.

Furthermore, the integration of artificial intelligence and machine learning into the analysis of gravitational wave data illustrates another dimension of this vision for science. Techniques that utilize AI to enhance signal detection and analysis increase efficiency and accuracy, allowing us to explore increasingly faint gravitational signals. This intersection of technology and scientific inquiry offers promising pathways for innovation and may lead to exciting breakthroughs in other fields of research.

As we look towards the horizon of 21st-century science, it becomes clear that the study of gravitational waves embodies the essence of exploration—a poignant reminder of humanity's enduring drive to unravel the mysteries of existence. The opportunities ahead beckon curiosity, inviting scientists, educators, and the wider public to engage with the cosmos in profound ways. This vision not only enriches the scientific community but extends to foster a sense of connectedness in our collective journey toward understanding the vast complexities of the universe.

In conclusion, the vision for 21st-century science emphasizes the exploration of gravitational waves as a central tenet driving modern astrophysics. These cosmic messages invite us to contemplate fundamental questions, expand our understanding of the universe, and unite as a collaborative collective dedicated to uncovering the mysteries of existence. By integrating diverse approaches, embracing innovative technologies, and prioritizing ethical considerations, we position ourselves to embark on an extraordinary journey of discovery. The whispers of gravitational waves resonate throughout the cosmos, urging us forward into a brighter future for scientific exploration where breathtaking possibilities await.

17.4. Challenges and Opportunities

The discovery of gravitational waves has ushered in a new era in astronomy, paving the way for profound insights and a reimagined understanding of the universe. In "Challenges and Opportunities," we reflect on the dynamic landscape of this evolving field, where intense scientific inquiry coexists with the complexities of real-world implications.

As we stand on the threshold of this new frontier, we face the dual challenge of improving detection capabilities while grappling with the philosophical and ethical implications of our findings. Gravitational waves are not merely fascinating phenomena; they symbolize the interplay of forces that govern celestial dynamics, serving as conduits through which we explore the fundamental laws of physics.

The initial challenge lies in the technological advancements necessary to capture the faint signals emitted by cosmic events. Existing observatories like LIGO and Virgo represent remarkable achievements, yet the next generation of detectors will need to push the boundaries of sensitivity even further. The planned upgrades and new instruments will usher in a new era of gravitational wave astronomy, opening avenues to explore even more distant galaxies and complex events that will enrich our understanding of cosmic evolution.

However, the journey is not solely about refined instrumentation. It also requires a careful examination of the ethical frameworks that guide our research. As we delve deeper into the tapestry of cosmic phenomena, we must engage with the societal implications of our discoveries. Gravitational wave astronomy offers critical insights into the lifecycle of stars and the processes that lead to the formation of black holes, but it also poses questions about our responsibility to disseminate knowledge and ensure that scientific advancements benefit humanity as a whole.

Moreover, engaging the public becomes pivotal in creating awareness and understanding of gravitational wave discoveries. Establishing ongoing dialogues between researchers and communities is essential for fostering interest in astrophysics and encouraging a sense of ownership over scientific exploration. This outreach not only enhances public understanding of complex scientific concepts but also inspires future generations to partake in the grand narrative of discovery.

In addition to the challenges ahead, we find an array of incredible opportunities to expand our grasp of the universe through collaborative efforts and interdisciplinary approaches. The convergence of gravitational wave astronomy with fields like dark energy, dark matter, and multi-messenger astronomy invites richer interpretations of cosmic events. The exploration of these connections reveals the interdependence of phenomena and challenges us to refine our existing models.

As we navigate the challenges and embrace opportunities in gravitational wave astronomy, we are reminded of the responsibility that comes with discovery. The waves we detect are not mere data points —they carry with them the stories of the universe, inviting us to contemplate profound questions about existence, the nature of cosmos, and humanity's place within it.

In conclusion, the journey of unraveling the mysteries of gravitational waves inspires a spirit of resilience, collaboration, and exploration. As we listen closely to the cosmic whispers carried through the fabric of spacetime, we embark on a journey filled with possibilities and challenges, weaving a tapestry rich with knowledge that expands our understanding of the universe. Through continued dedication to innovation, ethical engagement, and interdisciplinary exploration, we will continue to unveil the ever-evolving story of gravitation and the intricate connections that define the cosmos.

17.5. The Unveiled Universe

In the uncharted realm of gravitational waves, the veil between observation and understanding begins to lift, revealing the vast complexities of the universe woven into the fabric of spacetime. As we delve into this segment, "The Unveiled Universe," we reflect on how gravitational waves have reshaped our perception not only of celestial events but also of fundamental physical laws, cosmic evolution, and our own existence within this grand tapestry.

The journey to unveil the mysteries of the universe is deeply intertwined with humanity's insatiable curiosity—a driving force that propels scientists and explorers alike. Gravitational waves, initially seen as theoretical whispers, are now tangible signals bearing witness to cataclysmic events occurring billions of light-years away. The first detection in 2015 marked a historical moment, embedding gravity's spectral echoes into our understanding of cosmic life. What once existed solely in the realm of mathematics and speculation transformed into a narrative defined by observation and empirical evidence—the beginning of an unprecedented new chapter in astrophysics.

At the heart of this unveiling is the role of gravitational waves in bridging gaps in our comprehension of cosmic phenomena. These waves have illuminated events such as black hole mergers and neutron star collisions—cosmic occurrences that embody both destructive forces and profound opportunities for discovery. With each passing wave, we piece together data that affirms and challenges existing theories, revealing not simply the mechanics of individual events but the intricate relationships that govern stellar evolution, galaxy formation, and the distribution of matter throughout the universe.

However, the unveiling of the universe through gravitational waves is not merely a technical triumph; it is a fundamentally philosophical endeavor. Each discovery prompts deeper inquiries about the nature of reality itself—that elusive concept encapsulating time, space, and existence. The quest to understand gravitational waves serves as an invitation to reflect on the philosophical implications of our findings, urging researchers to engage not just with the scientific methods, but also with the ethical responsibilities woven into their work.

As gravitational wave astronomy continues to unfold, it unlocks a dialogue about the nature of humanity's relationship with the cosmos. Each wave detected represents not simply a data point, but also a question regarding the place we occupy in this vast universe—challenging us to consider our responsibility towards the knowledge we acquire and the moral implications of our scientific pursuits. Gravitational waves echo both stories of cosmic origins and warnings of existential crises; they serve as reminders of the interconnectedness of all entities within the universe.

Looking forward, the path of discovery stretched before us is both exhilarating and fraught with challenges. Future observatories promise to deepen our capacity for observation, bolstering our ability to discern fainter signals while attempting to bridge myriad disciplines toward a cohesive understanding of gravitational waves and their implications. As we venture forth, the spirit of collaboration and open inquiry will remain essential in refining our understanding of these cosmic whispers.

In summary, the unveiling of the universe represents a journey— a remarkable exploration shaped by curiosity, discovery, and ethical considerations. Through gravitational waves, we are reminded of the intricate balance between knowledge and responsibility, inviting us to contemplate the interconnected stories told across time and space. As we listen closely to the gravitational echoes that resonate from the heavens, we embark on a collective voyage into the mysteries of existence, ever prompted to explore, understand, and engage with the limitless expanse of the cosmos that surrounds us. Through this ongoing journey, we invite new explorers—those who will continue to investigate the profound enigma of gravitational waves and the universe's secrets, illuminating paths yet untraveled and mysteries waiting to be unveiled.

18. Ethics and Philosophy in Astronomical Discovery

18.1. The Philosophy of Scientific Exploration

The exploration of gravitational waves represents a profound intersection of science, philosophy, and ethics, intricately woven into the tapestry of modern astronomical discovery. Within this framework, the philosophy of scientific exploration emerges as a guiding principle, reflecting upon the methods, motivations, and implications of our quest to understand the cosmos. As we delve into the philosophical dimensions of gravitational wave research, we consider not only the principles that underpin scientific inquiry but also the ethical implications of our discoveries, the balance of knowledge with consequences, and the search for cosmological meaning that enhances human understanding.

At its core, the philosophy of scientific exploration seeks to illuminate the methodologies that drive our curiosity and inquiries into the universe. The pursuit of understanding gravitational waves exemplifies how the scientific method evolves through observation, experimentation, and the synthesis of theories. As we venture into the unknown, scientists employ diverse approaches to unravel the complexities embedded within gravitational wave signals—processes that reflect the dynamic interplay between theory and empirical evidence. The journey toward understanding these cosmic faint whispers invites reflection on the epistemological foundations of science, urging researchers to ponder the very nature of knowledge, inquiry, and exploration.

Ethical implications also arise as we navigate the milestones of scientific discovery. As gravitational wave astronomy advances our understanding of the universe, one must confront the broader societal ramifications of these findings. Questions surrounding the responsibility of scientists to share knowledge, consider the environmental impact of research, and effectively communicate discoveries to the public become increasingly vital. Ethical frameworks become indispensable in guiding researchers toward transparency, equity, and the conscious dissemination of knowledge, ensuring that advancements benefit society as a whole.

Furthermore, the balance between knowledge acquisition and potential consequences is a recurring theme within the narrative of gravitational wave research. As discoveries reveal not only the functions of dark matter and dark energy but also the origins of heavy elements and the life cycles of stars, we must remain vigilant about the ethical dimensions of these revelations. The knowledge gleaned from gravitational wave observations must be approached with care and consideration for the impacts it may have on societal constructs, public perceptions of science, and the evolving moral landscape.

The search for cosmological meaning permeates our quest to understand gravitational waves and their implications. Each detection serves as a reminder of humanity's connection to the universe—the quest for understanding is not merely a scientific endeavor, but also a philosophical pursuit that engages deep reflections about existence. Gravitational waves, as they ripple through spacetime, prompt scientists and inquisitive minds alike to confront questions about our place in the cosmos, the nature of time, and the laws that govern our reality. Engaging with these profound inquiries nurtures a greater appreciation for the interconnectedness of all beings and the larger narrative shared across the universe.

As we project into the future of gravitational wave astronomy, we envision pathways abundant with discovery and insight. The continued development of next-generation observatories, enhanced detection technologies, and interdisciplinary collaborations signal promises of unprecedented understanding of the universe. However, as these advancements unfold, the commitment to ethical inquiry and philosophical reflection must remain at the forefront.

In conclusion, the philosophy of scientific exploration emphasizes the intricate relationship between the methods of inquiry, the ethical implications of discovery, and the search for meaningful understanding of the universe. The journey into gravitational wave astronomy beckons us to explore deeper, engage with curiosity, and act with responsibility. Gravitational waves are our invitations to listen closely to the whispers of the cosmos, unraveling the mysteries woven through intangible threads of spacetime, ultimately leading to a rich and nuanced understanding of our existence within the grandeur of the universe. As we forge ahead into this new chapter of discovery, we embrace both the excitement of exploration and the profound complexity that informs our shared journey through the cosmic expanse.

18.2. Ethical Implications of Discoveries

The exploration of the ethical implications surrounding discoveries, particularly in the context of gravitational wave astronomy, is a pivotal aspect of contemporary scientific inquiry. As humanity stands at the forefront of groundbreaking revelations about the universe, the integration of ethical considerations into these scientific advancements invites researchers, philosophers, and the general public to reflect on the broader consequences of our discoveries. Gravitational waves, as subtle ripples in spacetime produced by some of the universe's most violent events, offer numerous opportunities to consider the ethical dimensions intertwined with the pursuit of knowledge and understanding.

One of the primary ethical implications of gravitational wave discoveries is the responsibility borne by scientists to communicate their findings transparently and accurately. As gravitational wave astronomy opens new doors to understanding phenomena such as black hole mergers and neutron star collisions, it becomes imperative to ensure that information is disseminated in a way that is comprehensible and relatable to the public. Misinterpretations or exaggerations of findings could lead to confusion and skepticism about scientific endeavors, undermining public trust in research and the scientific method.

Moreover, the knowledge acquired from gravitational wave research has the potential to influence societal and philosophical discussions about existence. By providing empirical evidence regarding the nature of the universe and its structure, researchers must be aware of the implications of their findings on various communities, fostering conversations on the significance of such discoveries within cultural, religious, and ethical contexts. As we unveil the mysteries of the cosmos through gravitational wave detection, we must also engage with the questions that arise about our place in the universe, the interconnectedness of existence, and the responsibilities that accompany human knowledge.

Additionally, the advancements made in gravitational wave astronomy will inevitably lead to inquiries into the ethical dimensions of emerging technologies. As researchers integrate machine learning and artificial intelligence into data analysis, the consequences of algorithmic decision-making must be carefully scrutinized. Ensuring that these techniques are developed with equity, fairness, and transparency at their core is essential for fostering trust in the scientific community and maintaining the integrity of the research process.

The concept of balancing knowledge with consequences further emphasizes the ethical responsibilities of scientists. Each discovery that expands our comprehension of the universe carries with it the potential for unintended consequences, including shifts in public perception about science, technology, and the balance of power within society. Ethical considerations should guide scientists to recognize these potential impacts and strive to ensure that new knowledge enhances the wellbeing of humanity while promoting a sense of moral accountability.

As we delve deeper into the realm of gravitational wave astronomy, we must also contemplate the philosophical implications surrounding our discoveries. Gravitational waves embody a rich narrative of existence that invites exploration beyond mere empirical inquiry. The questions that arise from our investigations prompt a deeper understanding of the nature of reality, the relationship between time and space, and the mysteries surrounding the origins of the universe. Engaging with these philosophical inquiries holds the potential to reshape not only scientific understanding but also humanity's collective quest for meaning in the broad expanses of existence.

Looking ahead, a bright future for gravitational wave astronomy awaits, filled with both challenges and opportunities. As next-generation observatories emerge and technology continues to evolve, the potential for new discoveries looms on the horizon. However, it will be imperative for the scientific community to navigate these developments with vigilance, ensuring that ethical considerations remain at the forefront of inquiry and interpretation.

In summary, the ethical implications of discoveries in gravitational wave astronomy serve as a reminder of the interconnectedness of human knowledge and responsibility. As we listen closely to the whispers of the universe and unravel the intricate stories woven through the fabric of reality, we must remain committed to fostering dialogue about the broader consequences of our work. This engagement not only deepens our understanding of the cosmos but also reinforces our responsibility to act with integrity, humility, and creativity as we navigate the expansive journey of scientific exploration. By embracing both the ethical implications and the cosmic narratives that emerge from our discoveries, we pave the way for a future defined by discovery, inquiry, and a shared commitment to understanding the beauty and complexity of the universe we inhabit.

18.3. Balancing Knowledge with Consequences

In the exploration of gravitational waves, the intricate relationship between knowledge and consequences emerges as a central theme —one that has profound implications for science, society, and ultimately, our understanding of our place in the cosmos. The journey of discovery surrounding these enigmatic ripples in spacetime demands not only a rigorous scientific approach but also a vigilant consideration of the moral and ethical dimensions that accompany such advancements. As we peel back the layers of knowledge unveiled through gravitational wave astronomy, we must confront the responsibilities that arise and the balance needed to navigate the complex interplay between knowledge gained and its far-reaching consequences.

The unfolding story of gravitational waves invites scholars and scientists to tread carefully, especially given the potential societal impacts of newfound knowledge. The ability to detect these waves—originating from cataclysmic events such as black hole mergers or neutron star collisions—represents a transformative leap in our understanding of the universe. However, this transformative power carries implications that extend beyond academic circles, prompting discussions about public perception, the trust placed in scientific discoveries, and the broader implications of such knowledge.

Central to this balance is the imperative for transparency and public engagement. As discoveries are made, scientists have a responsibility to convey findings in ways that resonate with and are comprehensible to the broader community. By fostering a dialogue that connects empirical evidence with public curiosity, we can ensure that the excitement surrounding gravitational wave detections translates into understanding and appreciation rather than confusion or skepticism. Engaging with the public helps demystify complex concepts and cultivates a culture that celebrates scientific inquiry as an inherently human endeavor, fostering a sense of shared ownership over our collective journey through discovery.

Moreover, the implications of gravitational wave research invite philosophical reflections regarding our knowledge of the universe. As we unravel the dynamics behind massive cosmic events, we humbly acknowledge that our understanding remains incomplete. Gravitational waves pose profound questions regarding the nature of existence itself—themes that intertwine with notions of time, space, and the interconnectedness of all things. By contemplating these themes within the context of our discoveries, we enrich our insights and open pathways for deeper existential exploration.

The balance between knowledge and consequences also extends into the ethical realm, demanding continuous scrutiny as new technologies and methodologies emerge. The application of artificial intelligence and machine learning in gravitational wave detection has opened avenues for unprecedented efficiency in data processing; however, we must remain vigilant in ensuring that these technologies are developed transparently and ethically. Biases in algorithms could undermine the integrity of the research, emphasizing the need for rigorous assessments, validation, and public discourse about the ethical implications of technological innovations.

As we embrace the challenges ahead, the future of gravitational wave astronomy resonates with the promise of new discoveries that will shape not only our understanding of light and dark but the very revelations about the universe's fundamental workings. The continued growth of collaborative efforts among international observatories reinforces a shared spirit of exploration—one that transcends borders and disciplines. By pooling our resources, knowledge, and expertise, we create a rich tapestry of scientific inquiry capable of tackling complex challenges with vigor and unity.

Ultimately, the journey through gravitational wave astronomy and the reflections on balancing knowledge with consequences provide an open invitation to all seekers of understanding. It speaks to the essence of scientific inquiry—a relentless pursuit characterized by curiosity, adaptability, and respect for the profound mysteries that lie in the cosmos. As we carry forward this legacy of discovery, we recognize the importance of grounding our efforts in ethics and philosophy while remaining curious and engaged.

In conclusion, balancing knowledge with consequences lies at the heart of our endeavor to decipher the echoes of the universe. The interplay between understanding and morality underscores the importance of fostering a culture of scientific inquiry that celebrates discovery while responsibly addressing the implications of our findings. As we continue to listen to the gravitational waves that ripple through spacetime, we embrace the beauty of exploration, recognizing that we are part of something larger—a shared cosmic narrative that invites us to understand our place in the universe and the intricacies that connect us all. Each gravitational wave detected becomes more than a scientific observation; it represents the power of discovery, an invitation to ponder, and a moment that bonds humanity in the pursuit of knowledge.

18.4. Cosmological Meaning and Human Understanding

In the expansive narrative of cosmic exploration, the subchapter on cosmological meaning and human understanding speaks to the profound implications of gravitational wave detection on our perception of the universe and our place within it. The ability to detect and interpret these fleeting ripples in spacetime has not only provided insights into cosmic phenomena like black hole mergers and neutron star collisions but has also invited us to engage with deeper existential questions about the nature of reality, connection, and the universe's fabric.

Gravitational waves serve as cosmic messengers, carrying with them unprecedented information about the dynamics of massive celestial events. Each signal detected offers glimpses into moments of cosmic history that occurred billions of light-years away, prompting us to reconsider what we thought we knew about the universe. The exploration of these waves has the power to reshape our understanding of fundamental forces, stellar life cycles, and the dynamics governing galaxies. With every event analyzed, researchers are reminded that meaning is not static; it evolves with discoveries and challenges existing paradigms.

One crucial aspect illuminated by gravitational waves is the interconnectedness of cosmic systems. The waves emanating from merging black holes or neutron stars reveal intricate relationships between celestial bodies, shaping the larger narrative of cosmic evolution. This web of interaction—where gravity, mass, and energy converge —underscores our growing appreciation for the complexity of the universe. When we interpret these signals, we are not merely observing isolated events; we are piecing together a broader story, recognizing that everything in the cosmos is interlinked, part of an intricate tapestry woven through time and space.

The philosophical implications of these discoveries challenge us to reflect on the nature of existence itself. As we unravel the cosmic narrative, profound questions arise: What does it mean to exist in a universe governed by the laws of physics? How do gravitational waves challenge our understanding of time, causality, and the fabric of reality? These inquiries offer fertile ground for dialogue between scientific exploration and philosophical thought, enriching our understanding of the universe while prompting introspection about our place within it.

Furthermore, the potential for gravitational waves to unveil secrets about dark matter and dark energy adds yet another layer of complexity to our understanding. As we seek to deduce the roles of these elusive components within the cosmos, gravitational waves serve as vital tools, providing empirical data that informs our insights into the universe's structure and evolution. The study of gravitational waves consequently interlaces with broader cosmic questions, compelling researchers and the public alike to consider the fundamental aspects of existence and the mysteries that linger just beyond our comprehension.

As we turn our attention to the future of gravitational wave astronomy, we anticipate a bright horizon filled with discovery and revelation. The establishment of next-generation observatories, improvements in detection methodologies, and global collaboration all promise to enhance our ability to listen to and interpret the signals from the cosmos. With each wave detected, we will continue to engage with the inherent beauty of scientific inquiry while nurturing a culture of curiosity, critical thinking, and a shared sense of responsibility.

The journey into gravitational wave astronomy and its impact on cosmological meaning thus reflects a collective aspiration—a commitment to unraveling the intricacies of the universe while recognizing the profound connection between knowledge and ethics. As we explore, we embrace the cosmic narrative that binds us, inviting all intrigued souls to join in this quest for understanding, engaging with the fascinating stories etched into the fabric of reality. Each wave detected is not merely a measurement; it is an invitation to peer deeper into the cosmos, celebrating the awe and wonder it inspires as we seek to unveil the extraordinary mysteries that lie beyond our horizon.

In this endeavor, the fullness of human understanding is enriched with each gravitational wave detected, and our consciousness expands as we connect with the cosmos—a reminder that we are participants in this grand exploration, forever drawn to listen, learn, and discover the whisperings of the universe. Through this pursuit, we seek not only knowledge but also a deeper connection to existence itself.

18.5. A Bright Future for Gravitational Astronomy

A bright future awaits gravitational astronomy, a field that has already rewritten cosmic narratives with its groundbreaking discoveries. As technological advancements continue to unfold and our understanding deepens, the exploration of gravitational waves promises to unveil even more profound mysteries than we have yet encountered. The path ahead is illuminated by the glow of possibility, inviting researchers, students, and the public alike to engage with the universe in unprecedented ways and to ponder the implications of these signals that ripple through spacetime.

Central to this promising future is the continual refinement of detection technologies. The next generation of gravitational wave observatories aims to achieve improved sensitivity and broaden the frequency range of detectable signals. Such advancements will enable astronomers to capture waves emitted from even more distant cosmic events, bringing forth an avalanche of new data that will deepen our understanding of the dynamics of black holes, neutron stars, and their interactions within galaxies. Emerging initiatives such as space-based observatories like the Laser Interferometer Space Antenna (LISA) will open new avenues of exploration, allowing researchers to probe phenomena like supermassive black hole mergers that remain largely elusive with current ground-based facilities.

Moreover, the power of collaboration will continue to shape the landscape of gravitational wave astronomy. The international network of observatories fosters a spirit of unity, allowing scientists across continents to combine their expertise and resources to enhance the understanding of gravitational waves. As researchers leverage data from multiple observatories, they will build a more integrated narrative about dark matter, dark energy, and the evolution of cosmic structures. The synergy of shared knowledge and diverse perspectives will play a pivotal role in driving forward the quest for understanding the universe.

The journey through gravitational wave astronomy will also inspire ethical reflections that guide scientific inquiry. As discoveries are made, the responsibilities tied to our newfound knowledge deepen. Engaging with public discourse about the implications of gravitational wave research will be crucial in ensuring that scientific advancements are communicated transparently and responsibly. Fostering scientific curiosity and inclusivity in the dialogue surrounding gravitational wave discoveries will enable communities to engage meaningfully with the contributions of research to societal and philosophical discussions.

Furthermore, the character of cosmological exploration will be shaped by interdisciplinary approaches that bridge diverse fields. The convergence of physics, mathematics, computer science, and even the humanities will foster an environment ripe for innovative discoveries and enriched interpretations of gravitational wave signals. This collaborative approach will augment our ability to interpret the data collected, helping us piece together the intricate stories behind the cosmic events and enhancing our comprehension of the universe at large.

As we look forward, the implications of gravitational wave research extend far beyond mere observations; they challenge the very foundations of our understanding and provoke larger existential inquiries. With each wave detected, we begin to glean insights into the nature of reality, the origins of existence, and our place within the cosmos. Gravitational waves beckon us to listen closely and embrace their stories, carving paths toward an expanded narrative that reflects both the complexities and beauty of the universe.

In summary, the future of gravitational astronomy lies in its commitment to continuous exploration, inclusivity, and the pursuit of knowledge. As we strengthen the connections between observational practices and theoretical frameworks, we prepare ourselves to delve deeper into the mysteries of gravitational waves. For every wave detected echoes an invitation—an opportunity to explore the cosmos, unlock hidden narratives, and engage in the grand adventure that defines humanity's quest for understanding. Through the lens of gravitational waves, we chart a course into uncharted territories, forever intrigued by the whispers of the universe that invite discovery and inspire the journey of exploration.

19. From Observation to Understanding

19.1. Piecing Together the Cosmos

In the quest to piece together the cosmos, we embark on an intriguing exploration that transcends traditional boundaries of observation, theory, and understanding. As we delve into the realm of gravitational waves, we are presented with unique insights that illuminate the vast expanse of the universe and deepen our comprehension of its complexity. This narrative intertwines the efforts of astronomers, physicists, and explorers of all ages, as they work together to unravel the stories encoded within the signals that ripple through spacetime.

At the heart of this endeavor lies the synthesis of theories and observations, which form the backbone of our understanding of gravitational waves. The groundbreaking insights of Albert Einstein, whose general theory of relativity predicted the existence of these cosmic whispers, laid the groundwork for decades of inquiry. Yet it is the subsequent observations of gravitational waves that breathe life into these theoretical constructs, enabling scientists to validate, refine, and even challenge existing cosmological models. Through the meticulous detection of gravitational waves from merging black holes and neutron stars, researchers glean critical information about the properties of these celestial bodies and the dynamics that drive the universe's evolution.

While the synthesis of theory and observation is essential, it also presents challenges in interpretation. Each detected wave bears a unique signature, reflective of the event from which it originated. The complexities embedded within these signatures demand rigorous analyses and advanced modeling techniques, as scientists seek to unravel their implications. For instance, the challenge of distinguishing between similar gravitational wave signals from different types of events requires careful scrutiny of waveform characteristics—a task fundamentally reliant on collaboration and communication among experts, enhancing the depth of inquiry that can be brought to bear on these mysterious cosmic messages.

Interdisciplinary approaches further enrich our understanding, as gravitational wave research encompasses a breadth of fields—from astrophysics and cosmology to engineering, computer science, and even philosophy. The collaborative spirit inherent in gravitational wave astronomy exemplifies how diverse expertise can come together to tackle complex questions about the universe. As we bridge disciplines, the dialogue nurtures creative problem-solving and innovative thinking, revealing new avenues for inquiry that extend beyond the confines of traditional scientific frameworks.

Looking forward, the path ahead is filled with opportunity. The launch of next-generation observatories, equipped with advanced technologies and enhanced sensitivity, heralds a new chapter in gravitational wave detection. The ability to explore previously inaccessible regions of the universe promises a wealth of discoveries, deepening our understanding of cosmic events, the interplay between matter and energy, and the fundamental forces governing existence.

The journey toward understanding the cosmos through gravitational waves invites all who are curious to partake in this grand endeavor. From seasoned scientists to inquisitive minds of all ages, an open invitation to explore, learn, and engage with the knowledge gained reinforces the notion that exploration is an inherently human pursuit that transcends barriers and unites us in our quest for knowledge.

In conclusion, piecing together the cosmos through the lens of gravitational waves serves not only as a scientific pursuit but as a cosmic narrative that binds humanity together in a shared journey of discovery. As we navigate the complexities of observation, interpretation, and interdisciplinary collaboration, we continue to uncover the profound stories woven into the universe's fabric. The whispers of gravitational waves beckon us forward, inviting us to listen closely, engage deeply, and explore the vast expanses of knowledge waiting to be unveiled. The cosmos, in all its grandeur, stands as an open invitation for exploration—a canvas of mystery, where each wave detected reveals the intricate tapestry of existence that connects us to the wonders of the universe.

19.2. Bridging Theories and Observations

Bridging Theories and Observations

In the realm of scientific inquiry, the act of bridging theories and observations creates a dynamic interplay that not only advances our understanding but also enriches the narrative of discovery. In gravitational wave astronomy, this bridging is paramount, as it links the abstract predictions of theoretical physics with the tangible phenomena captured by sophisticated observational tools. The integration of theoretical frameworks, empirical evidence, and the relentless pursuit of knowledge defines the essence of gravitational wave research, providing a pathway toward deeper insights into the universe.

At its core, the theory behind gravitational waves traces back to Albert Einstein's General Theory of Relativity, where gravity is articulated as the curvature of spacetime in response to mass. This groundbreaking shift in perspective illuminated the possibility of ripples propagating through spacetime—waves generated by the acceleration of massive objects. The theoretical underpinnings laid the groundwork for profound inquiries into the fabric of the cosmos, yet the challenge remained: how does one empirically validate these weighty concepts?

The transformation from theory to practice began in earnest with the establishment of detectors, most notably LIGO and Virgo. These facilities harness laser interferometry—an ingenious technique that utilizes coherent light to measure infinitesimal changes in distance caused by passing gravitational waves. The precision required to discern these subtle signals is extraordinary, demanding an acute understanding of both the theoretical models and the engineering complexities inherent in detection. Each wave captured represents not merely a fleeting cosmic event but rather a moment where theories crystallize into observable reality.

However, the journey of discovery does not end with detection; it necessitates a rigorous interpretation of the observed waveforms. Each characteristic of a gravitational wave signal—the frequency, amplitude, and duration—encodes critical information about the astrophysical events that produced it. For instance, the distinctive "chirp" pattern from binary black hole mergers offers insights into the masses and spins of the black holes involved, while the intricacies of neutron star mergers provide a narrative concerning element formation through rapid neutron capture processes. This analytic endeavor exemplifies the challenge of translating the theoretical and mathematical constructs of gravitational waves into substantive astrophysical knowledge.

The process of bridging theories and observations accentuates the importance of interdisciplinary approaches. In grappling with the complexities of gravitational wave data, researchers pull from various fields—astrophysics, physics, engineering, computer science, and even philosophy—to form a richer understanding of the phenomena. This collaborative spirit fosters innovative methodologies, as experts with diverse backgrounds come together to develop new models and tools for interpreting gravitational wave signals. The integration of computational techniques such as machine learning has further transformed the landscape, enhancing the efficiency and accuracy of signal detection and categorization.

Moreover, the ethereal nature of gravitational waves opens avenues for cross-disciplinary exploration and insight. The discovery that these waves encode information about black holes, neutron stars, and cosmic events invites conversations about fundamental physics, dark matter, and dark energy. Researchers must continually revisit existing paradigms, encouraging the scientific community to challenge established theories and embrace novel ideas in light of new discoveries.

The future of gravitational wave astronomy hinges on the continuing effort to bridge theories with observations. As new technologies emerge, and as next-generation observatories take shape, the potential for richer, more nuanced understandings of cosmic phenomena will expand immeasurably. The pathway forward will demand rigorous questioning, deep collaboration, and an unwavering commitment to unveiling the stories embedded within the gravitational waves as they traverse the expanses of spacetime.

In conclusion, bridging theories and observations in gravitational wave astronomy exemplifies the dynamic process of scientific discovery. Through the synthesis of theoretical insights with empirical evidence, researchers enhance our understanding of the universe while further shaping the narrative of exploration. This endeavor encourages scientists to listen closely to the whispers of gravity as they unveil the complexities of existence, inviting a collective journey into the profound mysteries that the cosmos has yet to reveal. Each wave detected serves not just as a scientific achievement; it is a call to deeper inquiry—a reminder that the quest for knowledge is perpetual, encompassing both the known and the unknown in our beautiful, expansive universe.

19.3. Challenges in Interpretation

The exploration of gravitational waves represents one of the most exciting frontiers in modern astrophysics, yet the journey toward comprehending this profound phenomenon has not been without its challenges—particularly in the realm of interpretation. As the scientific community seeks to decipher the implications of gravitational wave detections, various hurdles emerge, each demanding rigorous analytical approaches and interdisciplinary collaboration.

One prominent challenge in interpretation arises from the complex waveforms captured by gravitational wave observatories. Each signal can possess intricate characteristics that encode detailed information about the massive celestial events which generated them—ranging from black hole mergers to neutron star collisions. Understanding these waveforms necessitates sophisticated theoretical models that accurately predict the expected shapes and features of the signals. However, the mathematical complexity of these models can make it difficult to extract meaningful conclusions, as different scenarios could yield similar waveform characteristics.

Moreover, the detection of gravitational waves often occurs against a noisy backdrop of environmental factors and instrumental artifacts, complicating the process of pinpointing genuine signals. Each observatory is equipped with advanced noise filtering techniques designed to sift through the cacophony of vibrations stemming from seismic activity, thermal fluctuations, and even human activity. Despite these measures, the potential for confusion between gravitational wave signals and background noise remains a challenge that requires careful consideration and meticulous data analysis. Distinguishing between authentic signals and false positives demands concerted efforts among scientists, resulting in a collaborative exploration of methodologies that enhance signal interpretation.

Additionally, the meaning derived from gravitational wave observations can also be influenced by the limitations of current astrophysical models. As researchers analyze waveforms and draw conclusions regarding the properties of merging black holes or neutron stars, they must remain vigilant in reassessing existing theories. The unexpected trends observed in recent gravitational wave detections have prompted fresh inquiries into the nature of stellar populations and black hole demographics, encouraging scientists to reconsider established frameworks and explore new avenues of thought.

To address these challenges, researchers increasingly emphasize the importance of interdisciplinary approaches in interpreting gravitational waves. By drawing upon expertise from diverse fields—including astrophysics, computer science, data analytics, and even philosophy—scientists can collaboratively advance their understanding of gravitational wave phenomena. This synergy not only enhances the accuracy of interpretation but also encourages innovative methodologies that allow for richer analyses, ultimately leading to more comprehensive insights into cosmic events.

Furthermore, the successful interpretation of gravitational waves intertwines with public engagement and education. As scientists communicate their findings, they must present the implications in a manner that resonates with wider audiences, fostering interest and understanding among the general public. Meaningful dialogue about the discoveries made in gravitational wave astronomy invites individuals into the conversation, deepening societal appreciation for the complexities of the cosmos and inspiring curiosity about the universe.

As we envision the path forward in gravitational wave research, the interpretation of signals will continue to be a focal point of inquiry. The deployment of next-generation observatories, enhanced data collection technologies, and advanced analytical techniques will provide opportunities to refine our interpretations of gravitational waves and address the challenges that emerge in this domain. Collaborative efforts will be vital, fostering a spirit of unity that links scientists from various backgrounds together in their pursuit of understanding.

In conclusion, the challenges in interpretation represent pivotal moments in the journey of gravitational wave astronomy. By navigating the intricate nature of waveforms, addressing the complexities of noise, and embracing interdisciplinary collaboration, the scientific community is poised to unravel the profound implications of these cosmic signals. As we continue to listen closely to the whispers of the universe, we not only uncover insights into the fundamental forces that govern existence but also invite the next generation of explorers to engage in the vibrant quest for knowledge that transcends the boundaries of understanding. The journey ahead beckons us all to embrace the challenges and opportunities that lie within the gravitational waves, illuminating the cosmos and guiding us toward greater discoveries.

19.4. Interdisciplinary Approaches

Interdisciplinary approaches in the field of gravitational wave astronomy represent a critical evolution in scientific inquiry, showcasing how collaboration across various disciplines can enhance our understanding of the universe. As we venture into the complexities of gravitational waves, the integration of knowledge from physics, engineering, computer science, and even the humanities illuminates new pathways for exploration and discovery. This chapter delves into the transformative power of interdisciplinary collaboration, examining the ways in which it enriches our comprehension of gravitational waves and impacts the broader narrative of cosmic understanding.

At its core, gravitational wave astronomy epitomizes the convergence of theoretical physics and experimental research. Theoretical predictions regarding the existence of gravitational waves stem from Einstein's General Theory of Relativity, fundamentally reshaping our understanding of gravity, mass, and spacetime. However, translating these theoretical frameworks into tangible observations necessitates the expertise of researchers across various fields. Physicists work hand-in-hand with engineers to design sophisticated instruments capable of detecting gravitational waves, demonstrating how the intimate relationship between theory and practice enhances the scientific process.

The collaborative efforts extend beyond the confines of physics, encompassing data science and computation as crucial components. The vast datasets generated by gravitational wave observatories present significant challenges for analysis and interpretation. This complexity invites computer scientists and data analysts to develop algorithms and machine learning techniques that can sift through immense amounts of information, identifying gravitational wave signals amid the noise. The synergy between astrophysical research and computational innovation not only streamlines data processing but also raises the prospect of uncovering hidden cosmic events that may have eluded detection through traditional methods.

The role of interdisciplinary approaches further extends to fields like mathematics and philosophy, inviting scholars to engage with the foundational questions surrounding gravitational waves and their implications. Mathematics serves as the language through which the complexities of gravitational waves are expressed and modeled, providing the tools necessary for characterizing the waveforms produced by cosmic events. Meanwhile, the philosophical implications of these discoveries open avenues for reflection about existence, reality, and our relationship with the cosmos. This intersection encourages a holistic understanding of gravitational waves that transcends discipline-specific boundaries, fostering dialogue that enriches our collective comprehension.

The importance of interdisciplinary collaboration is evident in the educational initiatives that arise from gravitational wave research. Programs aimed at engaging students from various academic backgrounds promote curiosity and foster a spirit of inquiry that transcends traditional scientific education. By exposing students to the collaborative nature of scientific research, we cultivate a new generation of thinkers eager to engage with the complexities of the universe, ready to question, explore, and contribute.

Looking towards the future, the potential for expansion in interdisciplinary approaches is boundless. As the global network of gravitational wave observatories continues to grow, the opportunities for collaboration across countries and disciplines increase exponentially. The development of next-generation observatories promises to elevate our ability to capture gravitational waves, amplifying inquiries that connect black holes, neutron stars, and the very fabric of space-time.

Furthermore, the alignment of gravitational wave astronomy with other scientific realms—such as cosmology, nuclear physics, and even artificial intelligence—will foster a richer tapestry of exploration. Researchers will be poised to tackle the fundamental mysteries surrounding dark matter, dark energy, and the origins of cosmic structures through interdisciplinary inquiry that engages diverse perspectives and methodologies.

In summary, interdisciplinary approaches serve as cornerstones in the field of gravitational wave astronomy, illuminating pathways that deepen our understanding of the universe. By embracing collaboration across diverse fields—physics, engineering, computer science, mathematics, and philosophy—we create a more holistic inquiry that enhances our grasp of gravitational waves and their implications. Each discovery becomes an invitation to explore further while building connections across disciplines, ultimately enriching the grand narrative of cosmic exploration. As we continue this collaborative endeavor, we remain steadfast in our pursuit of knowledge, driven by the profound curiosity that defines the human experience and our relentless quest to decipher the mysteries of the universe.

19.5. The Path Forward

The quest for understanding the universe through the lens of gravitational waves has been a remarkable journey, profoundly reshaping our perception of reality and the forces that govern the cosmos. As we have embarked on this exploration, we have encountered moments of triumph, grappled with challenges, and celebrated the stories woven into the fabric of existence. This book, "Gravity's Ghosts: Unveiling Gravitational Waves," serves as a reflection of that journey —a narrative that weaves together the history, breakthroughs, and implications of gravitational wave astronomy, while acknowledging the human element and the call for future inquiries.

The journey of discovery in gravitational wave astronomy is framed by the extraordinary contributions of visionary scientists and researchers who have dedicated their efforts to translate theoretical concepts into tangible realities. From Einstein's groundbreaking predictions to the triumphant detection of gravitational waves by observatories like LIGO and Virgo, this path has been marked by collaborative efforts that reinforce the interconnectedness of knowledge and human curiosity. Each wave detected not only confirms existing theories but also invites exploration of new questions— further enriching our understanding of the universe and our place within it.

The future paths and predictions in gravitational wave astronomy brimming with potential call for continued innovation and collaboration. Next-generation observatories are set to enhance our detection capabilities, allowing us to probe previously unreachable cosmic phenomena. As technology advances and methodologies evolve, the potential for now unseen cosmic events becomes increasingly tangible. The integration of gravitational waves with insights from disciplines ranging from astrophysics to philosophy will encourage new perspectives and deepen our comprehension of the cosmos.

However, the journey ahead is not solely about technology; it remains intricately interwoven with the human element. As researchers pursue gravitational wave discoveries, the responsibility to engage with society, to communicate findings effectively, and to nurture public curiosity becomes paramount. Encouraging scientific literacy and fostering a culture of inquiry will empower future generations to participate actively in cosmic exploration—enabling individuals from all backgrounds to connect with the mysteries of the universe.

Reflecting on the cosmic journey reminds us that science is not just an enterprise of knowledge; it embodies the quest for understanding that drives humanity forward. The gravitational waves we detect serve as echoes of cosmic events—inviting us to listen closely, to ponder, and to embrace the mysteries that lie beyond our understanding. Each signal detected from the vast expanse invites curiosity, propelling us to ask fundamental questions about existence, time, and the profound interconnectedness of all things.

In closing, let this book serve as an open invitation to new explorers —those who seek to engage with the gravitational waves that ripple through the cosmos and those who yearn to uncover the intricate narratives hidden within these whispers. As we continue to listen, learn, and discover, we foster an enduring journey of exploration that transcends the boundaries of knowledge and time. The path forward is illuminated by the glimpses of understanding we have gained, beckoning all inquisitive minds to embark on a shared cosmic quest —forever driven by the echoes of gravity that invite us to explore the beauty, complexity, and profound wonder of the universe we inhabit.

Each wave serves as a reminder that our adventure does not end here. The universe teems with untold stories waiting to be unveiled, each whisper of gravitational waves a call to exploration, an invitation to understand the profound secrets that reside in the vast expanse of the cosmos. The journey of discovery continues—let us embrace it together.

20. Gravity's Ghosts: Conclusion and Reflections

20.1. The Journey of Discovery

In the expansive narrative of gravitational wave astronomy, the journey of discovery is characterized by a blend of scientific exploration, technological innovation, and philosophical engagement with the mysteries of the universe. As we delve into "The Journey of Discovery," we reflect on the remarkable path that has led to the detection of gravitational waves, an endeavor that stands as a testament to human ingenuity and curiosity.

The groundwork for this journey was laid in the theories of the early 20th century, with Albert Einstein's predictions of gravitational waves transforming our understanding of gravity and spacetime. However, it was not until decades later that the ambitious dream of detecting these waves began to materialize. This quest required persistent effort and collaboration among scientists, engineers, and researchers, culminating in the construction of groundbreaking observatories like LIGO and Virgo. Each successful detection of a gravitational wave event—signaling the cataclysmic merger of black holes or neutron stars—has validated Einstein's long-standing theory, marking milestones in the narrative of modern astrophysics.

Yet the journey does not solely consist of triumphs; it is equally defined by the challenges and uncertainties encountered along the way. The path of discovery has involved grappling with complex waveforms, navigating environmental noise, and confronting questions about the implications of findings on our understanding of dark matter, dark energy, and the broader cosmos. These challenges demand an adaptive mindset and a commitment to interdisciplinary collaboration that invites scientists from diverse fields to contribute their expertise toward a common goal.

As we look toward the future paths and predictions inherent in gravitational wave research, the prospects are vast. The continued development of next-generation observatories will enhance our ability to detect fainter signals, expanding our knowledge of the cosmos and refining our models of stellar population dynamics. Space-based detection initiatives like LISA hold the promise of probing previously unreachable frequencies, offering a richer understanding of cosmic phenomena and challenging existing paradigms. Each new gravitational wave detection will propel us further into the narrative of cosmic exploration and invite new questions about the nature of reality.

Central to this journey is the human element—recognizing that it is people who imbue science with meaning, curiosity, and engagement. The stories of researchers navigating the complexities of gravitational wave astronomy, collaborating across borders, and inspiring inquisitive minds highlight the significance of our collective endeavor. As we share discoveries and connect with the public, we emphasize the importance of transparency and inclusivity, fostering an appreciation for the beauty of scientific inquiry.

Finally, in reflecting on the cosmic journey, we acknowledge the profound interconnectedness of existence that arises from our discoveries. Each gravitational wave detected becomes more than just a signal; it represents an invitation to explore the universe's grandeur and a reminder of the delicate balance between knowledge and responsibility. The philosophical inquiries sparked by our findings continue to inspire deeper reflections on our place within the cosmos and the responsibilities we hold as stewards of knowledge.

This journey of discovery is far from complete; it is an ever-evolving narrative that beckons future explorers to engage with the gravitational whispers of the universe. As we stand at the threshold of new horizons, we remain committed to our pursuit of understanding and discovery. The echoes of gravitational waves resound throughout the cosmos, speaking of stories yet to be uncovered, and inviting us all to participate in the rich exploration of our universe.

As we conclude this narrative, let us embrace the open invitation to new explorers—those who are curious, who seek answers to the profound questions of existence, and who yearn to unravel the complexities woven into the very fabric of reality. The journey continues, and as we listen, learn, and discover together, we cultivate a shared understanding of the cosmic tapestry that defines us all. The gravitational waves whisper of mysteries untold, urging us onward into an exciting future brimming with discovery.

20.2. Future Paths and Predictions

Future paths in gravitational wave astronomy are poised to evolve in exciting directions, shaped by advancements in technology, collaborative efforts, and a commitment to inquiry that transcends traditional boundaries. As we stand on the cusp of this new era, the patterns of the cosmos beckon us forward, inviting us to explore phenomena previously hidden from view and to seek answers to the profound questions that lie at the heart of our existence.

One of the crucial elements of this future involves the deployment of next-generation observatories. As technology progresses, we anticipate the launch of sophisticated instruments capable of significantly increasing sensitivity and expanding detection capabilities. The establishment of models such as the Laser Interferometer Space Antenna (LISA) will allow us to probe the low-frequency regime of gravitational waves, unlocking a treasure trove of events including the mergers of supermassive black holes and exploring the dynamics that have shaped the universe since its inception.

Moreover, advancements in artificial intelligence and machine learning will facilitate the processing of the vast amounts of data generated by these observatories. By employing cutting-edge algorithms to filter and classify signals, researchers will enhance their ability to discern genuine gravitational waves from terrestrial noise. This integration of AI in gravitational wave astronomy exemplifies the broader movement toward automating data analysis, accelerating the pace of discovery, and enabling researchers to focus on interpreting the implications of their findings.

In addition, the collaborative spirit of gravitational wave research will continue to flourish, as the global network of observatories emphasizes the significance of shared knowledge and multidisciplinary approaches. The convergence of diverse scientific perspectives will enrich our understanding of cosmic phenomena, forging connections between gravitational wave detections and other astronomical observations, such as gamma-ray bursts and other electromagnetic signals. The spirit of unity and collaboration will be vital as we collectively tackle the complex inquiries that arise from these discoveries.

However, the future paths of gravitational wave science are not without challenges. As we expand our understanding of the universe, we must remain attuned to the ethical dimensions of our findings. The implications of discovering new and unexpected phenomena—particularly those related to dark matter, dark energy, and the dynamics of cosmic evolution—will require ongoing dialogue about the responsibilities of scientists to share knowledge transparently and engage with societal values. The intersection of ethical considerations and scientific inquiry will shape the narrative of our discoveries, reinforcing the importance of balancing knowledge with consequences.

Furthermore, as the gravitational wave frontier continues to unfold, we must take into account the potential public engagement strategies that will cultivate curiosity and appreciation for the cosmos. Educational efforts aimed at demystifying themes related to gravitational waves through outreach programs, public lectures, and participatory initiatives will play a key role in forming connections between scientists and various communities. By fostering a culture of inquiry and inclusivity, we engage the public in appreciating the wonders of the universe.

Lastly, the human element of this journey is paramount. Behind the instrumentation and data analysis lies a rich tapestry of stories— the scientists, engineers, and citizens who dedicate their efforts to unraveling cosmic mysteries. Their drive, passion, and collaboration form the essence of our exploration, reminding us that the quest for knowledge is a shared human endeavor.

In conclusion, the future paths of gravitational wave astronomy hold immense promise and excitement. As we harness the advancements in technology, uphold a spirit of collaboration, and engage the public, we embark on a journey that transcends the boundaries of knowledge. The whispers of gravitational waves call us forward, inviting all inquisitive souls to participate in this grand exploration of existence. By listening closely and embracing the narratives woven into the fabric of reality, we open ourselves to the richness of discovery that lies ahead—each wave detected representing an invitation to deeper inquiry and an understanding of our place in the cosmos.

20.3. The Human Element

In the grand tapestry of gravitational wave astronomy, the human element is a key thread, integral to understanding not just the science but also the stories that underpin this remarkable journey of discovery. As we probe into the cosmos, unraveling the complexities woven into the fabric of spacetime, it is imperative to reflect on the individuals who have dedicated their lives to this pursuit. Their passions, challenges, collaborations, and triumphs illustrate the heart of scientific exploration—an endeavor marked by human curiosity, creativity, and resilience that propels us toward the mysteries of the universe.

At its core, the journey of gravitational wave detection is defined by the collective effort of scientists, engineers, and researchers from diverse backgrounds and disciplines. From early theorists like Albert Einstein, who dared to challenge the status quo with the bold predictions of his General Theory of Relativity, to contemporary pioneers who work tirelessly at observatories, each person contributes to an evolving narrative aimed at unlocking cosmic secrets. This collaborative spirit is essential; it not only drives technological advancements but also fosters an ethos of unity that transcends geographical and disciplinary boundaries.

Throughout the years, the journey toward the detection of gravitational waves has been filled with both excitement and obstacles. The initial skepticism surrounding the feasibility of capturing such faint signals led researchers to endure years of rigorous engineering, innovation, and experimentation. Every challenge faced—from technical shortcomings and funding limitations to the intricate calibration of detectors—reflected the determination and ingenuity of those involved. The story of LIGO, whose successful detection of gravitational waves in 2015 marked a historic moment in science, encapsulates the spirit of perseverance that characterizes the pursuit of knowledge.

The emotional landscape within the scientific community is not to be overlooked. Celebrations of milestones, such as the first detection, brought together individuals from far and wide, all united by a shared vision and collective success. These moments of triumph emphasize the power of community in science—where collaboration, mentorship, and passion converge to create an enduring legacy of discovery.

As gravitational wave research continues to flourish and inspire curiosity, the need for public engagement becomes increasingly apparent. The complexity of the concepts involved can alienate audiences; however, proactive outreach initiatives serve to bridge this gap. Educators, scientists, and science communicators are tasked with translating intricate ideas into accessible narratives that resonate with people of all ages. Through workshops, public lectures, and participatory projects, they create pathways to engage with scientific inquiry, inspiring future generations to explore the wonders of the cosmos.

The human element in gravitational wave astronomy also extends to the ethical responsibilities that accompany scientific discovery. As researchers unveil the mysteries of the universe, they must engage with the potential societal impacts of their findings. The dialogue surrounding ethical considerations ensures that advances in knowledge are thoughtfully integrated within a wider societal context, ultimately benefiting humanity through a deeper understanding of the universe and our place within it.

Looking ahead, the journey of gravitational wave astronomy remains ripe with opportunity, inviting new explorers—students, enthusiasts, and inquisitive minds—to embark on this cosmic quest. The legacy of those who have paved the way serves as an open invitation for all to engage in the wonder of the universe. Each gravitational wave detected carries a message, urging us to listen attentively and contemplate the intricacies of existence.

In conclusion, the human element is the lifeblood of gravitational wave astronomy, shaping every aspect of research, discovery, and understanding. The intertwining stories of pioneers, collaborators, and learners encapsulate the spirit of exploration as we delve into the cosmos. As we continue to unveil the mysteries hidden within gravitational waves, we embrace the rich narratives that emerge from our shared journey—reminding us that we are not just observers of the universe, but active participants in a grand exploration that transcends time and space.

So let us embark together, each wave a note in the symphony of existence, inviting every curious soul to listen closely, explore deeply, and contribute to the ever-evolving understanding of the cosmos. The journey of discovery is far from over—an open invitation to new explorers awaits, beckoning us into the depths of space, where the whispers of gravitational waves echo through the fabric of our reality, revealing the magnificent stories of the universe waiting to be told.

20.4. Reflections on the Cosmic Journey

As we conclude our exploration of gravitational waves and their profound implications for understanding the universe, we find ourselves reflecting on the cosmic journey that has brought us to this point. The study of gravitational waves embodies not just technological advancements and scientific endeavors, but also the spirit of inquiry and curiosity that drives humanity's quest for knowledge. Each ripple in the fabric of spacetime tells a story—of cataclysmic cosmic events, of collaborations that span the globe, and of the intricate relationships that bind us to the universe.

The journey has been marked by milestones: the prediction of gravitational waves by Einstein, the construction of sophisticated observatories, and the historic first detection by LIGO. Each of these moments represents a paradigm shift, a validation of theories that were once considered abstract, and a testament to human perseverance and ingenuity. Yet, as we celebrate these achievements, we must also acknowledge the challenges that lie ahead. Whether it is refining detection methods, addressing the ethical implications of our discoveries, or engaging the public's interest in science, the road to understanding the cosmos is filled with opportunities for growth and collaboration.

The quest for knowledge in gravitational wave astronomy reflects a broader narrative of humanity's relationship with the universe. It urges us to consider profound questions: What does it mean to exist within a cosmic tapestry where gravity shapes the destinies of stars and galaxies? How do our discoveries influence our understanding of existence itself? These contemplations enrich our understanding and challenge us to think critically about the implications of our findings.

In this light, we extend an open invitation to new explorers—those who are captivated by the mysteries of the universe and eager to engage in the quest for knowledge. Whether you are a student, a researcher, or simply a curious observer, your contributions matter. The narrative of gravitational waves is not solely the domain of scientists; it embraces anyone with a passion for curiosity and a desire to unravel the cosmos's secrets.

As we stand at the threshold of new discoveries and continued advancements in gravitational wave research, let us remember that the journey is ongoing. The universe continues to unveil its wonders, and the gravitational waves that ripple through spacetime serve as a reminder that we are all interconnected in this grand cosmic dialogue. Each wave detected is an invitation to listen closely, explore boldly, and contribute to the ever-expanding tapestry of knowledge.

The story of gravitational waves and the insights they provide will inspire future generations to question, to explore, and to discover. Together, we embark on this journey—a journey that transcends the boundaries of space and time, inviting us to uncover the intricacies of existence and connect with the mysteries woven throughout the fabric of the universe. With each step we take, we honor the legacy of those who have come before us, while embracing the curiosity that leads us toward the endless possibilities that lie ahead.

In this cosmic journey of discovery, let us remain attentive to the whispers of the universe, ready to engage with the wonders that await us, and eager to chart a course that enriches our understanding of the extraordinary reality in which we reside. The future is full of potential, and together, we can navigate the cosmic landscape, forging a path towards enlightenment and a deeper comprehension of the complexities that define our existence.

20.5. An Open Invitation to New Explorers

The universe, in all its grandeur, beckons a new generation of explorers to join the collective quest for knowledge as we stand on the cusp of unprecedented discoveries in gravitational wave astronomy. An open invitation is extended to curious minds who wish to engage with the profound mysteries that lie beyond our world—those who are eager to listen to the whispers of the cosmos and participate in the journey of unveiling the secrets encoded in gravitational waves.

Throughout this narrative, we have traversed the remarkable path paved by the pioneers of gravitational wave research. From Einstein's theoretical foundations to the spectacular detections made by observatories like LIGO, Virgo, and KAGRA, we have witnessed the evolution of a field that has transformed our understanding of cosmic events. Each wave detected serves as a cosmic messenger, revealing intricate details about the interactions between massive celestial bodies, inviting us to explore the dynamics that shape the universe.

As aspiring explorers, your role in this narrative is vital. The community of gravitational wave astronomy is not merely composed of scientists and researchers; it flourishes because of the curiosity and engagement of individuals from all walks of life. Whether you are a student, a teacher, an enthusiastic citizen scientist, or simply someone captivated by the wonders of the universe, your contributions can significantly influence the trajectory of this exciting field. By joining the movement to explore gravitational waves, you become part of a narrative that transcends traditional boundaries, where each voice is essential to the quest for understanding.

The opportunities for engagement are numerous—be it through hands-on citizen science projects, educational initiatives, or public outreach events designed to dismantle the barriers between professional scientists and the public. Your involvement may lead to discovering unseen signals, contributing to the analysis of data or simply furthering discussions that shape the collective understanding of gravity and the cosmos.

In a continuously evolving landscape marked by technological advancements and collaborative efforts, the possibilities for discovery are boundless. Each advancement—from next-generation observatories to the integration of artificial intelligence in data processing—enchants those already engaged in scientific exploration while inviting the broader public to share in the excitement of inquiry. The gravitational waves from cataclysmic events give rise to fascinating questions about the fabric of the universe, dark matter, dark energy, and the very essence of existence.

With each wave detected, the adventures in gravitational wave astronomy deepen our connection to the universe, reminding us that we all share the same cosmic heritage. The stories contained within these waves resonate through time, urging us onward in our exploration. Each ripple signifies not only an event isolated in time and space but a narrative that intertwines our understanding with the larger tapestry of existence.

As you take the first steps into this domain, remember that the journey is not merely about seeking answers. It is about the connections you forge, the discussions you have, and the curiosity you cultivate. Each inquiry, every moment spent questioning the intricacies of the cosmos, enriches the narrative and leads us toward deeper truths.

In closing, consider this an open invitation to new explorers. Gravitational wave astronomy awaits those willing to engage with its wonders, challenge existing paradigms, and explore the ethereal waves that ripple through the fabric of reality. Embrace the spirit of inquiry, listen closely to the whispers of the universe, and immerse yourself in the awe and beauty of discovery. The cosmos is vast and filled with mysteries, and together, we can embark on a journey that expands our understanding of existence, nurturing a legacy of exploration that transcends the boundaries of time and space. Welcome to the adventure that awaits—an exciting cosmic odyssey filled with potential and promise.

www.ingramcontent.com/pod-product-compliance
Lightning Source LLC
LaVergne TN
LVHW051445050326
832903LV00030BD/3242